THE FORESTERS

JAMES MILLER

THE FORESTERS

THE STORY OF SCOTLAND'S FORESTS

BIRLINN

First published in 2009 by
Birlinn Limited
West Newington House
10 Newington Road
Edinburgh
EH9 1QS

www.birlinn.co.uk

The Publisher gratefully acknowledges the assistance
of Forestry Commission Scotland and the Forest Life
Picture Library in preparing this book for press.

ISBN: 978 1 84158 833 9

British Library Cataloguing-in-Publication Data
A catalogue record for this book is
available from the British Library

Designed and typeset by Mark Blackadder

Printed and bound by Bell & Bain Ltd, Glasgow

CONTENTS

PICTURE CREDITS

The illustrations in this book are present because of the cooperation of a large number of people to whom I owe a great debt of gratitude, namely: Norman Davidson – for the pictures on pages 100 (with Pat McAuley), 101, 118 and 124 (with the family of the late David Anderson, Huntly), 126 (with Ronnie Legge), 132, 134, and 144 (with Roy Neish); John Keenleyside – for those on pages 99, 100, 108, 163, 184, and 189; Ian Ross – for page 77; Mairi Stewart – for pages viii and 195; Graham Tuley – for pages 12, 96, 130, 137, 162, 176, 186, 204, 205, 207 and 213; the custodians of the Gair Collection for pages 27, 35 and 36; Dorothy Kidd, Margaret Wilson and the Trustees of the National Museums of Scotland for pages 10–11, 14–15, 22, 23, 25, 26, 38–39, 40–41, 43, 55, 58, 56–57, 133, 140, 160, and 172; the British Library Newspaper Section, and Bill McLoughlin of DC Thomson & Co Ltd (courtesy and © The People's Journal) for pages 65, 69, 70, 71, 79 and 179; Lesley Junor and the Highland Photographic Archive, Highland Council, for pages 32 and 33; Giles Durocher and the Canada Dept. of National Defence/Library and Archives Canada, for the CFC pictures on pages 72 to 76; and Forestry Commission Scotland for the map on page xiii and the pictures on pages ii, xiv, 59, 81 to 84, 87, 90 to 91, 95, 111, 112, 119, 121, 125, 126, 127, 128, 129, 131, 135, 138, 139, 145, 146, 148, 154, 155, 157, 158, 161, 171, 173, 176, 180, 182, 196, 197, 198, 199, 200, 201, and 211. Every reasonable effort was made to identify and clear copyright.

FOREWORD

Since trees provide the backdrop to our lives, it is easy to take them for granted. How much more so when we view them from a car or train window. Forests are such a given that we have forgotten, if we ever knew, how Scotland comes to have the landscape it has today.

Once, forests covered a huge percentage of our land area. Only small remnants of that old Caledonian forest remain. But we still have forests, and mostly they are not there by accident.

These woodlands have been created by generations of dedicated individuals whose commitment to their work has delivered the Scotland we see today. That commitment cannot be overestimated, because it takes a rare individual to be able to deal with the reality that the work they do today might not bear fruit in their own lifetime. From the earliest days, the foresters described in this book were people for whom a capacity to think into the long-term was essential, and the results of their work are evident for all to see. We owe them, then and now, a debt of gratitude which cannot ever be adequately expressed.

Since becoming the Minister whose remit includes the work of the Forestry Commission, I am only too aware of the extraordinary efforts still being made by those who work in and for our forests. It is my ambition to ensure significant growth in Scotland's forests in our own time, and for that to happen there must be new generations of foresters taking up the mantle of their predecessors.

We should salute them all!

Roseanna Cunningham MSP,
Minister for the Environment

INTRODUCTION

In his novel *The Heart of Midlothian*, Sir Walter Scott has the comic character, the laird of Dumbiedikes, advise one of his servants as follows: 'Jock, when ye hae naething else to do, ye may be aye sticking in a tree; it'll be growing, Jock, when ye're sleeping. My faither tauld me saw forty years sin', but I ne'er fand time to mind him.' What Dumbiedikes had failed to do had become during his creator's life a standard pursuit among lairds the length and breadth of the country, and it was no surprise when a version of Dumbiedikes's words were adopted as the motto of the Scottish Arboricultural Society, now the Royal Scottish Forestry Society, when it was founded in 1854. Our countryside has undergone great changes in the last two centuries but one of the most obvious has been the spread of afforestation. Although by no means free from controversy, this has hardly been as dramatic as some other great shifts in human affairs – emigration, war, the rise and decline of the fishing industry, the changes in farming – but it has altered the very face of the land in a quiet and steady way.

There are many books about trees, the natural history of woodland and forestry as a science but it has been only very recently that some attention has been turned to the people who have been most directly involved in afforestation – the foresters themselves. In 2007 Forestry Commission Scotland joined other institutions in the support of the Touchwood project to collect memories of the work in forestry in a few communities. Two volumes have appeared so far from this effort. Both have been written by Mairi Stewart of the UHI Millennium Institute Centre for History. The titles are *Smell of the Rosin, Noise of the Saw* – about mid-Argyll – and *The Forest Is a Beautiful Place To Be* – about the Great Glen. There is also a website www.forestry memories.org.uk devoted to the theme. Alongside the Touchwood project, which still continues, can stand the individual memoirs of a few foresters who have chosen to set down in print their experiences. Among them have been Donald Fraser, John McEwen, Kenneth Mackenzie, Don MacAskill and Brian Denoon, and I am grateful to have been able to quote from their writing in these pages, in my attempt to capture the story of forestry and the foresters in Scotland, and especially in the Highlands, through the recent centuries, in the context of changing times and political or economic frameworks. The Royal Scottish Forestry Society's journal, now called *Scottish Forestry*, has documented the last century and a half of forestry, and the older issues are available as an archive on the Society's website www.rsfs.org.

It is in part a story of loss and recovery. It is also the story of generations of men and women dedicated to their occupation in often difficult and uncomfortable, occasionally dangerous, circumstances. It requires a special aptitude to be a forester, a patience and a willingness to recognise that one may never see the outcome of one's efforts, the life of a tree being so much longer than that of a human being. It is also a complex story with many strands running in parallel and to try to encompass it in the space and time available I have had to resort to a broad-brush approach at times and in general focus more closely on the Highlands, where forestry has been accorded great social and economic importance since the beginning, than on other parts of Scotland. If the reader wants more detail or another man's view, I can happily advise them to look in the two-volume *History of Scottish Forestry* by M.L. Anderson, the lively and evocative *Landscapes and Lives* by John Fowler, or any of the other publications in the Bibliography.

As ever I am very grateful to a number of people without whose generous help this book would not have been written. Malcolm Wield and David Jardine of Forestry Commission Scotland kindly put me in contact with retired colleagues and provided general support from the start. Norman Davidson (Huntly), Jimmy Henderson (Evanton), John Keenleyside (Forres), Colin Ploughman (Golspie), Willie Lindsay (Macduff), Allan Macdonald (Fort Augustus), Alastair Macleod (Ardersier), Hamish Fraser, Alastair Kirk, Harry Obern, Bryce and Elizabeth Reynard, Donald Stewart and Graham Tuley (Inverness), Finlay Macrae (Dingwall), Charles Scott and Bill Sutherland (Edinburgh), and Don and Margaret West (Cabrich) recalled their experiences for me and provided not only hospitality beyond the call of duty but also the heart of this narrative. Malcolm Wield and John Keenleyside also consented to read the typescript and made many valuable suggestions for its improvement. James McDougall and James Ogilvie at

Forestry Commission Scotland brought me up to date with the many and varied FCS policies at the present time.

The staff of the public libraries in Inverness, Perth, Lochgilphead, Dumfries and Peebles, the Scottish Natural Heritage library in Inverness and Aberdeen University Library also provided much valued support and help. Many people generously helped with finding interviewees and answering specific queries, among them Alasdair Cameron, Rachel Chisholm, Jean Escott, Sheena Fraser, Susan Garnsworthy, Sandy Maclure, Cliff Pike, Elspeth Ross, Fiona Scott, Richard Toleman and Gordon Urquhart. If I have omitted anyone I apologise.

I am deeply grateful to everyone who helped me in the task of writing this book and I must add that none of them is responsible for any errors in the following pages. Thanks must also go to Hugh Andrew, Andrew Simmons and their colleagues at Birlinn, and to my agent Duncan McAra for their elastic patience.

James Miller
Inverness
May 2009

NOTES ON UNITS

Older documents on forestry deal in miles, acres and other Imperial units. To my mind the acre and the shilling are as much part of our heritage as the axe and the cleek, and carry in their usage an echo of earlier days. Generally I've left the old units as used at the time. To convert between old measures and the metric system, readers may find the following useful:

1 hectare = 2.471 acres
1 kilometre = 0.621 miles
£1 = 20 shillings (20s)
1 shilling (1s) = 12 pence (12d)

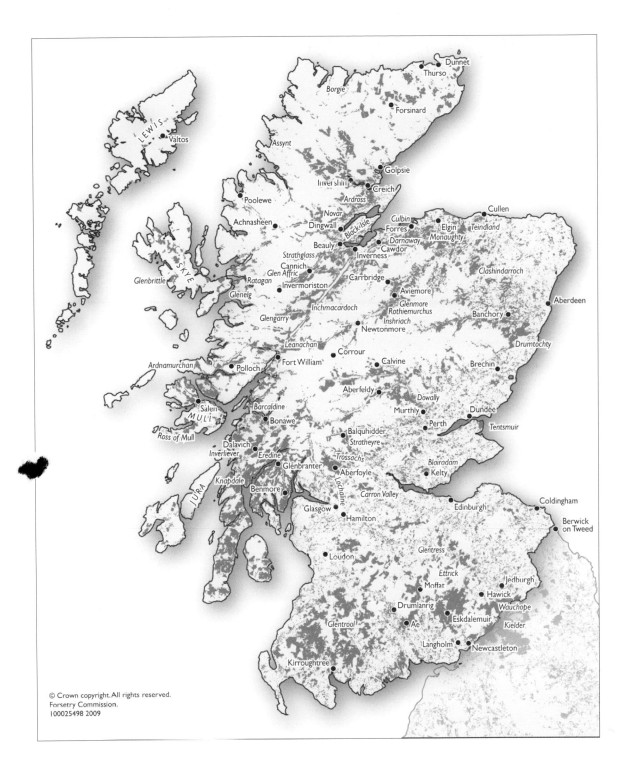

LEWIS
• Valtos

Borgie

Dunnet
• Thurso

Forsinard

Assynt

Golpsie

• Poolewe

Invershin
Creich

• Achnasheen
Ardross

Novar
Culbin
Cullen

Dingwall
Black Isle
Forres
Elgin
Teindland

SKYE
Beauly
Darnaway
Monaughty

Strathglass
Inverness
Cawdor

Glenbrittle
Cannich
Carrbridge
Clashindarroch

Glen Affric
Ratagan
• Invermoriston
Aviemore
Aberdeen

Glenelg
Inchmacardoch
Glenmore
Rothiemurchus
Banchory

Glengarry
Inshriach
Newtonmore
Drumtochty

Leanachan
Corrour
Calvine
Brechin

Ardnamurchan
• Polloch
Fort William
Aberfeldy
Dowally
Dundee

Salen
Barcaldine
Murthly
Tentsmuir

MULL
Bonawe
Perth

Ross of Mull
Balquhidder
Stratheyre

Dalavich
Trossachs
Blairadam

Inverliever
Eredine
Glenbranter
Aberfoyle
Kelty

Knapdale
Benmore
Lochaline
Carron Valley

JURA
Glasgow
Edinburgh
Coldingham

Hamilton
Berwick
on Tweed

Loudon
Glentress

Ettrick

Moffat
Jedburgh

Drumlanrig
Hawick
Wauchope

Glentrool
Ae
Eskdalemuir
Kielder

Langholm
Newcastleton

Kirroughtree

CHAPTER 1
'ALL BUT A LOST ART'
FORESTRY BEFORE 1919

The logging truck is a familiar sight on Highland roads. Rumbling along with creaking loads of stacked trunks, their cranes recumbent on top like the necks of ungainly birds, they carry the harvest from the plantations of conifers that are standard features of the landscape in almost every glen and strath. They are so commonplace that it takes an effort to recall that, apart from in a few localities and on some estates, large-scale forestry has been around for less than a hundred years, in effect since the Forestry Commission was set up at the end of the First World War. Monaughty Forest is a fairly typical product of the Commission's younger years. Its hectares of conifer bristle thickly over more than 5 miles of the long ridge of Heldon Hill between Elgin and Forres and make up only one forest in the well-wooded county of Morayshire. It has, however, a claim to be noticed, as it was somewhere on the flank of this ridge that early in December 1919 Lord Lovat planted the first Forestry Commission sapling in Scotland.

The newly formed Commission had just held its first meeting in London, with Lovat as its chairman. After adjournment, Lovat and one of the commissioners, Lord Clinton, agreed on a friendly competition to see who could get home first to plant the new body's first tree. Lovat did not really have much of a chance as Clinton lived in Devon, much nearer to the metropolis than the Highland laird's native heath. The story goes that Clinton got off his train and hurried with some colleagues to Eggesford, some 20 miles from Exeter, where they notched and heeled beech and larch seedlings into the ground. When Lovat stepped down to the platform at Elgin he was handed a cable with the victor's news. Undeterred, he carried on with his plan. It was the necessary small beginning.[1]

Scotland as a whole now has 13,000 square kilometres of forest and woodland, representing over 17 per cent of the land area. Most of the forests

Monaughty Forest stretching along the ridge of Heldon Hill

1

are in the Highlands – some 240,000 hectares (594,000 acres) – though such is the relative extent of the northern region that this is scarcely 10 per cent of its land area. The prize for being Scotland's most wooded region falls to Dumfries and Galloway where over one-fifth of the land is under forest. To the east, 14 per cent of Borders region is forested but the trees form a continuum with the vast Kielder Forest, the largest man-made forest in Britain, in Northumberland. Argyll and the north-east also have extensive forests and the densely peopled central belt is steadily acquiring more woodland. The vast bulk of this divided national forest is given over to conifers, with ownership divided roughly equally between the state, in the form of the Forestry Commission, and private landlords.[2]

Taking a long-term view the country is reverting in part to the well-wooded landscape of the distant past. The existence of grey, preserved pieces of timber in the layers of peat with which much of our land is covered is an eloquent memento of these ancient forests. How they were degraded and destroyed, by humans and by other agents, will be summarised later in this book; indeed, how we view our forests now is influenced by our view of these past ages. Here it is only important to note that once there must have been a rural population at home in a world of predominantly wild forest. They would have lived in what could be termed a forest-dwelling culture, a way of life in rhythm with the forest, much as the lives of the fisherfolk were tied to the rhythms of the sea. Between prehistory and now, however, the forest cover of Scotland diminished to a marked extent. In around 1800, for example, Heldon Hill was bare of anything save heather and rough grass and in this was typical of much of the country. Before the First World War, forestry in the Highlands was described as 'a long neglected and wasted resource'.[3] Only some 6 per cent of Scotland was then forested.

In ecological terms Scotland is part of the forest belt stretching across northern Europe. Although woodland became severely restricted on this side of the North Sea, in Norway, for example, it remained an important economic asset. 'The principal vegetable production of Norway is wood,' stated William Guthrie in a geography book published in 1812, 'The extensive forests of this country consist of fir, pine, oak, elm, ash, yew, birch, beech and alder trees . . . The sums received from foreign nations for timber are very great . . . The annual export of deal alone is reckoned at £175,000.' Sweden, Finland and Russia also retained vast pine forests, as did parts of Germany. The same author remarked of Scotland, 'The nudity of the country in many parts . . . is generally observed by the traveller from the south' before adding that the 'extensive plantations of trees continually making by the nobility and gentry must, in a few years, greatly remedy, if not entirely remove, this defect.'

In 1882, another observer noted that in Norway 'Most farms have a more or less extensive stretch of wood attached to them, and where this is the case the peasant proprietor derives from this part of his property not the least important part of his income'.[4] The contrast with Scotland in 1882 could not have been more marked, where peasant proprietors were very thin on the ground. During the inquiry chaired by Lord Napier in 1884 that led to the setting up of the Crofters Commission, and again during the inquiry carried out by a Royal Commission in 1892, forestry is mentioned only by the very occasional witness; eyes were almost entirely on agriculture and the status of small holdings and tenancies. In the opening session of the 1892 Commission, the chairman summarised their remit as 'to inquire whether any . . . land presently occupied for the purposes of a deer forest, grouse moor, or other sporting purposes, or for grazing . . . may be cultivated to profit, or otherwise advantageously occupied by crofters or other small tenants'.[5] Forest in the context of these inquiries meant open moorland, and afforestation the setting aside of open hill ground for deer stalking. When asked by the Napier Commission in what sense he used the word 'forester', Sir John Ramsden MP, the owner of Ardverikie estate, said, 'I use the word forester as a man simply employed in a deer forest as distinct from a woodman'.[6] Sir John agreed that at 'at some very remote time no doubt' the land had been under forest but added that the moss would not grow 'any timber at all' in the present. He also thought there had been no extensive timber industry, but he was now planting 'every acre I can spare for the purpose' although he did not expect personally to profit much from it.

When forestry was revived, it was almost entirely an initiative by the owners of larger estates: they had the resources and were open to innovation, whereas the farmers and crofters, tenants for the most part, had enough on their hands with straightforward crop- and livestock-rearing, and could not afford to invest anything in tree planting, even if such a venture should ever have occurred to them. Alexander Stewart, a crofter in Strone in Strathspey, told the Napier Commission in 1884 how he and his neighbours had lost hill grazing when the landlord had planted trees.[7] In the 1920s, when the newly formed Forestry Commission was much in the news and the first acres of state forest were being planted, it was reported that the pro-crofting lobby still regarded it with active hostility. It was something lairds did and was therefore tantamount to another weapon of oppression. 'They [crofters] had lost all tradition of the relationship of forestry to a peasant population' wrote A. MacCallum Scott.[8] In the crofters' defence, it has to be said that none of them had spare acres to play with.

Travellers in the eighteenth century were struck by the bareness of the landscape and the lack of old woodland. On his famous journey through the east in 1773, Samuel Johnson commented on a bleak prospect: 'From the bank of the Tweed to St Andrews I had never seen a single tree which I did not believe had grown up far within the present century.' 'A tree might be a show in Scotland as a horse in Venice,' he added, before noting that his companion, James Boswell, had found a tree – only one – at St Andrews that his guide had thought worth pointing out, before making things worse by assuring Johnson that this one was 'nothing to another a few miles off'.[9]

Johnson was never one to let the truth cloud a good opinion. His comments were only partly justified and he admitted that landowners were now creating small plantations around their properties. He saw little of the wilder parts of the country where there were extensive forests. William Roy carried out a military survey of Scotland between 1747 and 1755, publishing the results in a great atlas. Roy's father was a gardener near Carluke, and he was still a civilian when he joined the team to map the north in the wake of the defeat of the Jacobites in 1746. The important aspect of his mapping for our purposes is its recording of forest across much of the central Highlands: there were extensive woods at Altyre and Darnaway, south-west of Forres, and around Cawdor, along both shores of Loch Ness and extending up the glens to the west; likewise Strathspey and glens around the Cairngorms were well wooded.

Although the parish ministers and others who contributed to Sir John Sinclair's monumental *Statistical Account of Scotland* (*OSA*) in the 1790s bear out the general observation that much of country was denuded of woodland, they also record for many districts the reverse. 'There is a great quantity of natural wood in this parish, consisting chiefly of oak and birch,' noted the minister of Creich beside the Dornoch Firth on the east coast of Sutherland, 'but there is every probability that there was much more formerly. Several oak woods have been cut down within these 30 years . . . several young woods have been cut lately, and are growing again and in a thriving state. There are also considerable plantations of firs [Scots pine] in different parts of the parish. The largest is at Rosehall . . . of great extent, and in a very thriving condition'.[10] 'Where dismal bleakness lately prevailed,' noted the Revd

Charles Calder about the valley of the Conon draining into the Cromarty Firth, 'the eye is now presented with refreshing verdure'.[11] Of the peninsula of the Black Isle, Sir John Sinclair wrote in 1795 that 'plantations of firs, oaks, ash, elm, birch, beech, etc etc will most certainly thrive, in like manner, as they are already seen to do upon the different properties . . .'[12] He noted that the first man to exploit forests in the district had been Graham of Drynie who had supplied timber for the building of Fort George in the late 1740s. Sir John lamented a lack of good forestry practice: 'Our care and mode of management of woods consist chiefly in the preservation of them from cattle until they are beyond dangers, which eight, or ten, or twelve years time insures; and after-wards . . . in thinning . . . which in general is (very unwisely) too long neglected. Pruning, or any other such modes of improvement, we have given very little or no attention to.'

In the south of Scotland the overall picture in the *OSA* was of a landscape where much of the natural forest had disappeared and was only slowly being restored through the efforts of landowners. In the parish of Loudon in Ayrshire there remained only 95 acres of natural wood, in the author's estimation, and 250 acres of plantation. Before the Earl of Stair had been inspired to plant trees on his estate in Inch parish in Wigtownshire, the land had been 'naked'; in 20 years he planted an annual average of 20,000 trees – chiefly Scots pine but also larch, ash, beech and other species – and by the 1790s it was 'clothed and adorned'. The famous Ettrick Forest, though, was almost gone; as early as 1695, Sir Robert Sibbald had noted how Ettrick 'formerly wholly covered with woods . . . [was] to a great measure destroyed'.[13] Clearance of land for sheep grazing during the eighteenth century apparently saw off what remained of woodland in the adjoining parish of Eskdalemuir.[14] In the *OSA*, John Renton, however, observed in the parish of Coldingham in Berwickshire that 'there are a good many natural woods near the head of the water of Eye . . . chiefly of oak, hazel and birch'.[15] In Jedburgh the minister Thomas Somerville stated that the parish had 'abounded' with wood some 50 years before but now only 'a few old oaks, elms, beeches, plains [sycamore] and weeping willows still remain'.[16]

In contrast to the bare northern and southern moors, the broad mountain heartland, from the eastern foothills of the Grampians to the glens of Argyll, from the Ross-shire straths to the edge of the Highlands above the Forth valley, was relatively well wooded. Historical records are scanty but clearly the forests had provided a valuable resource, both for domestic and industrial use, for a long time. There are references to ships sailing from Inverness with cargoes of timber in the fourteenth century as well as to shipbuilding that must have used the local product. The records of the Parliament of Scotland from the fifteenth century onwards show that several measures were enacted to conserve forests and woodland but these did not have any lasting effect and the trend of over-exploitation continued until there was a severe shortage of timber resources in many districts by the seventeenth and eighteenth centuries. Apart from obvious uses as fuel and as a construction material, timber in the Highlands was used for roof crucks or couples; in the districts bereft of woodland, it had naturally become a valuable commodity and the peasantry were known to take roof timber with them when they flitted to a new dwelling. The factors in Assynt were instructed to preserve the woods along the Inver river and around Loch Assynt for the houses of the tenants. Balquhidder, which tradition held to have been well wooded, could afford by the 1790s little more oak and birch than served the locals for roof timber. On the Argyll estates use of timber was regulated by wood rangers. In October 1779 the chamberlain of Mull was instructed to obtain from the wood rangers annual 'full and regulated accounts of the timber given to the tenants'. It seems that the rangers were local men, tenants themselves, with this respon-sibility in their own districts.[17] As an instance of a more unusual use for trees, we can cite that in 1755 in the Black Wood of Rannoch, and possibly elsewhere, there were experiments in making soap from the ash of burnt *fearn* [alder].[18] A more exotic exploitation is recorded in the *OSA* for the parish of Kirkmichael on the north-west slopes of the Cairngorms: in the spring the birch trees were tapped and the sap was made into an alcoholic beverage known as *fion na uisg a bheatha*, the wine of the water of life or of the birch, life and birch being similar words in Gaelic, and a term only later transferred to whisky, in the opinion of Revd John Grant.

Large-scale exploitation of forest ranged from the making of charcoal for the iron-smelting industry to logging. Several operations devoted to using charcoal to smelt iron ore sprang up around Scotland in the seventeenth century and what may have been the earliest charcoal-fired blast furnace in the country was established at Poolewe in Wester Ross by Sir George Hay before 1610. The remains of many small bloomeries where iron ore was smelted have been found among the Loch Lomond oak woods.[19] Most of the iron-smelting sites were in the Highlands where the wood supply was sufficient, but one – the Tarrioch Ironworks – existed in the Cumnock and Doon Valley from about 1732, when it was founded by the third Earl of Cathcart. The extensive remains of the Bonawe furnaces on the southern shore of Loch Etive are now in the care of Historic Scotland. In this instance, the iron ore was imported from central Scotland and from Furness in Lancashire, the home of the parent company, and cast iron was exported. The demand for charcoal was very high. Coppiced oak was held to produce the best and it has been reckoned that the Bonawe furnaces needed at least 10,000 acres of woodland to keep them burning.

In many forests where oak was common the bark was harvested for use in the tanning of leather, already a dying trade by the 1790s by which time the natural woods in Clunie were 'much decayed' through careless husbandry and cattle grazing. In Dowally the men employed to peel the oak bark were paid a shilling a day – the women received 7d – and the bark was sold for 1s 3d a stone to the tanners. The *OSA* account of Torosay in the east of Mull notes that 'several woods . . . mostly birch, with some oak and ash . . . [are] occasionally sold for charcoal to the Lorn Furnace Company'.[20] At least 40 woodcutters and dyke-builders laboured in the woods in the parish of Kilchrenan and Dalavich, halfway down the west side of Loch Awe, 'inclosing, cutting, barking or peeling' trees. The men were paid one shilling or 1s 6d a day, the women who toiled alongside them 6d to 9d.[21] Oak woods at the junction of the Tummel and the Garry were cut down every 20 years for their bark and were valued for this at £4,500.

The seventeenth and eighteenth centuries saw a resurgence of interest in woodland and silviculture, both as a leisure pursuit and as an economic resource. This enthusiasm, especially as it was displayed by a few landowners, brought with it a need for foresters with the required knowledge and skills to tend the new woodlands. A range of forestry skills had survived from more distant days and the most likely place for these to be strongest was Strathspey and the surrounding districts, where a thriving logging industry sprang up in the eighteenth century. Pine, oak and birch were felled and floated down the Spey in vast rafts for export and to supply extensive shipbuilding yards at Garmouth on the Moray Firth.

This advertisement in the *Inverness Journal* on 4 September 1807 offers Scots pine forest for sale in Strathspey.

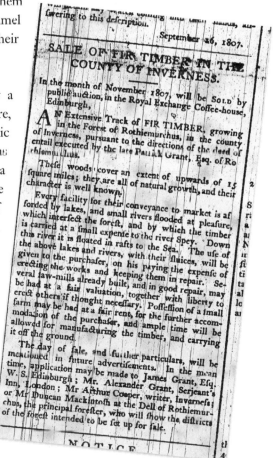

In about 1784 two merchants, a Mr Dodsworth from York and a Mr Osbourne from Hull, bought the Glenmore forest from the Duke of Gordon. 'They employ a great many hands . . . in felling the trees, and manufacturing them to plank, deals, masts, etc,' wrote the Revd James Gillan, minister of Speymouth in 1792. 'The planks, deals and masts are sent down the Spey in rafts, conducted by two men, at the rate of 30s the raft. The logs and spars are, for the most part, floated down the river loose, to the number perhaps of 20,000 pieces at a time, with men going along the side of the river with long poles, to push them on, as they stick to the banks. These men have 1s 2d a day, besides whisky; and there will sometimes be from 50 to 80 employed at once in the floating.'[22] The business of Messrs Dodsworth and Osbourne, known as the Glenmore or the Hull Company, built two sawmills at Garmouth for processing the lumber, one a windmill powering 36 to 40 saws. Some of the masts were 60 feet long and were said to equal Baltic timber for quality, and in 1791–92 no fewer than 82 vessels sailed away with cargoes of this valuable commodity. John Grant, the minister of the parish of Abernethy and Kincardine, also describes the rafts from Glenmore but gives a different figure for their size: 12,000 pieces of timber once a year.

According to Elizabeth Grant of Rothiemurchus, the Spey floaters, as they were called, lived mostly near Ballindalloch in Morayshire.[23] Certain families had followed the trade 'for ages' and knew all the 'holes and shoals and rocks and shiftings' of the river. At the first sign of a spate they came upstream to the forests where the felling had been going on and lived in a bothy at the junction of the Druie with the Spey, sleeping in their wet clothes on heather spread around the fire, their feet towards the flames, 'a circle of wearied bodies half stupefied by whisky' in Mrs Grant's words, who nevertheless thought them 'a healthy race, suffering little except in their old age from rheumatism'. A series of sluices on the tributary streams of the Spey was used to control water to induce artificial spates when required. To handle the logs in the river each man used a long pole called a clip, with a strong iron hook and spike on the end, and ran along the banks to ease stoppages and keep the mass moving. The poles were also known as cleeks, from the general Scots word for any such hooked implement. Specimens of the iron end pieces, termed 'dogs', from the late nineteenth century survive in the Highland Folk Museum. Steering logs downriver was tough, wet, dangerous work but it moved Mrs Grant to recall it in terms of delight: 'The many light forms springing about among the trees, along banks that were sometimes high, and always rocky, the shouts, the laughter, the Gaelic exclamations, and above all,

the roar of the water, made the whole scene one of the most inspiriting that either actors or spectators could be engaged in.'

Extensive forests in the upper reaches of Strathspey belonged to Sir James Grant and were known collectively as the fir woods of Abernethy.[24] Sixty years of logging had kept it, in the opinion of John Grant, from producing trees of great size; 'Before then, the making of deals by saw-mills was little known and less practised,' he wrote, noting that in Castle Grant some floors could be seen made from deals cut and dressed in the old way by the adze and the axe. At the beginning of the eighteenth century felling seems to have been done only on an ad hoc or intermittent basis; 'It is not a very long time back since the Laird of Grant got only a Scots merk (13s 4d) a year for what a man choosed to cut and manufacture with his axe and saw'; the rent for this had risen gradually to 5s sterling a year and a pound of tobacco. Attempts at logging on a larger scale had been unsuccessful – Brigadier Alexander Grant, who had died in 1719, had tried to sell mast timber in London but had given up for 'want of roads in the woods, skill in the country people, and all kinds of necessary implements' – until a branch of the York Building Company had launched in about 1730 a timber operation that earned John Grant's severe censure 60 years later. He called them profligate, vain and a corrupting influence, with abundant horses and equipment and a habit of opening hogsheads of brandy for the locals 'by which five of them died in one night'.

Mixed native woodland, predominantly Scots pine and birch, in Glencarron, Wester Ross.

Overleaf.
A view of Glenmore drawn in about 1780 by Charles Cordiner, an Episcopal clergyman who died in Banff in 1794.

Scots pine and rock – characteristic features of the Central Highlands. This picture was taken in Glen Feshie.

This extravagant venture lasted for about seven years before the incomers disappeared in a cloud of debt. 'But yet their coming to the country was beneficial in many respects,' recorded the minister, 'for, besides the knowledge and skill which was acquired from them, they made many useful and lasting improvements. They made roads through the woods. They erected proper saw-mills. They invented the construction of the raft, as it is at present, and cut a passage through a rock in Spey, without which, floating to any extent could never be attempted.' The introduction of the practice of rafting timber has been credited to Aaron Hill, the York Company's secretary and a poet,[25] but something akin to it may have always existed. John Grant says that before the York Company's short-lived venture, the rafting of timber down the Spey had been a 'very awkward and hazardous' business, some ten or twelve dozen deals 'huddled together' and conducted downstream by a man paddling a hide currach. This pilot led the raft with a rope tied round his knee with a slip knot so that he could quickly let himself loose when the timber snagged, whereupon he had to land, carry the currach upstream, launch and free the stuck raft. Grant describes the later rafts as consisting of 'two or three branders of spars in the bottom, joined end to end, with iron or other loups [loops], and a rope through them, and conducted by two men, one at each end, who have each a seat and oar, with which they keep the raft in the proper direction.' Grant agrees with James Gillan in giving the expense of a raft as

£1 10s. Mrs Grant says that the Ballindalloch floaters bored the logs with an auger and inserted iron plugs as tie-fasts for the wattles used to bind the raft together.

There are many records of the rafting of timber, a common practice wherever the proximity of forest and river made it feasible and one that continued over many decades. In 1742 a consortium of Lowland and English businessmen signed a contract with Roderick Chisholm of Comer and Alexander Chisholm of Muckerach, both in Strathglass, for 50,000 'firr trees' at one shilling each. The plan was to float the timber down to ships lying off Inverness, and the consortium also reached an agreement with Simon Fraser, Lord Lovat, to pay £2,500 for the passage of the logs through his stretch of the river. The plan fell through and in 1744 the consortium began proceedings to nullify the contract with the Chisholms. The outcome remains unknown, but the surviving documents give some details of a trial floating of close to 400 logs. It seems that this consignment was cut and 'thrown in two heaps in the river in time of a great storm when the water was all Ice . . . As the thaw came the waters swell'd raised the timber . . . a great many came down the ice being then a coming down . . . the timber could not miss to break some of them, yet notwithstanding some of the trees of the longest dimensions are come down haill & sound . . . without any attendance or help.'[26] The York Building Company considered floating logs from the Black Wood of Rannoch down to Perth in the late eighteenth century but the Tummel proved too rocky and turbulent. On 4 September 1807, the *Inverness Journal*, the newly founded newspaper in the district, carried an advertisement for a sale of timber at Amat in Strathcarron, timber that could be floated down the Carron river to Bonar Bridge. In the same issue Patrick Grant of Rothiemurchus was also advertising for sale by auction in the Royal Exchange Coffee House in Edinburgh 'an extensive track of fir timber . . . these woods cover an extent of upwards of 15 square miles . . . every facility for their conveyance to market is afforded by lakes and small rivers flooded at pleasure which intersect the forest, and by which the timber is carried at a small expense to the river Spey. Down this river it is floated in rafts to the Sea.' The floating of logs down the Dee to timber yards in Aberdeen in the nineteenth century was restricted once the threat to stone bridges became important.[27] A more recent instance of timber floating occurred in the 1930s when an Inverness contractor rafted trees during the construction of the Loch Ericht–Tummel hydro-electric scheme.[28]

The Strathspey logging industry peaked during the Napoleonic wars,

Overleaf.
The exact location of this picture is unknown, but it is thought to have been taken on the Druie river in Strathspey in about 1900 by Walter Dempster, headmaster of Rothiemurchus school between 1891 and 1923. The long poles with the hooked dog or cleek on the end for guiding the logs can be clearly seen.

when home-grown timber attracted attention as never before. Elizabeth Grant says the timber on her family estate, Rothiemurchus, became marketable in the 1790s: 'three or four thousand [trees] a year could easily have been cut out of that extensive forest for ever, and hardly been missed,' she enthused. The Grants of Rothiemurchus enjoyed an expensive lifestyle – Elizabeth's father bought one of the first three houses built on Charlotte Square in Edinburgh's New Town – and the natural product of their home braes enabled its pursuit. 'The forest was at this time so extensive there was little room for tillage through the wide plain it covered,' wrote Elizabeth, 'Here and there upon some stream a picturesque saw-mill was situated, gathering its little hamlet round; for one or two held double saws, necessitating two millers, two assistants, two homes with all their adjuncts, and a larger wood-yard . . . The wood manufacture was our staple, on it depended our prosperity. It was at its height during the war [Napoleonic war] when there was a high duty on foreign timber; while it flourished so did we, and all the many depending on us; when it fell the Laird had only to go back to black cattle again "like those that were before him". It was a false stimulus, said the political economists. If so, we paid for it.'

The forester during Elizabeth Grant's youth was a Duncan Macintosh – 'a handsome, clever, active little man of low degree,' in her words – who was brought to Rothiemurchus from lower on the Spey by Mr Osbourne, who at first supervised the felling and then left Duncan to get on with overseeing the work gangs. Duncan had a female companion, 'Mary, of a certain age, and not well favoured', to comfort him during the first lonely winter, and they had an illegitimate son, Sandy, who later became factor. Duncan, however, left Mary to woo and win the daughter of the tacksman at Pityoulish, much to the chagrin of this girl's father and the excitement of the community. A long, happy marriage ensued for the forester. He was also a consummate fiddler for the dancing and probably played at the big social event of the year, the Floaters' Ball at Christmas time. 'As the harvest-home belonged to the farm, this entertainment was given to the forest – all engaged in the wood manufacture, their wives and families, being invited,' wrote Elizabeth Grant. The day of festivity began with a game of 'ba' – an early version of shinty – and wound to its close with feasting on mutton and beef, the consumption of drams and punch made in the washing-tubs, and dancing in the lofts.

'The number of people employed in the forest was great. At the winter season little could be done beyond felling the tree, lopping the branches, barking the log . . . before the frost set in. Most of this indeed was done in the autumn . . . The logs prepared by the loppers had to be drawn by horses to the nearest running water, and there left in large quantities till the proper time for sending them down the streams.'

The Highland engineer, Joseph Mitchell, recalled the logging in the second volume of his memoirs, published in 1884: 'Formerly the vast forests in Strathspey, which produced the finest timber in Britain, were managed very primitively and unprofitably. The timber was cut down . . . afforded very considerable employment to the tenants, whose horses dragged it down to the river side. The tenants were paid by ticket from the wood department, and the amount due to them was placed by the factor to the credit of their rents . . . About three hundred people were employed . . .'[29] After the end of the Napoleonic war, in 1815, trade with the Baltic resumed and there was no longer the same need for timber from Strathspey. Logging and floating went on but gradually the scale of the activity fell away. In his later years, Duncan Macintosh began a new career farming the arable land around the Grant home, the Doune. Elizabeth Grant says that he was 'quite invalided' by 1820 but does not specify the nature of his disability. Her brother William gave up his career in the law to manage the estate, including the forest. He put a stop to the old practice of general felling, though it is not exactly clear what Elizabeth meant by this, and instituted clear felling of defined sections. 'William made a plan of the forest, divided it into sections, and . . . allotted one portion to be cleared immediately, enclosed by a stout fencing, and then left to nature, not to be touched again for fifty or sixty years. The ground was so rich in seed that no other course was necessary . . . in a season or two more, a thicket of young firs would be found there, thinning themselves as they grew . . .' William's reforms extended to systematizing the use of horses to drag felled logs to the streams and the processing of timber. One large sawmill was built near the junction of the Druie with the Spey, where pine trunks were cut into deals and the thinnings from the birch woods turned into staves for herring barrels.

The accounts of the Strathspey parishes for the *New Statistical Account*, written in the mid 1830s but published in 1845, make no mention of floating rafts of timber downstream. The description of the parish of Speymouth says, however, that around 120 floats came down the Spey in 1834 and that shipbuilding was still thriving at the mouth of the river, although 'The timber trade of Garmouth is now far from being what it once was. The forest of Glenmore was exhausted upwards of twenty years ago and all the natural timber brought here since was from the forest of Abernethy . . .

Rothiemurchus . . . and Glen Feshie'.[30] The author adds that since 1818 foreign timber had been more generally used for 'extensive jobs', which presumably included shipbuilding. The course of the Spey at its mouth was changed in 1860 to save the village of Kingston from erosion and it has been suggested that floating timber ceased after that date; but another source says it continued on a small scale into the early 1900s.[31] The rafting of logs happened in Sutherland in the 1920s to bring timber down to Bonar Bridge, and no doubt other unrecorded occurrences have kept the custom alive.

For the space of a century Strathspey was a part of Scotland where a sub-culture of forestry workers emerged, comparable to other rural or village communities devoted to farming, fishing or mining which depended on a single occupation and which passed on accumulated lore and skills through the generations. This 'forest sense' must at one time have been much more common and widely spread, before it diminished and barely survived at all until it was nurtured by the lairds who took an interest in woodlands. 'In this country forestry was all but a lost art,' said A. MacCallum Scott in 1926,[32] 'But on Lord Lovat's estate, and in one or two other isolated cases, the secret of successful forestry was preserved. The lessons of successive generations . . . the potentialities of each variety of tree on different kinds of soil were recorded in the estate books, and a small nucleus of highly trained foresters survived.'

When the Forestry Commission was formed in 1919, it had to re-create almost from scratch a cadre of foresters, including in its activities not only the planting of trees but the training of the people it needed and a more general promotion of the importance of its task. Sir John Stirling-Maxwell, one of the pioneers of the new pursuit, spoke in 1930 of the need to create 'a forest sense'. In reviewing the first ten years of the Forestry Commission's existence, he admitted 'that the task of placing forestry on a proper footing in this country is proving more formidable than we expected'.[33] This he attributed to the poor amount of investment in forestry by private landowners – woods were being felled but not replanted – but perhaps behind his remarks lay a realisation that, present economic conditions apart, forestry had still to be widely accepted as a normal part of country life. The Commission had the task of setting rural life on a new course.

James Grant, the minister of Cromdale, gave in to local pride when he boasted in 1835 that his parish had the biggest plantations in the country; the laird, the Earl of Seafield, had planted over 2,500 acres during the previous 26 years.[34]

A popular claim was that the earl had trees from Carrbridge to Cullen, but it was nevertheless a risky one since planting trees had become a regular component of the package of measures that lairds throughout Scotland implemented on their estates. Sometimes climate, soil and lack of knowledge conspired to bring about failure but on the whole the seedlings and saplings grew. Planting on some scale had been going on for a very long time. William Blair, cellarer to the abbot of Coupar Angus, established a tree nursery for the Forest of Ferter in 1460, and he probably was not the first to have one. In the late 1500s, the Earl of Gowrie and Sir Duncan Campbell of the Breadalbane family both planted extensively and were reputed to have been fond of walnut and chestnut. The Campbells carried on this practice, and one of them planted the woods around Cawdor. There are also records of sawmills from these centuries. The lairds' interest in trees encouraged the establishment of many nurseries; for example, Robert Dickson had one at Hassendeanburn near Hawick from 1729.[35] John Evelyn's book *Sylva*, published in London in 1664, primarily in connection with the supply of timber for the Royal Navy, influenced many landowners to adopt his ideas on tree propagation. The first Scottish book on the subject, *The Scots Gard'ner* by John Reid, appeared in 1683 and was republished in 1756. Little is known about Reid except that he was born at Niddry and was employed as a gardener and forester by Sir George Mackenzie of Rosehaugh on the Black Isle. Sir George, however, had another estate near Edinburgh and it is believed that Reid worked here and never came north of the Highland Line.[36] Most of *The Scots Gard'ner* is devoted to what is suggested by its title but it has one chapter on 'How to propagate and order forrest-trees.' Reid advised raising trees from seed and described how to make and maintain a nursery. He commented on many trees, including oak, elm – noting that 'extraordinary clean and smooth barked elms' were now available from Holland, ash, the 'great maple, commonly, but falsely called plane', beech, gean and 'Scots firre'. To Reid pine cones were 'husks'. He said nothing about what could be construed as commercial forestry but had in mind decorative groves and avenues.

In the wider European context, care of forests was already well established; laws against clearing woods exist for Germany from the twelfth century and systematic forestry had its beginnings there in the 1500s. Scotland had her own

This advertisement for saplings from a nursery on the Black Isle appeared in the *Inverness Journal* on 4 September 1807.

NURSERY TO BE SOLD AT ALLANGRANGE.

A VARIETY of FOREST TREES, Oak, Ash, Elm, Beech, Plane, Lime Tree, Spanish Chesnuts, Geens, Mountain Ash, Larch, Spruce of different ages and sizes, also, a number of Apple, Pear, and Plum Grafts of the choicest sort, with a variety of Flowering Shrubs. These Plants to be Sold on the most reasonable terms.

Application to be made to James Forsyth, Gardener at Allangrange, who will shew the Plants and treat with any desirous to purchase.

laws for the conservation of woodland, but it was not until the last decades of the eighteenth century that the passion for improvement of estates gave forestry the lasting boost that developed into our present practices. The *OSA* and other sources record it in many parishes, right across the country. Fraser of Belladrum planted in the environs of Kiltarlity, west of Inverness, for over 30 years; and his kinsman, Lord Lovat, also had a nursery. Mackintosh of Mackintosh had 'very considerable plantations', and the Earl of Moray planted over 500 acres in the parish of Petty between 1770 and 1790. An old rhyme had been passed down in the parish of Banff – 'From Culbirnie to the sea,/You may step from tree to tree' – but this memory was not matched by the reality until Lord Fife began planting in 1756. Lord Fife also planted extensively in Mortlach, starting with pines at Tininver in the 1730s.

The activities of the Perthshire lairds may have encouraged Perth burgh council to launch a rare public initiative in January 1714. The burgesses decided to take the unusual step of enclosing and planting the burgh muir, an area of about 70 acres. The provost bought 14,000 Scots pine seedlings and Alexander Reid, described as 'ane old qualified gardner', was placed in charge of the work. He died in 1716 to be succeeded by Daniel Murray. Large sums were invested in planting, drainage and other work over the succeeding years, and it was some time before income from the plantation began to accrue. The burgh fell into a recurring dispute with the Duke of Atholl over where the march fell between their respective properties. By the time of William Roy's survey the whole muir appears to have been tree-clad, mainly with pine but also with oak, ash, birch, elm and sycamore. The income from the wood reached the impressive average of £530 per year in the 1780s, dropping slightly to £445 per year in the 1790s. Income peaked at £1,205 13s 0½d in 1796–97, ironically the wood's swansong as the council decided at that time to examine alternate uses for the land. By the autumn of 1804 almost all of it had been auctioned for agriculture.[37]

Beside the Moray Firth, the shifting sand-dunes of Culbin were still bare but nearby, on the west bank of the Findhorn, stretched the 900 acres of the ancient forest of Darnaway. Some sessile oaks here, examined in 2001, were found to be true veterans, the largest three trees ranging from 399 to 727 years old, possibly dating from 'the once vast ancient semi-natural oak forest of Tarnua' that became a royal forest in 1346. In more recent times, Francis Stuart, the ninth Earl of Moray, began to plant the open areas in the Darnaway forest in 'about 1767'; by the 1790s, John Macdonnel the minister reckoned he had clothed more than 3,400 acres, in Petty and Dyke but mostly in Edenkillie.[38] 'The nurseries from which these plantations have been made,' wrote Macdonnel, 'except a little at the beginning, have been all raised at Darnway. Scotch firs, planted out at two years old, from the seed-bed, are used as nurses; and as soon as they are fit to afford shelter, the more valuable kinds of forest trees, principally oaks, are planted amongst them.' By methods such as these, the Earl of Moray's efforts had resulted in the planting between 1767 and 1791 of 596,000 oaks and 308,000 ash, beech, elm, sycamore, Spanish chestnut, spruce and larch; and between 1767 and 1787 of 9,687,000 Scots pine. In 1924, the nineteenth Earl of Moray told his fellow members of the Royal Scottish Arboricultural Society about the afforestation efforts of his forebear, who had been nicknamed 'the tree planter' for his efforts, and gave similar figures: 11.3 million trees between 1767 and 1807 in the county of Elgin [Morayshire] and 1.8 million on other family estates. He also mentioned how the Comyns, the custodians of the Darnaway forest in the reign of Edward I, had been ordered to supply 400 oaks for the building of Dornoch Cathedral, and described a roup of timber in May 1729 when wood from part of the estate was sold for £6,900 Scots.

In the parish of Fossaway and Tulliebole, to the west of Loch Leven, the minister noted that 'planting is now become very fashionable and is proceeding with rapidity. Within the last eight years about 800,000 trees have been planted . . . The Scotch fir are in the greatest number; and the larch grows quickest'.[39] Around Hamilton in Lanarkshire, Alexander Hamilton the laird was a keen planter 'covering and adorning a country which before was sterile and naked'.[40]

The number of workers employed must have run into the thousands. Presumably the many gardeners and labourers enumerated in the reports to the *OSA* from the parish ministers did the hard graft and filled the role of today's professionals. The term 'forester' was in use, although such a man often approximated to a gamekeeper in his duties, in keeping with the practice of calling any stretch of uncultivated ground set aside for hunting a forest irrespective of its tree cover. In a letter in February 1762 to the Duke of Gordon, his factor, William Bell, mentions salaries paid to foresters; it seems to have been normal for them to receive five or six bolls of oatmeal and 30–40s per year. The letter names the forester in Glenmore as James Stuart.[41] The forestry practised by the lairds produced a cadre of experts who found themselves in demand in other parts of Britain.

The lands belonging to the clan chiefs and lairds who had chosen to support the Jacobites in the Rising of 1745–46 were confiscated by the British

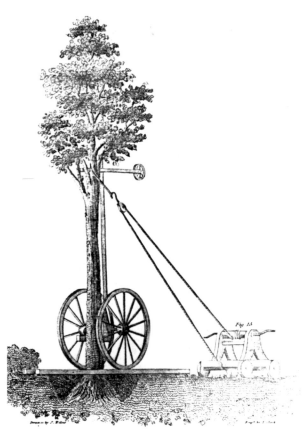

government and assigned to the care of a body known as the Commissioners for the Forfeited Estates, in whose hands they remained for nearly the next 40 years. The Commissioners took an interest in all the possibilities for developing the resources of the Highlands, to bring the region into the fold of the mainstream economic life of the country and thereby exercise what they saw as a civilising influence. Forests were a resource and forestry was one of the activities they encouraged wherever the land held promise of success.[42] The estate papers record the condition of forests – a letter in November 1770 refers to the exhausted state of the Stratherrick woods, to the south-east of Loch Ness, through cutting by the tenants, bark peeling and grazing by goats – and describe the practices of the time. For example, in 1766 Captain John Forbes, the factor for the Lovat and Cromarty estates, planted 151 acres on Blairnakylach north of the Morass of Cunnan [Conon]. The cost was 15s per acre, and the carting of what is described as the firs, presumably Scots pine seedlings, from Aberdeen to the site a further £15 8s. Forbes arranged a series of plantings in the area in the late 1760s, the work being overseen by George Cumming the gardener at Brahan Castle. On the Arnprior estate in March 1760 John Buchanan from Bochastle near Callander petitioned the Commissioners to be allowed to continue his cutting of the Strathyre woods that he had purchased in 1757 for a three-year period. It was noted for the Strowan estate in the parish of Fortingall in 1755 that an 'immense deal of birch and alder wood' grew on Rannoch but that the only valuable timber was the pines in the Black Wood. Planting took place, and by March 1765 the young pines were doing well within the fences put up to exclude grazing cattle. A letter from Robert Menzies the factor in February 1783 gives the name of the forester – John Cameron – and says he is to be allowed £20 to employ men to repair fences, gather cones, sow seed and cut young birch to make space for the pines.

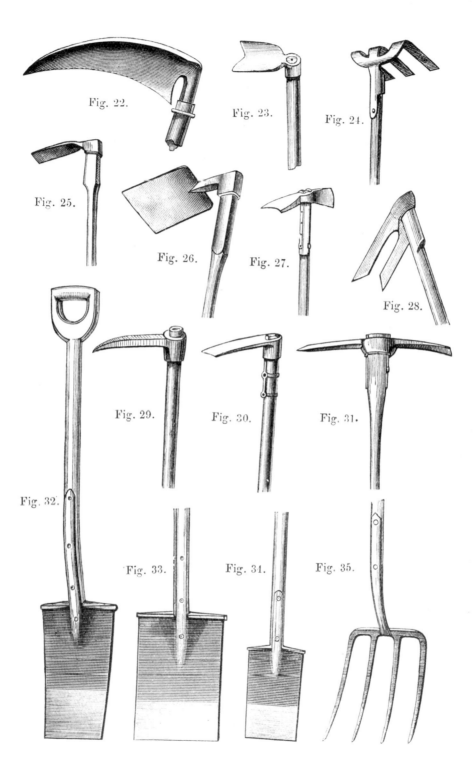

Fig. 22.

Fig. 23.

Fig. 24.

Fig. 25.

Fig. 26.

Fig. 27.

Fig. 28.

Fig. 29.

Fig. 30.

Fig. 31.

Fig. 32.

Fig. 33.

Fig. 34.

Fig. 35.

The appearance of the larch among the species planted by the lairds is a reminder that the eighteenth century saw the introduction of many exotic tree species. One tradition has it that the larch was first planted in Scotland in 1725 at Dalwick in Tweeddale, but a record exists that puts the date much earlier – in around 1670 – and the place Lee in Lanark.[43] A Colonel Menzies of Culdares in Glenlyon is credited with bringing them first to Atholl in 1737; he gave some, perhaps 16, to James, the second Duke of Atholl, who planted them out in the following year and followed this with several hundred more over the next 20 years.[44] John Duke of Atholl who succeeded in 1764 planted another 11,400 larches.[45] By the 1790s the Atholl dukes had set over 4,000 acres under mostly larch, reckoned the fastest growing among the species available.[46] Other trees also made their debut. For example, Monymusk had an avenue of Norway spruce planted in about 1720, and still there in 1851, when they had reached 90–100 feet high. More introductions followed in the nineteenth century, most spectacularly perhaps from the North American continent in the form of the Douglas fir in 1827, the giant redwood in 1853 and the Sitka spruce, now the most productive conifer in the country.

In 1819 James Duff, fifth Earl of Fife, took over part of the old priory at Pluscarden as a nursery and grew larch, Scots pine and beech to plant out on Heldon Hill. Thanks to the efforts of him and his fellow lairds, by the time of the publication of the *New Statistical Account* in 1845, forestry had become an established feature of the country estates. The Scottish Arboricultural Society, now the Royal Scottish Forestry Society, was founded in Edinburgh in February 1854. The first president was James Brown. Born probably in the Lothians, he became forester on the Arniston estate and, in 1847, wrote *The Forester*, destined to go through several editions and become the standard reference work for his fellow professionals in the Victorian period, a distillation of theory and practice up to that time.

In the Victorian period the forester became an important person in the rural hierarchy. One of them, Christopher Young Michil, at Cullen House, took it on himself to submit to the Society's journal his views on how junior staff should be trained.[47] These are very much of their period – pedantic and pompous – and one is forced to wonder if any of Michil's readers shook their heads with amusement as they considered his advice. Michil was of the firm opinion that forestry could be done properly only where a duly qualified forester was in charge. 'A person passing rapidly through a country by railway, whose eye is accustomed to observation, and whose mind is imbued with the true spirit of forestry, can very well determine as to the competency or otherwise of the forester in charge of the wooded estates passed through,' he wrote, '. . . how often are the most shrewd and observing of men misled and deceived on engaging their servants by misjudging their qualifications.'

In Michil's view, a forester did not have to be able to speak or write well as 'The culture of forest trees is a subject amply sufficient to occupy and engage all the time and talents of the most gifted and energetic men of the age' and other talents were of lesser importance. He was also convinced that there was much still to do to establish properly qualified foresters in the countryside, and went on to detail his ideal system of training. It should begin, he believed, with an unwritten agreement – to avoid any argument later over the correct working conditions – to provide employment for three years. He recalled that in his own case 'the agreement was only a verbal one, and fully met all the

Woodcutters with tools, thought to have been photographed in Inverness-shire. Among them is an adjustable levering implement used to roll over logs.

A janker, the high-axled cart used to carry logs. The photograph was taken at a sawmill at Edgerston, Roxburghshire.

requirements of the case'. His starting wage had been 9s per week, rising to 10s in the second year and 11s in the third, the same wage as the general estate workmen at the time. After his three years, the apprentice should work in a public nursery for four months to gain further experience before rejoining the estate and working once more alongside his former colleagues but now taking on more skilful tasks. Thereafter the apprentice progressed through the rank of journeyman to foreman and finally, after some eight years, might be considered a reliable, honest worker.

For Michil a man's moral character was as important as his technical skill and his physical strength. To ensure the first, his leisure had to be supervised to ensure no time was ever wasted. In summer the man should rise at five o'clock – 'the practice of lying too late in bed is both a general, pernicious and hurtful habit . . . From this evil a thousand others spring', have porridge for breakfast, spend ten minutes reading some improving literature, offer a prayer 'for the night's rest and joys of the morning' and go to work at six. Two ten-minute breaks broke up the morning and afternoon, and an hour was allotted for dinner, although Michil stressed that only a quarter of this time should be spent eating to allow further opportunity for study. The worthy forester laid down precepts for every minute and every activity – he even digressed to consider the pros and cons of drinking tea, and suggested a reading list of improving works for the young man to study on the Sabbath. How far Michil's scheme was taken up by other landowners and, therefore, how many foresters were trained under his exacting regime remain unknown.

A more typical career may have been that of Malcolm Dunn, who was given a long and effusive obituary in the *Transactions of the Royal Scottish Arboricultural Society* in 1901.[48] Dunn was born in Methven in 1837, the son of a farm grieve, and began work as an apprentice gardener at Strathallan Castle when he was 13 years old. Thereafter, as he advanced in his career, he moved around the country – to Yorkshire, Worcestershire, Chelsea and County Wicklow – before being appointed chief gardener at Dalkeith Palace in 1871. He developed a special interest in pomology but also was prominent in the development of forestry, helping to organise a forestry exhibition in Edinburgh in 1884, promoting a lectureship in forestry at Edinburgh University and campaigning, albeit unsuccessfully, for a government-owned model forest area. He was indefatigable in leading the annual excursions of the Arboricultural Society and in the obituary's wording – 'Himself an untiring walker, he had little sympathy with those who sought to shirk any item in the day's programme, and at such times he was wont to comment on the degeneracy of modern legs' – the reader detects memories of exhaustion on the anonymous writer's part.

Forestry and horticulture seem to have been inseparable among the Victorian profes-sionals but gradually a degree of specialisation emerged. John Grigor founded a tree nursery in Forres in 1828; in 1840 he sold trees to the burgh council for the replanting of New Forres moor at the cost of £163 16s 10d (the town had plantations valued at £800 in 1838). In 1868 Grigor

It's all hands to the task to heave this heavy stump on the cart in this image captured at the Reelig estate, west of Inverness, in around 1880.

published a practical treatise on forestry, dedicated to the Highland and Agricultural Society of Scotland 'whose operations have greatly extended and improved the woods and forest throughout the kingdom', bringing into one volume the experience and knowledge he had acquired. What he terms a 'calendar of operations' gives a picture of the forester's year. January and February were to be devoted to felling, thinning, pruning, cleaning ditches and drains, and planting when the weather permitted; and nursery plots had to be dug to expose them to frost break-up, and then there was sowing and collecting of ripe pine seeds. The thinning of the plantations should be completed by the end of March, and transplanting of pines, grafting, and sowing of conifer seed should be done in April. The spring and summer months were an endless round of sowing, weeding, draining, fencing, clearing whins and pruning hedges. More thinning, pruning and preparation for planting went ahead in September and October, when felling began and seed such as beechmast could be collected. Much the same range of activity kept the forester active during November and December, with the extra task of gathering leaves for compost.

Forestry in Scotland was still lagging behind the practice in neighbouring countries. Two French visitors in 1886, blamed the poor state of Highland forests more on stalking and sheep farming than on the skills of foresters: 'they are powerless to cause ideas to triumph, the simple notion of which does not exist even in the most enlightened public. They have to struggle all the time against grazing, against force of habit . . . [and] with the fantastic folly of the sportsmen of two worlds'.[49]

The first formal education for professional foresters was organized for recruits to the Indian Forest Service in the 1880s. Although Parliament recommended in 1887 the formation of forestry schools, nothing happened. Degree courses at Oxford eventually began in 1909. The campaigning of the Royal Scottish Arboricultural Society led to the establishment of a lectureship at Edinburgh University in 1889 – the inaugural lecture by the first incumbent, Dr William Somerville, was published in the Society's journal. Edinburgh began to offer a bachelor of science degree course in forestry in 1906, by which time three agricultural colleges financed by the Scottish Education department were also training in forestry.

The Victorians looked to Germany as the place to find the best and most relevant practice of scientific forestry. In 1901, the assistant factor of Innerleithen, Fraser Story, wrote an account of his sojourn in Eberswalde, north-east of Berlin, and in other parts of the Kaiser's empire.[50] With another

Scot, Eric Nobbs, Story spent four months in the Eberswalde forest academy, attending lectures and learning practical management on excursions into the surrounding 40,000 acres of state forest, where the prevalent tree was the familiar Scots pine. For the next four months, Story and Nobbs toured through other German forests where variations in soil, topography and climate favoured different tree species. On the Baltic island of Wollin (now in Poland) they saw how shifting sand dunes could be fixed and turned into woodland; similar methods were to be employed to forest the Culbin Sands in the 1920s. A graduate of the Edinburgh University forestry course, Story observed that a forester's training was much more thorough in Germany than at home. A would-be *Förster* had to excel in high school, serve an apprenticeship with a district forest officer for two years, do three years in the army and, after passing required examinations, become an assistant. After another eight or nine years and a final examination the lucky man could move to the next step in the ladder. It could take eighteen years to become a fully fledged forester. The home-grown foresters had per force to be more of the self-taught variety, acquiring knowledge through published works, experience and working under a regime such as the one advocated by Mr Michil from Cullen. Most would have spent their working lives in one place, a custom that persisted for a long time. In 1926, when John Sutherland retired as a foreman forester on the Skibo estate after having worked there for almost 50 years, he was described, perhaps unkindly, as 'passing like an heirloom from one proprietor to another'.[51]

The heartland of the Frasers of Lovat lies to the west of Inverness around the lower reaches of the Beauly river, the watercourse down which the English consortium proposed to float Chisholm timber in 1742. Beaufort Castle, until recently the Fraser family's seat, rises above the river in the centre of a broad acreage of parkland, forest and field between higher hills to east and west. In the late nineteenth century the estate comprised over 181,000 acres, the tenth largest landholding in the country. For the Frasers forestry was as much a part of the life of the Highland gentleman as salmon and game, and Simon Joseph Fraser, fourteenth Lord Lovat and third Baron Lovat, who inherited the lands and titles in 1887, had long had an interest in it, encouraged, it is said, by John Dewar, the head forester.[52] Like other Highland landowners in the nineteenth century, Lovat's father and grandfather had also practised forestry. As Lovat said at a lunch for a group of foresters visiting Beaufort in 1923: 'For three generations my family have been planters of trees. We have the estate accounts

The rugged forested landscape near Lord Lovat's home, where the Beauly river cuts through the Aigas gorge.

for over 100 years relating to the forests, and these accounts have been of the greatest value to the [Forestry] Commission. We have the family tradition and the family recorded experience . . . my grandfather . . . he planted about 10,000 acres . . . on the average I used to cut 70 acres a year which brought me in £5,000: but of that I spent £2,000 on replanting.' He found forestry satisfying: 'Your work does not perish each year. It endures for generations . . .'[53]

According to Sir Francis Lindley his biographer, Lovat set about replanting much damaged woodland in 1909 after a plague of red squirrels had wrought havoc among 30- and 40-year-old pine, a plague that may have resulted from Victorian persecution of the pine marten, and came into contact for the first time with experts from whom he learned that forestry in Britain was a long way behind that in other countries. He set forth his views on the need for afforestation in an article that same year in the *Transactions of the Royal Scottish Arboricultural Society*, an article that began as a response to the report of the Royal Commission on Coast Erosion but turned into his own proposal for state forestry.[54] He found the afore-mentioned report to be dismissive of the rural population, as well as ill conceived on other matters, and called for a board to be appointed to investigate the practicality of state forestry in Britain. There was even a shortage of basic data on the total acreage that might be put down to growing trees on a commercial basis. Lovat knew that afforestation would have severe knock-on effects on sporting activity (mainly deer stalking), sheep farming, the rural people and even the rates (property taxes) in poorer districts. But he also revealed where his heart lay when he wrote 'I yield to no man in my belief in a well-thought-out scheme of afforestation as a check to rural depopulation.'

The government had acquired Inverliever Forest and other lands beside Loch Awe in 1907. These properties, running to some 12,600 acres, became a Crown forest, run by the Office of Woods, the first state-owned forest in Scotland, where the first two years were spent in setting the place in order and preparing for forestry operations. This venture was a harbinger of the future, but it did not appear so to Lovat. Scathing about the government's apparent ignorance of what was involved in state afforestation – he was a Unionist peer during the Liberal administration of Herbert Asquith – he attacked the lack of progress at Inverliever. 'To build up an industry requires brain, application, thought,' he wrote, 'to destroy one, a little wind in Parliament and the stroke of the permanent official pen suffice.' He argued that it was easier for the state than private individuals to initiate a forestry scheme and called for a central forestry body, the acquisition of experimental areas, the establishment of training centres, a survey of the whole nation, and the state to start planting in mountain and heathland, and begin to cooperate with landowners and provide them with financial incentives to the same end.

Lovat was not alone in his general views. They had been around for some time, and earlier correspondence in the *Transactions* of the RSAS had expressed similar opinions. In the same year – 1909 – Aberdeen and North of Scotland College of Agriculture sought from the government an area of forest that it could use for teaching and demonstration purposes, and appealed to local authorities in the north to support their request; Inverness County Council, aware of the suitability of the county for forestry, at once fell in behind this plea for 'a national forest for experimental purposes'.[55] This was still at a time when the word 'forest' more readily meant the bald moors of a deer forest on a sporting estate than country planted with trees.

Sir John Stirling-Maxwell, a Tory politician and the owner of the Pollok estates, addressed the Glasgow Highland Club in November 1909 on the subject of forestry: the first thing he said was that the art of forestry was 'almost completely lost' in Scotland.[56] 'At one time it was well understood,' he went on, 'but forestry was almost completely crowded out in the time of our grandfathers by agriculture and grazing. At the present time the price of

A sawmill in Strathdon, around 1910.

timber has risen; the price of mutton and wool has gone down. In many places, too many places, deer has taken the place of sheep, because deer forests yield more profit.' He recognized that the creation of plantations was a financial 'cold, dead loss for the whole lifetime of the planter' and saw that this had to be undertaken by three agencies – the state, the municipality and the family. In France, Germany and Belgium the cost was divided between all three. In Scotland he saw the state as taking the lead and families, by which he meant landowning families such as his own, being encouraged to follow through tax and other financial incentives. His conclusion was that forestry was likely to add to the population and welfare of the Highlands.

Forestry was now in the public arena as a topic of promise. Also in the autumn of 1909, John D. Sutherland, a lawyer with an interest in rural development,[57] described employment in forestry in Germany to the Foresters and Gardeners Society of Argyll in Oban, some of whose members had recently travelled to see for themselves how their neighbours managed things. A head forester with five staff worked full-time on a 5,000-acre forest in Germany, with some 40 or 50 more men 'besides many girls' in the right season, said

Mr Sutherland, whereas a Highland sheep farm of the same size needed only four men with a few extra hands in the harvest-time. The work was healthy, the wages were 2s 7d to 3s per day for the men (1s 6d for the girls), and clearly if forestry were to be extended in the Highlands 'there would not be the same fear of depeopled glens'.

Lovat's own forester, Gilbert Brown, looked after 10,000 acres and employed 50 men; another 30 worked for the merchants handling the timber. Forestry fitted well with crofting – the seasonal demands for labour did not coincide and complemented each other quite handily. Writing on the advantages of forestry in the *Inverness Courier*, a columnist identified only by his initials 'PTM' saw the crofter-forester as the way to go. Forestry was not the pet scheme of the opponents of smallholders, he asserted, but the twin sister of agriculture – 'the forester and the agriculturist must in the Highlands work together'.[58]

Lovat was repeating this message during the general election campaign that winter. As a Unionist peer, he had introduced a Land Bill in the House of Lords to allow, among other things, crofters to expand their range of economic activity, but nothing was going to happen while the Liberal

Woodcutters in Strathspey, photographed before the First World War.

government stayed in power. 'Nothing would be more beneficial to small-holders than the development of afforestation in the Highlands,' he told an audience in the village of Kiltarlity, literally on his own turf, on a snowy night in December, 'Much could be done for the benefit of crofters and others if suitable ground were planted with trees . . . Forestry would suit the crofter because it meant work between November and March, a time when the crofter had least to do'.[59]

Highland landowners were in general agreement with Lovat about forestry. In March 1911, Brodie of Brodie underlined the need for forestry by pointing out the possibility of a 'timber famine'. Britain was spending £25 million a year on imports of rough timber, £8 million on wood pulp and £2 million on manufactured wooden articles, he told an audience in Nairn. He also said that the forestry being taught in universities was not reaching the working foresters.[60] The domestic demand for timber had expanded considerably during the previous century, with vast quantities being used as railway sleepers and pit-props. In January that year, Lovat, Sir Ronald Munro-Ferguson MP, Sir John Stirling-Maxwell, John Sutherland and Captain Archibald Stirling of Keir gave their views on forestry to a committee of the Development Commissioners, a government body formed in 1910 to look into rural development. Six months later, Lovat and Captain Stirling, who was to become Lovat's brother-in-law, kept up the pressure by co-writing a report for the RSAS on afforestation in the Highlands. The editor of the *Inverness Courier* welcomed this as 'of exceptional interest and importance' and had no doubt the government would give it 'intelligent and anxious consideration'.[61]

The scheme Lovat and Stirling put forward was for the afforestation of Glen Mor, the Great Glen, and to explain their ideas they focused on one section of 15,000 acres they called the Fort Augustus block.[62] They considered the whole glen to have 60,000 acres of immediately plantable ground, much of it suitable for smallholdings and already containing tracts of natural woodland and plantation. Men of the time when the deer forest was the standard form of sporting estate, they recognized that they had to minimize the risk to what they saw as 'one of the few channels through which money flows into the Highlands' and paid special attention to how such land could be developed to allow forestry and stalking to go on side by side. Sheep farming was less important in the Great Glen; even when this was yielding its best return, rents for sheep farms were always much less than what the land could command as a deer forest.

When it came to the forestry labour force, Lovat and Stirling believed that the 'crofter class' would be the best suited to forest work and wrote that the central forest authority should aim 'to prevent the rural dwellers from going into the towns rather than to attempt to transfer town-bred men to the country'. The initial capital outlay for this theoretical forestry was estimated to be £17,600, most of it going on houses for the forestry workers. The head forester would have an annual wage of £250; the 'under foresters' £75; the 'forest guards' £52 – they would be responsible for general care of the woods, vermin control, fire protection and so on; and the 'flying squad' of rabbit trappers 22s per week 'less price of rabbits sold'. No daily wage was suggested for the force of labourers other than noting a cost of £3 or more per acre; clearly they would be given work as the need for their efforts arose. Fencers would be expected to erect 4 miles each of deer and sheep fence per year. These details and much more on the management of the forest block were published in the *Transactions* of the RSAS.

A few days after the Lovat–Stirling report appeared, the results of the 1911 Census laid added stress on the potential of forestry for the future of the Highlands: a falling rate of population growth and continual emigration were combining to lower the population of the Highlands and islands, and now it had dropped almost to the level last recorded in 1821, nearly a century before. Forestry implemented under the aegis of a central authority, as advocated by Lovat and Stirling, was seen as one way to stop this haemorrhage. Later that summer, visitors to the Highland Show in Inverness could admire an exhibition on forestry and hear Sir John Stirling-Maxwell, president of the RSAS, call on government to develop long-overdue forestry. The

Left.
The men and horses of the woodcutting squad on Reelig estate, near Inverness, in 1920.

Right.
A woodcutting squad at Lentran, near Inverness, 1922.

on Newtonhill, Duncan
m Mackintosh, Bob Macrae,
ld, Bonnie Willie, Rod
Cutting Squad Reelig

Jock Forbes, Duncan McCulloch, Bonnie Willie,
Davie McDonald, James Morrison (Newtonhill
Rod Mann, Bob Macrae, Tom Mackintosh Wood
Cutting Squad Lentran Sawmill 1922

Development Commissioners announced an intention to invest in forestry and forestry education.[63] Sir John Stirling-Maxwell gave further impetus to the drive to launch state forestry and again emphasized its promise to employ a rural population with a paper entitled 'The place of forestry in the economic development of Scotland', published in 1913 after the author had delivered it as an address to the Aberdeen branch of the RSAS.[64]

The outbreak of the First World War in August 1914 diverted the minds of the nation but also drove home the importance of state forestry. The stalemate of trench warfare on the Western Front in the First World War stimulated a tremendous demand for timber. Someone reckoned that every soldier needed five trees to provide him with the timber needed for his military task.[65] For decades Britain had been relying on imported wood from the Baltic, Scandinavia, Canada, Newfoundland and other countries, and only around 4 per cent of the national demand was met from home sources. In 1913 about half of the country's need for timber was met by imports from Russia. The attacks on merchant shipping naturally made the situation critical, as domestic forests were hopelessly incapable of providing enough timber. The government set up a committee under the chairmanship of Sir Francis Acland, parliamentary secretary to the Board of Agriculture, to solve the problem. Among its members, inevitably in view of their previous interest and experience, were Sir John Stirling-Maxwell and Lovat. The latter, however, was a professional soldier as well as a laird, and commanded the Lovat Scouts, the unit he had raised as mounted reconnaissance troops for service in the Boer War. He was with the Scouts in the Middle East when he was asked to take over in February 1917 as director of the forestry department formed to deal with military timber supplies. After a hasty episode of reorganisation and travel, he established his headquarters at Le Touquet near Paris in April 1917 and took command of all forestry operations on the Western Front. Forests had been acquired in the Jura mountains and throughout France, and contingents of Canadian lumbermen shipped in to work in them. As Lovat took up his new post, the French forests were turning out 50,000 tons a month for the war effort, and under his command the foresters took this total to 300,000 tons a month by July 1918.

Before then, however, contingents of Canadian and Newfoundland lumberjacks had made an impact on the Highlands. Most of the timber cut down in Britain during the war came necessarily from private plantations, and to get it out the British government asked in early 1916 for experienced foresters from Canada. The first draft of the 224th Forestry Battalion landed on these shores in the following April; the 238th Battalion followed in September, and the two units were soon combined into the Canadian Forestry Corps (CFC), under the command of Brigadier General Alexander MacDougal. By the end of the war, their strength climbed to almost 31,500 men and they met 70 per cent of the Allied need for timber. The Canadians were deployed mostly throughout Western Europe from Belgium down to the Pyrenees, but they also moved into two districts in Scotland – in Stirling and in Inverness. The men of the Newfoundland Forestry Corps, almost 500 strong, came over in the spring and summer of 1917.

Affectionately nicknamed the 'sawdust fusiliers', they were generally popular in Scotland. 'Tales of the backwoods have achieved tremendous popularity and the life of the lumberman has been surrounded with a halo of romance,' noted an anonymous contributor to the *People's Journal*.[66] Of course, many of them were Scots emigrants or the descendants of emigrants, and they brought into the conservative country byways of the motherland a breath of the new world which only added to their allure. They also brought new techniques. Near Craigvinean in Perthshire, the Newfoundlanders erected a 3,000-foot-long chute to flush logs from the felling sites to the sawmill. In Morayshire, the Canadians set up a camp at Broadshaw on the boundary between the Cawdor and Moray estates, where the government had bought large stands of mature forest. The journalist who observed the newcomers in action clearly knew something of forestry but was a little sniffy about Canadian practice. 'As to the superiority of their methods I am not convinced,' he said at one point. The fellers worked with hand-operated chain saws, using a simpler method of 'stumping', cutting so as to guide the fall of the trunk, than Highland foresters did. Likewise the Canadians' hand axes

Overleaf.
At this sawmill near Dowally in the early 1900s a steam engine supplies the power.

Previous page.
Hauling timber at Calter
Bog, Dumbartonshire.
The date of the picture is
unknown but it was
taken probably in the
early 1900s.

were lighter in weight than the home axe but allowed the newcomers to work faster at snedding, trimming side branches from the fallen trees. They also cut a trunk to leave a high stump, something Highland foresters definitely found odd and wasteful. A steam winch called the 'iron horse', with an enormous boiler and a furnace burning waste timber, allowed the logs to be dragged out on wire cables up to 1,200 feet long. The boiler also powered another winch operating overhead ropes and pulleys that slung 18-foot logs to the loading bank. Teamsters with pairs of horses drove four-wheeled wagonloads of this timber to another bank where they were cross-cut into 9-foot lengths, and these were then loaded on bogies to trundle along rail lines to the sawmill. This, noted the visitor, was 'a huge erection fitted with a sixty horsepower engine', with a 50-foot chimney for the smoke, for driving the circular saws. It also drove a dynamo to supply the camp with electric light. Affleck Gray remembered how the CFC's first felling in Strathspey was along the Sluggan Pass from Kincardine to Loch Morlich. They stayed at Glenmore until their camp was ready and built a light railway to carry timber from the Pass down two and a half miles to a sawmill.

No. 120 Company of the CFC produced a souvenir booklet of their stay at Kinsteary, south-east of Nairn, as it happened less than 10 miles from the birthplace of the father of their CO, a Major Sinclair. The statistics record their output from the century-old Scots pine, larch and beech of the Urchany woods – 4,925,066 FBM (foot board measure, the total is equivalent to roughly 42,100 cubic metres of stacked lumber) between June 1917 and the end of the following April. (There is more about timber measurement below.) The sawmill's record was 32,814 feet of timber in one day, with 30,000 feet frequently being achieved. The men also took out almost 167,000 feet of pit-props.

The CFC stayed in the Highlands for several months after the end of the war. Felling in Sutherland did not cease until February 1919 and the last Canadians did not withdraw until the following June. Sir John Stirling-Maxwell hosted a cheerful farewell dinner for them in the Royal Hotel in Inverness on 15 May; this was reported in detail in the *Inverness Courier*, where one can read the jocular hints in the Canadians' speeches about Sir John being caught between two millstones, one being the pushy Canadians keen to get on with their job and the other some foot-dragging lairds.

Various methods have been used over the years to measure the amount of timber in an area of standing woodland. Nature rarely cooperates in providing

trees of standard sizes or dimensions but the value of an estate very often depended on the volume of growing timber on the land. Foresters spent considerable amounts of time in learning the techniques for the calculation of this all-important total and had ready-reckoner tables to help them. 'These were based really on calculations of the volume of a cone,' explained Norman Davidson. 'The tables referred to average breast-height diameters – usually 3 feet 9 inches from the ground – of trees and also the height of the tree. You could ascertain the volume of a stand of trees without a lot of difficulty, by measuring a portion of them with tapes and extrapolating to the stand. You had to fell a number, perhaps one per cent, to confirm the top heights and the general shapes of the trees. Depending on the locality, trees could be tall and

This timber bridge was constructed to allow the extraction of logs across the Whiteash gulley near Fochabers, 1916. Three carthorses are dragging loads across the bridge. It is thought that the work was done by the firm of A.G. and W.J. Riddoch.

thin, or short and fat. The procedures became well established over centuries. Tons were calculated but volume tended to be used much more as we had no simple way of actually weighing timber. We used a hypsometer to measure tree height but a quick way, if you could see the base and the tip, was to do an ocular measurement with a person standing beside it scaled up. Mensuration is a whole topic on its own. To gauge the volume of 1,000 acres of trees was simple but time-consuming if you wanted to be reasonably accurate, within 10 or 15 per cent, or even 20 per cent, of the actual figure. In days gone by 20 per cent accuracy was quite reasonable.'

The old measure of the Hoppus foot fell out of use. Named after an English surveyor Edward Hoppus in the early eighteenth century, this unit used length and girth measurements to calculate volume, confusingly recorded as so many Hoppus feet. Fifty Hoppus feet gave one Hoppus ton. This system was officially abandoned in 1971 and metric measures were adopted throughout forestry in this country. To complicate matters, Americans and Canadians had their own units, for example the foot board measure mentioned earlier and the cord, the latter used especially in relation to firewood where one cord represented a stacked pile, four feet by four feet by eight feet.

The war effort lent a new urgency to forestry. Newspaper editorials frequently repeated the lesson – there had to be state afforestation and, in Scotland, the obvious place for such an effort was the Highlands. There, thanks to the industry of the Canadians and others, much of the mature timber had been felled by the time of the armistice in November 1918. The Timber Supply Department of the government summed up the state of the country's woodland in 1918–19: there were only 950 square miles of woods over 20 years of age, 100 square miles had been cleared since 1914, another 110 cleared and not replanted, and the rest, totalling 620 square miles, was made up of young woods, coppice, scrub and woods either sold or already exploited.[67] The *People's Journal* warned returning Highland soldiers that 'Timber felling has so changed the aspect that in parts the country is almost unrecognizable. Tracts . . . which waved with pine and larch now present a bleak, desolate appearance . . . Rutted highways and broken fences, hutments and old plant speak of the way of the woodman'.[68] The war had denuded Perthshire of forest, complained the *Perthshire Constitutional and Journal* on 6 August 1919. The Highland Railway Company and the Great North of Scotland Railway Company proudly reported that they had carried 403,550 and 238,328 tons of timber respectively in 1918, many times the pre-war loads.[69] But there was also the often-repeated hope for the work forestry would bring. Some of this was already underway, for example, at Glencruitten, near Oban, the Women's Land Army planted thousands of nursery seedlings in 1919.[70]

'There is very little known about women working in the woods in World War I,' noted Affleck Gray in his account of the Women's Timber Corps in the Second World War, 'but there did exist in Scotland at least one small group which was sponsored by the Duke of Atholl and accommodated in the old inn at Inver, Dunkeld, which had been turned into flats. It was referred to as the Ladies' Forestry Corps.' Gray also recalled that three of the women were drowned in a bathing accident in the Tay near Dunkeld in 1918.

The recruitment of women into the labour force was a feature of wartime Britain. The Board of Agriculture sought government aid of £2000 to recruit 200 women in May 1917, a sum that included provision of £600 for clothing. Mary Sutherland must have been one of the few women graduates in forestry in the country in 1918 when she published an article in the *Transactions* of the RSAS called 'Women's labour in forestry'.[71] She pointed out how this was a recent innovation brought on by the shortage of workers but reminded her readers that women had commonly worked in the past in tree nurseries and planting and could still economically undertake much of the lighter work on estates. 'This would naturally make an increase in the wages bill,' she noted, 'as women's labour should be on the same basis as men's, i.e. equal pay for equal work – but this expenditure would be returned in the increased profits.' Sutherland then went on to detail investigations into the relative value of the work of the two genders. She found that women worked 'more rapidly and carefully' than men in light work 'requiring careful manipulation and patience', such as handling seedlings, but that male labour alone, or male and female workers cooperating in a team, were more economic when it came to heavier operations. At one point she inserted 'the girls [*sic*] proved that they could stand severe weather conditions without interruption to their work' and reached the general conclusion that 'the labour of women will be a valuable factor in the future of British forestry'.

CHAPTER 2
'THE CREATION OF A FOREST SENSE'
THE EARLY YEARS OF THE FORESTRY COMMISSION

In November 1918 the government set up an Interim Forest Authority to bring some order to forestry in Britain and prepare for afforestation by carrying out the task of drafting a new forestry bill and generally acting as midwife in the birth of its successor. Sir Francis Acland was appointed as chairman. A Liberal member of parliament, he had held several seats since his first election in 1906 and had been since 1915 parliamentary secretary to the Board of Agriculture and Fisheries. The other members of the new authority included Lord Clinton and Lord Lovat. Sir Francis and his colleagues had been recommending a single forest authority for Britain against the opposition of the Department of Agriculture, who felt that forestry should be part of its responsibility, and this became the government's own view. In July 1919 the bill to create a forestry commission was debated in the House of Lords; its only critic was Lord Haldane, who was sarcastic about a central authority, and his opinion was easily rebutted by the many who favoured the proposal, including Lord Clinton, Lord Lovat and the Duke of Sutherland. After collecting a few amendments the bill passed its third reading in the House of Commons on 12 August and came into force on 1 September. The new body was given a grant of £3.5 million to see it through its first ten years.

The chairmanship was offered to Sir Francis but he recommended that the post should go to Lord Lovat. Sir Francis did stay on as one of the seven commissioners. The others were Charles Forbes-Trefusis (Lord Clinton) who united in his name and his person a Scottish-Devon ancestry; Sir John Stirling-Maxwell; L. Forestier-Walker, a Welsh landowner from Monmouth; Thomas Brabazon Ponsonby, an Irish ex-soldier and high sheriff with experience of agriculture; the copiously named Walter Thomas James Scrymsoure-Steuart-Fothringham, heir to Grantully and Murthly in

Perthshire; and Roy Lister Robinson. Most of them shared the background common to holders of high office at the time – country estate, public school, Oxbridge – but Robinson was the odd man out: he had been born in Australia in 1883 and had come to Oxford as a Rhodes scholar, before entering the civil service as secretary to Acland's 1916 committee. Sir William Schlich, professor of forestry at Oxford and one of the foremost teachers of the subject in England at the time,[1] thought Robinson his most brilliant student, and, with Lovat or possibly more than him, he was to be the directing influence on the early decades of the Commission. After his death in 1952, he was to have his ashes scattered in the forest from which he had taken his title when he was ennobled in 1947 – Baron Robinson of Kielder Forest and Adelaide.

Assistant commissioners were placed in charge of the home nations. John Donald Sutherland was appointed as the first assistant commissioner with Scotland as his remit. Sutherland, who was to be knighted in 1935, had been born in Inverness in 1865; before the war, in which he served with distinction and reached the rank of colonel in the Royal Engineers, acting as assistant director of forestry in France under Lovat, he had shown a keen interest in rural development. Sutherland is commemorated by a grove of Douglas fir in the forest at Barcaldine. His staff back in 1920 comprised forest officers, foresters and other personnel ranked in a graded structure reminiscent of the military with its officers, NCOs and other ranks; forest officers were university graduates, with the others coming from forestry schools. John McEwen, a forester who was also politically a radical, described how at a conference in the mid 1920s in Fort Augustus the three attending commissioners stayed in one hotel while everyone else was placed in another where the divisional and district officers were assigned single rooms whereas the foresters had to share: 'Officers and foresters were kept away from each other at meals and had no contact whatever in the hotel. That was Lovat's army procedure.'[2] The military aspect of the grading was reinforced by the issuing of uniforms, a practice that was to persist into the early 1980s.

Scotland was divided into four areas each with its own divisional officer. The Glasgow division had only a brief life, leaving three regional headquarters in Aberdeen, Inverness and Edinburgh. John F. Annand, whose background included wide experience in the north of England and a period in Eberswalde, was appointed as divisional officer in Aberdeen. South-west Scotland came under the supervision of divisional officer John Murray, whose father had been head forester at Murthly. Frank Scott was placed in charge in the Inverness office with the north-west as his remit.

The first job facing these men was the acquisition of land, and Heldon Hill was an early forest under Annand. In the autumn of 1920, John McEwen was appointed the forester in charge and told to plant 500 acres in his first year. 'There was not a man nor a tool in the place, and others, e.g. in Inverness, had never been asked to plant more than 100 acres,' recalled McEwen,[3] 'I told Annand I thought it was impossible but the figure had been settled in headquarters in Edinburgh.' McEwen set to, organising work squads to clear the ground of branches left from wartime felling, engaging the 'the most noted poacher in Morayshire' to keep down the rabbits, and organising draining and planting. Unemployment meant easy recruitment of over 40 men, most of whom were assigned to planting once the preliminaries had been done to prepare the ground. McEwen set a target of 650 trees per man per day 'and I had no difficulty in attaining that figure'. The saplings came from all over the country – nursery work was in its infancy – but the bulk was Norway spruce from southern England, barely acceptable, thought McEwen, for the task to be performed.

McEwen brought varied experience to his new role. Born in Keltneyburn in Perthshire, the son of a shepherd-forester, he had had his first job in forestry on Cullen estate in 1905, where he had worked in a hedging squad for a year, tending all the hedges on the estate. 'It was a painful job . . . swinging the hedge bill for six or seven hours a day,' he wrote in his memoir. 'We had to be at the starting point in the shed at 7 o'clock in the morning, and were back at 6 o'clock at night, 6 days a week. We had no half day. The hours were shorter in the winter, but not much . . . I was paid 12/- a week for my first year . . . 14/- was the maximum for a working man at that time, and Cullen House paid better than some of the other landlords . . .' In 1907 he had moved to another estate, Altyre near Forres, where pay was better at 17 shillings a week, a woman cooked for the men in the bothy, and Saturday afternoons were free. 'We had to get in 1,000 plants a day, on rough ground, full of stones and roots, unploughed. We simply had to find a place where a plant could get in reasonably well, lift a piece of turf and stick it in, it didn't matter how.' McEwen went on a training course for gardeners and foresters at the Royal Botanic Gardens in Edinburgh in January 1908 and later with his brother set up as felling contractors, working on wind blow and other felling in various parts of the country for timber merchants. It was hard work for not very good piece rates of pay. 'One contract was for clear-felling medium-sized timber at a certain price per tree for clear-felling, snedding, cross-cutting and clearing certain sections of those trees over a certain diameter. We were fighting for 7d a tree, but all we could get was 6d. It was sheer slavery . . .' This work had been followed by a spell in timber processing and the sawmilling industry.

There was an irony in the fact that McEwen's first job had been on Cullen estate, for in no way was this young man the kind of compliant worker preferred there decades before by Christopher Young Michil. As many were to find out, John McEwen was well read, radical in his politics and relentless in trying to improve the conditions of the forestry workers, forming a trade union for them. His left-wing stance and his antipathy towards landowners did not prevent him from becoming president of the Royal Scottish Forestry Society in 1960. When he died in 1992 at the age of 104, his obituary in *Scottish Forestry* noted: '. . . a man of enormous principle and vigour whose work helped create a climate in which landlords were more sensitive to access and to the requests of the ecologically oriented non-governmental bodies, than they otherwise might have been. In many respects, a man ahead of his time.'[4]

As the people thrust aside the restrictions of wartime and counted the tremendous cost of the conflict, the social and economic problems of the countryside returned to the fore and now there was a new impatience and determination to deal with them. The nation owed a moral debt to those who had fought but, judging from the newspaper editorials, the government seemed to be dragging its feet in meeting its obligations as it wrestled with an old social order trying to retain its grip. Forestry was imperative – 'small-holdings and forest areas are the chief hope of the Highlands', said one opinion piece in the *People's Journal*, and it was time to forget the 'wail' of such as the Duke of Roxburgh about the effects of supertax on forest owners' incomes.[5] The lack of progress in creating smallholdings for ex-soldiers, despite the passage of the Land Settlement Bill in November 1919, was to lead to land raids in the next few years. The *Perthshire Advertiser* thought in October 1919 that there were two to three thousand ex-servicemen looking for holdings but a meeting on the subject in the Perth City Hall later that month was described as having a 'disappointing' attendance.[6] In this uneasy atmosphere much hope was placed in forestry and the efforts of the fledgling commission. 'Trees mean men,' wrote A. MacCallum Scott in 1924, 'The path to the recolonisation of the depopulated Highlands is a forest path.'[7]

Lord Lovat was especially keen on what forestry could do to revitalize the Highlands. After his tree-planting excursion to Monaughty Forest, he settled down to the steering of the Commission through its first years. Thanks to the press, the public were now forest-conscious as possibly never before. The *Inverness Courier* carried a wildly optimistic editorial at the end of January 1920 – the Commission had acquired up to 100,000 acres for planting in Britain, and half of the Commission's afforestation effort was to be in Scotland. Progress on the ground was slower than these media hopes suggested. In February 1921, Lovat told the Highland Reconstruction Association that the Commission planned to plant up to 6,000 acres in 1921, and up to 18,000 acres per year by 1924–25.[8]

In 1921 the Commission bought land near Peebles, land that became Glentress Forest, the first state-owned forest in the south of Scotland. Planting with larch, Douglas fir and pine continued during the following years. The 1,000-acre estate of Eshiel was divided into holdings against the opposition of sheep farmers. The first estate in the north to become Commission property was Borgie in Sutherland, gifted to the state by the Duke of Sutherland, and several others in the Highlands – Inchnacardoch, Portclair at Invermoriston, South Laggan, Achnashellach, Slattadale, Ratagan and Glenelg – were acquired between 1919 and 1922. Glenmore was also identified as a site for development and 17,500 acres were obtained there. Two forestry schools were established at Birnam and Beaufort, and nurseries in several centres, including Craibstone (near Aberdeen), Murthly and Hairmyres (in Lanarkshire). Rumours and exaggerated reports of the Commission's acquisitions abounded. The Duke of Buccleuch told fellow members of the RSAS in Edinburgh in February 1921 that it seemed the Commission had acquired 60,000 acres to date of which 50 per cent was plantable. Half the Commission's planting programme would indeed take place in Scotland, but so far only around 17,500 acres in Sutherland, 15,500 in Inverness-shire, 1,500 in Moray, 5,500 in Argyll and 3,000 in Roxburghshire had come into Commission hands, although the aim was to plant 125,000 acres in the next ten years. Only 550 acres had been planted so far in Aberdeenshire, Forfar, Inverness-shire and Sutherland. On one deer forest the Commission was trying to exterminate the deer. One history of the Commission says it acquired only 48,312 acres in its first year and planted only 1,728 (618 in Scotland) at a cost of just over £7 per acre.[9]

The delegates to the British Empire Forestry Conference in London in July 1920 visited Scotland to see the new Commission's activities for themselves; they called at Murthly, the Seafield lands in Strathspey, Lovat's own Beaufort and the Novar estate belonging to Hector Munro Ferguson, another keen supporter of forestry. The laird of Novar had his own apprentice scheme, with 15 young men in training at the time of the delegates' visit.

There was a shortage of skilled labour in the immediate post-war period, with head and under-foresters difficult to obtain, according to the annual report in 1919 of the Landowners Cooperative Forestry Society, although this was likely to ease as training programmes had an effect. In the meantime, in some parts of the country, German prisoners of war were allowed to work in the woods, but there were objections from those who found this a painful reminder of the losses of men in the war.[10]

The wages for foresters were set by the Central Agricultural Wages Committee: men over eighteen years of age with three years' experience were awarded 36s per week, and at the low end of the scale girls younger than sixteen received 12s per week.

The Beaufort school for foresters enrolled its first students in 1920, all ex-servicemen between 19 and 25 years of age, housed in a group of converted army huts on the Lovat estate beside the Beauly river, with a lecture room, museum, dining room, kitchen and sleeping accommodation. There were no fees; all meals, accommodation, books and tools were provided, and the students also received a weekly allowance of 10 shillings. This must have been an attractive package at the time. A native of Dingwall and a lecturer in forestry, James Fraser was appointed as the principal, and a Mr Leslie from Aberdeen taught trade skills. Beaufort's head forester was said to think the two-year course would enable diligent students 'to fill positions of trust in forests anywhere'.[11] For their practical training, Lord Lovat gave the students exclusive use of 1,000 acres of woodland.

The early 1920s was not a good time to start a venture that depended on government funding. The brief post-war economic boom had evaporated, and the country was faced with economic stringency, unemployment and recession. Industrial unrest in the minefields resulted in a dearth of coal and in rural areas this stimulated what one newspaper called 'amateur forestry', the felling of trees for fuel; one victim was an avenue of beeches planted in Glen Nevis to commemorate the victory at Waterloo.[12] Inevitably the government was forced to cut back on public spending and a committee chaired by Sir Eric Geddes reported early in 1922 on where cuts could be made. This programme was nicknamed the Geddes Axe. It struck a glancing blow at the fledgling Forestry Commission. The acquisition of land for afforestation ground to a halt and existing planting was curtailed; newspapers carried gloomy reports of staff being reduced by 50 per cent. The threat was greatest in the Highlands where the promise of state forestry had been so keenly anticipated and where private planting initiatives by landowners, although welcome for the work they brought, were less likely to be of great impact. In some crofting areas, the formation of holdings and forestry was already underway. At times and in places where crofters feared the loss of part of their grazings for trees afforestation had started without much popular support but the advantages of forestry had become apparent. This favourable attitude was now likely to be undermined. The social problems spread; in June 1922 there was a land raid in Stratherrick on Lovat's own property. For a while there was a likelihood that the Forestry Commission would be abolished altogether, but Lovat managed to persuade enough friends and allies at Westminster to come to his aid to blunt the threat and limit the damage to the Commission to a smaller budget. The Royal Scottish Arboricultural Society repeated the claims for forestry. The Commission survived, battered but determined. Its direct expenditure of £289,619 in 1921 fell to £219,870 in the following year, although funds offered for employment relief allowed it to continue its work and, in effect, increase the spending on afforestation.

In November 1923, Sir Murdoch Macdonald, the MP for Inverness-shire, asked the Chancellor of the Exchequer, Neville Chamberlain, about the prospects for forestry to relieve the economic problems of the Highlands. Chamberlain thought that the Commission's programme for the Highlands had not been adversely affected by financial restrictions and said the government proposed to make an extra £50,000 available in winter for unemployment relief. Some alarming headlines were, however, appearing in the papers at this time, including one in the *People's Journal* on 22 December that read 'Grim shadow of famine darkens Highland glen' and pictured crofters as 'heart-broken by the weeping of their hungry children'. The same issue noted that the Forestry Commission had been anonymously donated proceeds from one individual's wartime investment to employ extra men.[13]

In 1923 the Commission took over responsibility for the Crown Woods; the forest at Inverliever was the only Scottish member of this group of woodlands, all the others being in England and Wales, but it was a sign that the Commission had weathered the financial storm. That year, Lovat, Lochiel, the Duke of Atholl and other lairds constantly argued that forestry was a national necessity as well as a practical solution to the depopulation of the Highlands. The warnings were given a poignant underlining when the newspapers carried reports and photographs of hundreds of Hebrideans taking ship for Canada. Ian Macpherson, MP for Ross and Cromarty, saw forestry as one of a trio of industries ideally suited to the Highlands, along with agriculture and fisheries.

In July 1923 the first batch of graduates sallied out from the Beaufort school. In the context of an article reporting the hopes for forestry extension in the north, the *People's Journal* recorded 'The initial class . . . in 1920 commenced with 13, and 12 of these completed their course. Eleven certificates were given, and the number of these students now employed by the Commission is five.'[14] All the ten students who began their studies in 1921 completed their course; seven of them joined the Commission's labour force. As planting efforts continued through the 1920s, the school developed its own nursery. 'Over half a million baby trees go out to the various afforestation areas . . . every year, and these are planted and reared by the students themselves under the supervision of Mr Harry Watson,' wrote a visiting journalist in 1928.[15] Watson was James Fraser's successor as head of the school. Peter MacDonald later met some of the graduates from Beaufort and found them to be very practical men: 'They looked at the new forestry school graduates as not knowing very much but they were slightly envious of the botanical knowledge of the new men, although they had practical know-how. What was important then is not necessarily so now, for example the selection of species for the ground.'

In 1929 the school closed and its role was taken over by a new establishment for training foresters at Benmore, 7 miles north of Dunoon on the Cowal peninsula, on an 11,000-acre estate gifted to the Commission by Harry Younger of Edinburgh. Younger, of the wealthy brewing family, developed a passion for trees and had planted extensively around the country house built in the centre of what had once been a deer forest and hunting ground for the Campbell chiefs in Argyll. The more central location would allow expansion of the training programme and easier attendance by university forestry students. Don MacCaskill went there in 1938 and described the course as a mixture of practical and theoretical training. The college had its own patch of forest where the students honed their skills and 'the afternoons were for lectures'.

The Commission embarked in 1923 on its first planting programmes in Galloway, beside Loch Ken, the beginnings of what was to grow into the largest national forest in the country at over 200 square miles. At the time the Commission was employing about one man for every 200 acres – villages at

Glentrool and New Galloway expanded to accommodate them – and it was reckoned that their wages would bring in some ten times the amounts earned by the keepers and shepherds who had been displaced by the new industry.

In February 1926 Lovat was able to stand before the Royal Scottish Arboricultural Society and describe the achievement of the Forestry Commission: despite the Geddes Axe the Commission was on track to fulfil its original ten-year programme within the budget. The Commission had also undertaken the policy to establish forest workers' holdings, in an attempt to emulate their counterparts on the Continent and – very important in Lovat's own view – maintain a viable rural population in the Highlands. The aim was to set down five holdings on every 1,000 acres of plantable land and ensure 150 days of work in the winter for the men and their horses, additional work for women and children in summer, and time for the families to work their own holdings. The problem was that a large proportion of the land the Commission had acquired was not suitable for tree planting, something not fully realized before. Only parts of deer forests and sheep runs could be put under trees, and many had only tiny parcels of the arable land essential for the forest holding. Lovat thought the Commission had to look outside the deer forests to find the arable acres. Despite these problems, the Commission had 147 holdings 'finished or occupied'. Most of the 'settlers' were country people, but a former miner took a holding in Glen Nevis in 1928 and Sir John Stirling-Maxwell held the view that numbers of unemployed miners could be absorbed into forestry.

The brutal realities that geography and climate imposed on Scotland were also being fully appreciated. Some land was felt to be just not fitted for forestry. 'Practically the whole of Sutherland and Caithness falls under this category,' said Lovat, 'The Borgie area . . . is a case in point. We have ceased to regard this property as an economic forest, and are using it under a modified planting scheme as an experimental area.'[16] 'Great tracts' of the Hebrides and the west coast had also been ruled out for forestry because of climate, altitude or soil, and in other areas of the north and east distance from rail, sea or canal rendered forestry uneconomic. Vast stretches of land under peat, however, were felt to be suitable for planting and a considerable research effort was being put into how to turn moor into forest. The chemistry of peat was being scrutinized in the laboratory and, in the field, experiments on drainage, manuring and methods of planting were in progress. 'It is quite possible that in the future the deer forests and poorer sheep farms, where today only one sheep or deer is grazed to five or more acres, may play their part in afforestation work,' warned Lovat gloomily, 'but as long as we are unable to treat the more refractory types of peat . . . that time is not yet.'

The fact that the poor quality of the soil was forcing the Commission to acquire arable land was starting to cause serious complaint. Lovat attempted to quash the criticism: 'It is true . . . that a few acres have been taken here and there as nurseries (our total nursery area in Scotland is only 250 acres, of which much has been reclaimed land). Any arable land . . . will be either wholly devoted to small holdings or . . . re-let to agriculturists for arable farms. It is not and never will be part of our policy to plant arable land.' But, argued Lovat, this did not apply to hill-grazing, where forestry was a more valuable pursuit for the nation than rearing mutton and wool and employed more people. Only three sitting tenants had been dispossessed in Scotland by the Commission's acquisition of sheep farms, he claimed.

The need for land drew much adverse criticism down on the Commission from the farming community, who saw the government body steadily swallowing good acres and threatening their own livelihood. The farming

Overleaf.
A railway laid for the extraction of timber in Dulnain forest in Strathspey, date unknown but possibly before the First World War.

A tree being felled by a steam-driven saw, it is believed somewhere in Renfrewshire, in 1922.

The men at this sawmill near Aberfeldy in 1924 make good use of the name of a popular song. According to the notes with the picture most of them came from Huntly.

organisations complained loudly and Sir Murdoch Macdonald, the MP for Inverness-shire, agreed that the Commission's activity had to be monitored. The *People's Journal* reported in August 1928 how the Commission had acquired from Lord Abinger some 3,000 acres between the Fort William–Spean Bridge road and the Caledonian Canal that included the farm of Auchendaul whose arable ground was noted for 'heavy crops' and pedigree livestock.[17] 'Only a few miles away, the same fate has befallen the farm of Glen Nevis', wrote the unnamed journalist, who also mentioned Inchree near Onich and part of South Laggan as other farms that had suffered the same fate. 'The question naturally arises – where is it going to end?' How would the growing population of Fort William be kept in milk and produce if the arable land went for forestry? Much better, thought the journalist, to leave the husbandmen to the soil 'into which many families have dropped the sweat of honest toil' and concentrate on the forestry that Sir John Stirling-Maxwell had shown to be possible on the high moors.

At Corrour Sir John had been experimenting on tree cultivation with some success. Whereas his friend Lovat was more interested in the social and

Some of the pioneers of forestry, photographed at Corrour Lodge in 1932 or 1933. Back row (l to r) J. Maxwell Macdonald, district officer in south-west Scotland; A.M. Mackenzie; J.F. Macintyre, retired head forester, Newcastleton District; A.M. Fraser, Forest of Ae and later district officer at Culloden; A.G. Morris, forester at Ayr County Council Waterworks, Glen Alton. Front row (l to r) Simon Cameron, head forester, Corrour; Sir John Stirling-Maxwell; J.A.B. Macdonald, conservator South Scotland. The Lodge was destroyed by fire in 1942.

strategic aspects of forestry, Sir John's passion was cultivation, and he has been called one of our greatest foresters.[18] From the early 1890s up until the outbreak of the war he had carried on his experiments to coax conifers from the thrawn soils of Corrour, around 1,500 feet above sea level on the north side of Rannoch Moor. By using fertilizers and a Belgian turf technique for planting on boggy ground, he had pioneered ways to overcome the obstacles nature had thrown in his path. In 1928 members of the Royal Scottish Arboricultural Society came to see this for themselves. By car and rail, they travelled over the sweeping distances of Rannoch Moor where they could see the nature of the landscape, daunting glacial moraines alternating with peat hags and dark lochans lying over ancient schists and granites. Much of it was boggy peat but on the north side of Loch Treig steep slopes of gravelly moraine allowed rough pasture to sprout. The whole region was drenched in 65 inches of rain each year. Buried in the peat were the relic trunks of ancient pine forest, which showed in the bleached, preserved wood how slow-growing the ancient woods had been – 50 annual rings in an inch of cross-section. The first modern attempts to cultivate Scots pine failed utterly on the peat but showed some slow growth on the drier morainic mounds. Sir John and his head forester, Simon Cameron, persevered, trying new techniques and patiently waiting for the passing of each season to know whether or not their latest idea was a success or a failure. The Society had first visited the area in 1910, when the earliest plantations were already 17 years old, and those who now returned saw the difference. By combining the right planting methods with the use of ashes, sand and slag to ameliorate the acid peat the pioneers had induced the trees to grow – Scots pine first to provide shelter, and then underplanted silver fir, Sitka spruce, Norway spruce and other species.

The spreading acres of saplings brought a new problem to the fore – that of pest control. Red squirrels were labelled vermin and squirrel clubs formed to hunt down the marauders; it was reported in May 1929 that the Highland Squirrel Club had accounted in a few years for 2,429 squirrels on various estates.[19] The first step in planting new areas was often to fence it to keep out rabbits, deer and livestock. The menace of fire was also becoming significant, with 120 fires in the year to 30 September 1928, 57 of them caused by sparks from railway engines; the cost of this damage had been £2,874.[20] The foresters also had political gripes: Lord Novar amused visitors to his woods in September 1928 by telling how he had found, on his return from Australia after the war, that rabbits had 'dug themselves in' along with the rate and tax collectors. He also thought the removal of death duties would allow the 'private adventurer' to compete with the Forestry Commission but he was still in favour of state forestry.[21]

By 1929, the Commission had 26 separate forest areas in the northern counties – 12 in Inverness-shire, 11 in Ross-shire and 3 in Sutherland. Of this total, 8 had been deer forests, 4 deer and sheep runs, 7 sheep farms, and 7 scrub or felled woodland. Now 250 men in winter and 350 in summer were employed in planting. A White Paper on the Commission published in the summer of 1929 revealed that 49,998,000 trees were planted in the year ending 30 September 1928: 45 per cent Scots and Corsican pine, 24 per cent Norway and Sitka spruce, 12 per cent European and Japanese larch, and 9 per cent Douglas fir. The Commission had acquired 434,471 acres in the UK, of which 275,913 were plantable (159,570 in England and Wales and 116,343 in

Scotland). In the period 1919–28 the cost per acre on the area planted had been £8 9s 9d in England and Wales, and £9 14s 10d in Scotland.

On their excursion in 1928, the RSAS went on from Corrour to visit Ardverikie, Gordon Castle on the lower Spey and the Culbin Sands. Here the problem was not peat but sand, acres of it in the form of unstable dunes shifting in the winds off the Moray Firth. A description of the area in the seventeenth century said 'nothing is met except fields covered with bent [marram] and low juniper, and countless herds of seals'.[22] Tradition had it that farms had been buried in the past by the onslaught of the encompassing sand and in 1694 dunes driven before a storm had overwhelmed the village of Culbin in a single night. The Commission had acquired in 1922 over 5,000 acres of this unstable coastal habitat, adjacent to the Binsness estate, whose owner had already had marked success in growing pine. About 2,000 acres of forest had been felled here during the war and had now been replanted, and experiments were showing the way to extend the planted area.[23] Clumps of marram grass were planted to bind the sand, with additional measures – thatching the ground with pine branches, and installing windscreens of brushwood – used where the scouring of the wind was more intense. With the fixing of the sand it was found that the trees grew well, with Corsican pine promising a better crop than the indigenous Scots pine. Similar use of trees to anchor shifting dunes was deployed in Luce bay in Wigtownshire.

As the first decade of its life drew to a close the Commission could give itself a little pat on the back. Though plenty remained to be tackled, much had been achieved and in the public mind forestry had become an accepted, generally welcome part of rural life. In passing, we should note that in June 1925 the *Forres, Elgin and Nairn Gazette* listed among lands purchased by the Commission '. . . a property known as Miltonduff . . . It lies into the larger forest scheme of Monaughty, the planting of which has been almost finished – 1,500 acres altogether. Besides Monaughty, at Pluscarden, large plantations are also being formed . . .'[24] The heathery ridge was planted with Scots pine and larch, with much Douglas fir and Sitka spruce going in on the steep slopes down to Pluscarden, some of which became large trees before they were felled in the late 1960s and early 1970s. Early trials with various tree species from north-west America were carried out in plots near Miltonduff. Lovat's first tree soon became lost among a host of neighbours.

In 1930, in an article in the *Scottish Forestry Journal*, Sir John Stirling-Maxwell, who had taken over as chairman of the Forestry Commission after

Lovat's resignation in 1927, looked back over the first ten years of the Commission and saw the decade as one of progress: 'Post-war conditions have been so unfavourable to private planting that our woodlands – smaller even before the war than those of any other European country – would by this time have been almost negligible. The Act has, I think, been justified by the bare fact that it has already resulted in the planting of nearly 150,000 acres by the State, and of about 50,000 acres by corporations and private planters assisted by grants.' He reckoned another 50,000 acres had been planted privately without assistance, making 250,000 acres in all, an impressive area but still nowhere near replacing the estimated 450,000 acres felled between 1914 and 1920. Sir John looked forward to the next decade, when another 333,000 acres were to be planted and no fewer than 3,000 families were to be settled in the forests. The success to date was attributable, he said, to the exceptional abilities of Lord Lovat, Lord Clinton and their colleagues, and to the work of societies such as the RSAS 'which kept the lamp alight during the dismal years before the war'.[25]

Sir John felt that private landowners, despite their economic straits and the break-up of large estates, could find planting to be one of their soundest investments. It should not all be left to the government. 'The only antidote I can see at the moment is the creation of what in some other countries is called a forest sense,' he told the members of the RSAS. He also emphasized that devoting land to silviculture increased employment. 'In one case, in the Loch Ness area,' he said, '78 to 80 men are now employed where only 5 men were employed before the advent of the Commission.' There were about 200 forest holdings in Scotland, and around 600 in England, but the Commission had the ambition to establish more at the rate of 350 per year for the next five years and 250 per year for five after that. Sir John thought this settlement policy had to be flexible – 'What succeeds in Norfolk may fail in Argyllshire' – but the Commission was keen to continue with the ideal of providing a viable rural population intimately connected with forestry.

Eight forestry holdings were set up near Fort Augustus at Auchterawe on the lower-lying part of the Inchnacardoch estate. Four of the holdings were quite small but the other four ran to between 10 and 15 acres each, roughly the standard size of a Highland croft and big enough to support a few cows and provide tillage for the usual crops of hay, oats, turnips and potatoes, and for a vegetable garden. The area of common grazing was limited, only enough for the wintering of hoggs – yearling sheep. One of the crofts was taken by Alexander Macdonald who had served in the Cameron Highlanders in the war and had had experience of forestry work before he had enlisted. Immediately after the war he found a job with a timber merchant in Inverness but when the opportunity to move back to the country arose, he was glad to take it and he and his family moved into their holding in the early 1920s. The youngest member of the family, Allan, was born there in 1940.

Among the recruits to the forestry labour force in the inter-war years were the men who were evacuated from St Kilda in 1930 on the fishery cruiser *Harebell*. No one missed the irony of this – people who had never seen a tree now starting a new life among them – but it was ready work for willing backs and hands with skills for which there was no demand in Argyllshire where many settled. Some began by cutting trees to make stabs and clearing land for planting at Savary near Lochaline and were reported to be quite pleased with their weekly wage of 38 shillings.[26]

There were only a few dissenting voices to the view that forestry was an instrument for rural regeneration. Macleod of Macleod told the Inverness Gaelic Society in April 1930 that looking to forestry as a means of solving Highland economic problems was nonsensical and ignorant, but he had no alternative to suggest. In general throughout the country numbers of men were finding employment in planting, at a time when unemployment was a common experience. The Ministry of Labour built a number of camps where unemployed men could be taught to plant trees and let loose on newly acquired Commission property. One such was erected on a hillside at Cairnbaan overlooking the Crinan Canal, a complex of over a dozen huts. Many of the residents came from the depression-hit industrial belt, shipbuilders, miners and fitters now laying aside their old trades for the spade and the planting bag. Many did not find the rural solitude to their liking but most stuck to it and played their part in the afforestation of Knapdale. There were over 1,300 men without work in Inverness in September 1932 and when the Commission began a planting programme on nearby Craig Phadrig, Ord Hill and Gala Hill many more applicants came forward in search of a job than could be taken on. Depression was worse in the peripheral districts; 65 per cent of the population of Stornoway was reported as unemployed in 1932 but here there was no forestry to offer even part-time work.[27]

Although it had little to offer as relief in an economic depression, by the end of the 1930s the Commission had started experimental plots on Lewis, at Balallan and Valtos, where Sitka, mountain pine and Japanese larch were reported to be showing considerable promise.[28] In 1931 Marcel Hardy had explored the possibility of planting on the Long Island and overcoming the twin problems of wind and peat, the latter often a yard deep over hard rock.[29] Hardy noted that there already existed a handful of plantations, pockets of battered trees that even on the sheltered east side of the island, in the grounds of the castle at Stornoway, were struggling upward at half the rate of growth of the same species in England. Conifers could thrive but, apart from birch and alder, it was no country for broadleaves. Hardy suggested minimizing the drainage problems by planting on east-facing, steep slopes, for example, in the east of Harris, which had the additional attraction of long sea lochs where timber could be floated out. He gave his readers detailed instructions on how to prepare drainage – horizontal head and foot collector drains, 2 feet deep and ramparted with turf, with a row of drains some 15 feet apart, running up and down the slope, again 2 feet deep and 18 inches wide. This was a recipe for much spade labour. In the patch so prepared, holes or 'pots' were dug to receive the saplings, and the turf from each one laid carefully on the upper, windward side to provide some shelter for the tree. Finally runlets were slashed on the down-slope side of the pot to encourage the rain to flow safely away.

Hardy emphasized the importance of shelter-belts of trees and gave as an example one he had seen in Caithness, in his words 'another wind-swept, treeless and mournful area'. Some people in Caithness, in fact, felt that the Commission was ignoring their northern county and began to reassure any who would listen that trees could grow there, witness the regular uncovering of bog pine. At least it was home to the best shelter-belt Hardy confessed he had ever seen. Much interest was being paid to the experiments on peat. The enveloping, soggy blanket that the members of the RSAS went to inspect at the Lon Mor near Fort Augustus in July 1930 was over 15 feet deep in places and it was proving very expensive to convert it to a condition where saplings stood a chance of survival. It became an open-air laboratory for experiments for over 50 years. The indefatigable Sir John Stirling-Maxwell had devised a method at Corrour that he called 'turf nurseries'. It involved turning over divots of peat in long lines, planting two-year-old seedlings on the upturned peat and encouraging their growth with helpings of manure and sand. Sir John said it was 'economical and successful', although it must have required many hours of spade work.[30] It held promise, though, for all the parts of Scotland where peat moors dominated the landscape.

The RSAS made another excursion to the hostile environment of Culbin in 1935. Over 3,000 acres of the dunes in the Commission's ownership were planted by this time, with Scots pine on the dry heath and Corsican pine on

the old shingle beaches. Severe sand storms had caused problems but the thatching of bare sand had allowed planting on even the blow-outs. The Commission's efforts to turn Culbin into a forest continued until the end of the 1940s, a 20-year struggle that underlined the long-term approach needed by those who grow trees. By 1949 some of the young pine, the thinnings, were being felled and shipped out to Fife for use as pit-props.

There were signs of a growing resurgence of a distinct way of life associated with forestry. The Highland woodsmen began to gather to hold annual competitions of skill, attracting entrants from all over the country. The writer who described the tree-felling contest at Dalcross in May 1931 turned eloquent for the readers of the *People's Journal*:[31] '. . . it has something about it that baffles description. Possibly it is the primeval instinct in man – the influence of the woods. Gleaming axes swish up and down in the feeble light that trickles through the branches; the rhythmic motion of the tree fellers, intent on proving their skill; tearing saws which bite their way through tough trunks with a steady monotone; and the crash of the mighty monarchs of the woods as they fall . . .' The judges awarded points according to eight criteria:

This picture was taken at the tree felling competition at Dalcross near Inverness, May 1931. The two men in short-sleeves were among the competitors and, according to the caption, it took about four minutes to fell the tree at their feet.

laying in, i.e. how the tree was cut at the foot; cutting as low to the ground as possible; axemanship; making the tree fall between markers four yards apart; a clean break with no damage to the trunk; snedding; the cooperation of the pair of fellers; and the time taken to do the job. A pair of skilled woodsmen could ply their axes and saw to bring down and sned a pine, 2 feet in diameter, in less than five minutes. Such competitions continue on a regular basis to this day, except that now the events include such novelties as chainsaw carving.

Highland forestry lost two of its prominent pioneers. Lord Lovat's brother-in-law, Archibald Stirling of Keir, died in 1931. Lord Lovat himself died in February 1933 and, as the cortege with Clydesdale horses bore his remains along snow-covered roads to the small church at Eskadale in Strathglass, his contribution to forestry was remembered far and wide. The *Inverness Courier* carried a fulsome obituary, referring to his frank and open character, and the respect in which he was held by all classes. His entry in the *Dictionary of National Biography* refers to his lack of pomposity, sense of humour and critical mind. In the memoirs of John McEwen, a man of strong left-wing views, the first chairman of the Commission is remembered as 'a powerful, domineering character' who made the lives of his senior foresters 'a pretty miserable one in the early days'. Lovat could have been all these things, depending on the viewpoint of the observer. Perhaps a forceful personality was needed to counteract what McEwen himself saw as the private landowners' attempt to keep a grip on the Commission. The author of Lovat's obituary in the *Scottish Forestry Journal* had no doubt: 'By rare good luck the leading part fell to him at the decisive moment, and we owe it to him, more than to any other, that among all the projects of reconstruction planned in the last year of the Great War the forestry scheme alone is found, fifteen years later, maturing on the lines originally laid down, and still enjoying the confidence of the country and support of all parties in Parliament.'[32]

Sir Francis Lindley claims in his biography of Lord Lovat that his subject was the first to realize the value of the Sitka spruce as a commercial tree. This would seem to be difficult to prove with certainty as Sitka has been grown in Britain since David Douglas brought it back from the north-west Pacific coast in 1831. Its potential for fast growth in wet conditions must have become apparent quite soon. This property and its long fibres, important for constructional strength and paper making, have made it the ideal species for commercial timber production in the Highlands, able to 'put on volume' at the rate of 14 cubic metres per hectare per year and reach maturity in 40 to 60 years. On the same scale, a hectare of oak can often manage only 4 cubic metres of growth in one year and take a century and a half to achieve its maximum potential. Sitka also produces good timber, and it is unfortunate that its habit of growing long branches that droop around the trunk to impose Stygian darkness underneath it, suppressing the ground cover, has earned it the reputation of forming dense, alien blocks on the landscape, a subject to which we shall return. In fact, only young Sitka, and young Sitka left unthinned, tends to form forbidding blocks. Lodgepole pine is another conifer of American origin that is widely planted in the north. 'It is a very variable species,' said John Keenleyside, 'The rate of growth depends upon its origin, where it came from. If it's from high up in the mountains, it's low, possibly as low as yield class 4. That means it's capable of growing at four cubic metres per hectare per annum. When you come down to coastal lodgepole pine the growth rate will certainly be more than 12 and maybe as much as 16. The tall coastal stuff grows rapidly but its form is poor and its stability is poor in windy situations. You can end up with a mass of stuff difficult to harvest and difficult to use, and in some places timber was converted to wood chips on site. The original aim of the Forestry Commission was to produce a resource of timber. If Sitka is growing, it's producing 12 cubic metres per year and with modern methods from improved material and seed-orchard seed you can get a yield class in the high twenties.'

On a map drawn in 1911 for afforestation around Fort Augustus and in Glenmoriston, Lovat showed a preference for larch. A much more attractive tree en masse than the forbidding Sitka, the larch in today's forests is often a hybrid between the European and Japanese species, more vigorous and hardier than either parent. This is our only deciduous conifer and the shedding of the needles in the autumn, after they turn a fine cinnamon brown, reveals plainly where this tree has been planted on a hillside, often in strips between and around blocks of Sitka or other conifers which, of course, remain dark green all year round. Many other introduced species of conifer are used in forestry. The Corsican pine has the ability to withstand drought, hence its use at Culbin, whereas the lodgepole pine can cope much better with the cold, wet conditions in the north-west. The Norway spruce produces timber similar to but at a slower rate than the Sitka. The Douglas fir needs good ground but grows rapidly in the right conditions to produce some very impressive specimens, including the tallest trees in the country. The grand fir, another import from America and a good timber tree, has the ability to thrive in shade and is often underplanted with birch or larch. The native conifer, the Scots pine, is also favoured in commercial forestry. Adaptable and tough, the species is found native in a belt stretching right across the Eurasian continent. Although exposed specimens in tough conditions can display highly contorted shapes, in sheltered forest the reddish trunks grow straight and tall, allowing plenty of light to reach the ground, encouraging often a rich, mossy cover of vegetation with a high biodiversity.

By the late 1930s the activities of the Forestry Commission and forestry in general had become established as a normal part of rural life. When the Highland Development League, formed in 1936, published a new five-year plan in 1939 the focus was on agriculture but the place of forestry was also recognized. Writing in the *Scottish Forestry Journal*, J. Hunter Blair acknowledged that 'At no time has interest in forestry on the part of politicians, the press, and the general public been greater than it is at present' but, he continued, 'It is a curious paradox that this greatly increased recognition of the value of forestry generally should have been accompanied by a simultaneous decline in the extent and importance of afforestation on private estates.' He blamed this state of affairs partly on a lack among landowners of the confidence to make long-term investment in forestry and partly on a lack of trained estate foresters. 'If the management of privately-owned forests is to rest upon a rational scientific basis, some means must be found of bringing it under the direction of fully trained forest officers,' he argued, before going on to suggest a scheme whereby a cooperative society could be developed as a kind of parallel Commission to act as an intermediary between state and landlord to encourage long-term planning and supervision of private forestry.[33] Before much could be achieved, however, another world war intervened.

Shortly after the outbreak of the Second World War, overseas woodsmen returned to Scotland. First to arrive, a week before Christmas 1939, were a contingent of 300 from Newfoundland, in response to an urgent appeal from the British government. Any repetition of the forming of a military forestry corps as in the First World War was abandoned to save time, and the Newfoundland Overseas Forestry Unit (NOFU), with men from Labrador as well as from Newfoundland, remained a civilian body of volunteers.[34] The terms of engagement were for six months at $2 a day or $12 a week, the minimum wage at the time at home. Four more contingents followed to arrive early in 1940, bringing over 2,145 men with such dispatch that the Forestry Commission was not quite ready to receive them. Base camps were set up in Kielder, Kershopefoot, Glenfinart, Glenbranter and Lochgilphead whence the men moved to smaller camps, some 70 in all, with sawmills, across the country. Three camps of Newfoundlanders were established in Inverness-shire and Ross-shire by February 1940. When the original six-month contract expired, many elected to renew for the duration once it was impressed on them that forestry was a more valuable contribution to the war effort than their joining the armed services. More Newfoundlanders came over in 1940 and 1941.

The signs of their presence remain. For example, the site of the NOFU camp is still visible in the Strathmashie forest between Newtonmore and Loch Laggan in the form of concrete platforms and pieces of ironwork overgrown with moss; aerial photography has revealed the large piles of sawdust where the sawpits were. In 1941, a journalist visited one of the camps and wrote about these 'Jack o' Tars' who came from such evocative sounding places as Trinity Bay and Spaniards Bay, and who built their own log cabins and wore distinctive red-and-black windbreakers and logan boots.[35] The men with whom the journalist spent time were probably French-speaking, as it seems

Members of the Newfoundland Overseas Forestry Unit around a camp fire, 1940.

Felling with a crosscut saw somewhere in the Highlands, February 1941.

The badge of the Newfoundland Overseas Forestry Unit.

that only they were known as Jack o' Tars. They received £12 a month, half of which had to be sent home, for their 8-hour days, except when they felt able to take on a contract and cut in 12-hour shifts for £20 to £30 per month. 'They cut through a tree as an ordinary man would cut a piece of cheese,' enthused the anonymous journalist, 'All bone and muscle they are and two of them working as a team can fell 120 trees per day.' The preferred implement was the salmon-bellied cut saw nicknamed the 'mankiller' because, as one jack said, 'it tears the life out of us'. The writer loved their rough humour and noted that they had given a stray collie they had adopted the name of 'Hitler'.

Donald Stewart, a schoolboy in Golspie, remembered them as 'a fine lot of hardworking fellows' when they arrived to occupy the camp vacated by the British Honduran foresters in 1943, of which more below. One of them was Colin Ploughman, from George's Brook in Trinity Bay, aged 19 when he volunteered. His brother had gone in the first contingent, and an uncle had served in the First World War forestry unit. 'Previous experience wasn't necessary,' he said, although in his case he had been in the woods 'since I was big enough to walk'. Colin crossed the Atlantic in the Royal Mail steamer *Antonio* in eight days and travelled on by train to Carrbridge, where he and his colleagues were to spend the next three months. 'The first meal we got was hard-boiled eggs,' he recalled, a puzzling introduction to the exigencies of wartime rationing. Carrbridge was followed by periods at Fairburn, Novar and Golspie. Many volunteered to join the Home Guard when it was formed in 1940 and comprised the entire 3rd Inverness Battalion in September 1942, turning one of their felling sites at Carrbridge into a rifle range and assault

One of the Newfoundland Overseas Forestry Unit camps in the Highlands, early spring 1943.

course and, in an exercise, 'capturing' Inverness. As a tractor driver and horseman, Colin's horse moved with him. In Golspie he met his future wife; like many Newfoundlanders who married Scotswomen, the couple returned to Halifax in 1946 but unlike many, the Ploughmans came back to Golspie in 1947 to escape unemployment.

Newfoundland was still a separate polity from Canada at the time – confederation took place in 1949 – and Canadians, from Ontario, Quebec, British Columbia and the other provinces, did not arrive here until February 1941, in the form of Company 1 of the Canadian Forestry Corps. They had a similar impact to that of their predecessors in 1916: Donald Fraser, the son of a gamekeeper on the Lude estate near Blair Atholl, saw them in their camp at Black Island – 'young uniformed swashbuckling big spenders, they created a wave of interest in the village, particularly with the young ladies.' The press also noted their performance skills in local concerts and that 'Even the wonted quiet of the Highland Sabbath is being broken by the sound of their axes'.[36] Bryce Reynard remembered hearing how they drove trucks to extract logs across a frozen Loch Morlich in the Cairngorms. Unsurprisingly, there were several weddings between the lumbermen and local women. In all, 30 companies of the CFC laboured in Scotland between 1941 and 1945, from Berriedale in Caithness – about as far north as there was timber to fell

Sergeant Marchand of the Canadian Forestry Corps sharpens a saw, at Forres in 1944.

– to Blair Atholl and Brechin, and the only camp south of the Highland Line, at Southesk. Headquarters was established in the heart of their area of operations, at Phoineas House, near Beauly, with several district headquarters and over 30 camps spread across the country. Most bore the name of the locality, but one near Balnagown Castle in Easter Ross was called Wilderness Camp and two south of Kiltarlity were known as Lovat No. 1 and Lovat No. 2. Some of the men were veterans of the wood-felling operations of the First World War, including the commanding officer Brigadier General J.B. White; he was succeeded in 1943 by Colonel C.E.F. Jones. Usually the work camps were ready to receive them, but one contingent arrived at South Cawdor to find unfinished facilities set down amid a devastated patch of ground where it was 'impossible to take five steps in any direction without falling over boulders into mud or over stumps'.[37]

Don West was a schoolboy in Eskadale beside the Beauly River when the Canadians arrived. 'They developed a sand quarry just across the road from our school, for making roads through the forest, and they came every day about nine o'clock in the morning and the first thing they did was light a fire,' he recalled. 'This was a great attraction for us, we would be with them lighting

Two men of the Canadian Forestry Corps in May 1941.

the fire. A big fire – this was in the winter to keep themselves warm. The first bulldozer I ever saw was theirs. We were entranced by the power of this thing, as we used horses and had no machines like that. It would push mountains of gravel and stones, heap it up, and the men would come with shovels to load the lorry. They would put in about four barrowfuls and off the lorry would go. The bulldozer driver, his name was Dave Webber. There was another Canadian chap called Jacko, an out-and-out gentleman. His forebears came

Three men of the Canadian Forestry Corps shifting logs, May 1943.

from the Highlands. We used the word "aye" a lot and I remember him saying "I just love to hear that word aye". Every day he came to the school – one day it would be chocolate, next day it would be chewing gum, next day another kind of sweeties. One time he came he gave the bigger boys a lovely knife.'

'Their equipment was way beyond ours. They had a janker – two wheels and a frame – and the winch on the end of the bulldozer would lift the tree by one end, the root end, and off the janker would go, dragging the log along. One of the saws in the their sawmill had "Henry Diston, Philadelphia, USA" written around the blade. You could take the teeth out and put new ones in – we'd never seen this before. The canthook, that was another thing they had.' The canthook was a pole with a large curved piece on the end, fitted with a spring lever, that the lumbermen used to grip and roll logs.

Opposite.
A high rigger atop a spar tree, the Canadian Forestry Corps, 1941.

A stack of timber cut by the Canadian Forestry Corps, 1941.

Two men of the Canadian Forestry Corps begin to fell a tree in the Forres area in February 1944.

'The Canadians were well liked. They would come round the houses with firewood, and they only wanted five or ten bob for the load, and they would get their tea and blether, and off they would go, happy as larry. At Christmas time they would send a lorry all round the strath, a canvas cover on it, and pick up all the children and take us to their camp for a lovely treat. Everybody got a toy of some sort, a lot of them made by themselves. There would be about forty children, maybe fifty, here in Eskadale. The school had three teachers. A lot of children were boarded out here during the war.'

Timbermen came from other parts of the world. Forestry units from Australian engineer regiments worked in the Lockerbie area, at Hoddam

Castle among other places, but it seems that they and units from New Zealand were most active in England. Norwegian troops carried out forestry operations in Glenmore. The first contingent of volunteers from British Honduras (now Belize) arrived in October 1941. They landed at Greenock only to find that their camp, at Traprain Law in the Lothians, was not ready, forcing them to stay at first in tents. The contrast between the tropical forests of their experience and the wet, cold conifers they found in Scotland could hardly have been greater. On the other hand, the spruce and pine to be felled seemed like broomsticks when compared to the mahogany to which they were accustomed. More contingents of the British Honduran Forestry Unit, to make up a final strength of around 900 men, came and were posted to camps at Golspie, Leckmelm, Kirkpatrick, Duns, Kinlochewe and Achnashellach, with their headquarters at Strathpeffer. According to Amos Ford, who wrote an

account of the BHFU,[38] they found the camps spartan and isolated but settled in as best they could, improvising some kind of social life. In Golspie, they found the pubs congenial: 'The people were grand,' noted Theo Lambey, 'the village was like our own.' 'The locals treated the Hondurans no different from anyone else,' said Donald Stewart. Often, though, the Hondurans, despite their being volunteers willing to accept the local pay rate of £3 a week, felt they were not well treated. The authorities were suspicious of them – although it seems ordinary people were far more welcoming, and there were some marriages. When some were seconded to Australian units, they were angered to be given menial work in sawmills, humiliating for men who back home felled giant tropical hardwoods. The combination of discrimination, bad weather, poor support and illness

Grave of the British Honduras forester at Golspie. Caption to come.

affected the men's work, leading them to be accused of low productivity. Some returned to British Honduras at the end of 1943, while others remained and settled in Britain.

Efforts were made to deploy 'home' labour in the forests as part of the war effort and forestry was made a reserved occupation. Bill Sutherland left school in Edinburgh in 1938 and spent a year at the Newcastleton Forest in Liddesdale in the west of Roxburghshire as his introduction to his chosen career. Here he worked in a squad of men at weeding, draining and planting, camping in tents in the summer and staying in the so-called foresters' loft in winter. Newcastleton was known as Forest Number 5 in the Commission's records, making it the fifth oldest acquisition, and it incorporated the pre-existing Dykecroft Wood. After his year's experience, Bill studied on the four-year forestry course at Edinburgh University. He was posted to the Dumfries area upon graduation to work on mainly planting. 'The top year we did 3,000 acres,' he remembered, nearly all Sitka with some larch and Norway spruce. There were also brashing experiments with handsaws and then with motor-driven mechanical saws. Horse extraction of thinnings soon gave way to the use of the sulky. The work force at Eskdalemuir included 20 conscientious objectors and some Newfoundlanders.

The Forestry Commission brought in a scheme to employ 17- to 19-year olds in the Cowal area, giving them a six-month course at Benmore before unleashing them into the woods, for a wage of 6 shillings a week. Schoolboys could do useful work – 900 were recruited across Britain in 1941 – but many found it hard and too low-paid to be attractive; for example, a drop in volunteering was noted in Inverness in June 1941. Charles Scott was one of the youngsters who stuck it out: 'I worked in the summers in the 1940s cleaning out the forests in Langholm in Dumfries-shire. The Dukes of Buccleuch had been into forestry in a big way, away back in the eighteenth century. They put up a lot of new forest with Douglas fir, you name it, and they were very progressive from that point of view. At the time we were getting these summer jobs; they had started planting Sitka and so on, commercial forest. We cleaned out the bracken, any plants taller than a young sapling, going up and down the rows between the trees. The trees were only two feet high. We had a sickle. The pay was not a lot, probably about 3s 6d a week. About four of us from the school for six to eight weeks. That was my introduction to forestry.'

A group of teachers at Trinity Academy in Edinburgh organised an expedition to work in forests each summer during the War. Alastair Kirk, aged 14, went along with some two dozen of his schoolmates in 1940 to a camp near Aberfeldy, where they slept in tents. 'We were paid 2s 6d a week, with all food and accommodation laid on,' said Alastair, 'That was for four weeks but by the time we went home the ten shillings we had earned would have been spent.' The school janitor came along as the cook, and the boys had the weekends off when they could explore the countryside on bicycles or on foot. Alastair's group returned to the woods in 1941, to Drumoak on Deeside, where they were given accommodation in the outhouses of the local school and palliasses to sleep on; in 1942 to Brechin; and in 1943 to Banchory. On the last occasion, they found themselves camping near a unit of the Canadian Forestry Corps, an encounter that gave them their first taste of Coca Cola. The work included

Schoolboys from Glasgow working in forestry in the Highlands, July 1940.

various activities – collecting brushwood to be burnt, peeling bark off felled logs, sawing trunks into 6-foot lengths, and snedding.

Hugh Morris found work on the high slopes of Craig Phadrig above his native Inverness when he left school in 1943: 'It was just ordinary forest jobs, felling, extraction, general maintenance. There were four of us in the squad, and we had cross-cut saws and bushman saws, which had just come in. It was very hard, physical work and we didn't dare leave a high stump.' The trees were up to 10 inches in diameter, mostly at the first thinning stage, but Hugh and his colleagues laboured from 8 a.m. until 5 p.m. with a half-hour for lunch at midday, bringing down 40 to 50 trees a day. The foreman, who had a croft nearby, had two Clydesdale horses that he hired to the Forestry Commission. 'I was the horseman for a while,' said Hugh. The wage was 30 shillings a week, fairly average at the time.

Opposite.
Lumberjills of the WTC
ready for work.

Once again, many women worked in the forests, in the Women's Timber Corps. This initiative came from Sir Samuel Strang Steel, a Borders laird who was the honorary secretary of the Royal Scottish Forestry Society for 25 years from 1930, and a commissioner from 1932 until 1949. Part of the Land Army, the WTC had a strength of 1,200 by the end of August 1942. Inevitably they attracted the nickname of 'lumberjills'. After a five-week training course at Park House, east of Banchory, or Shandford Lodge near Brechin, they went to work in the forests. The Ministry of Supply laid down their pay scale: the maximum, for those over the age of 19, was £2 6s for a 48-hour week, from which a considerable proportion was deducted for boarding in the work camp, resulting in a net 18 shillings a week in the pocket. The so-called 'leader girls' and camp supervisors were later given rises of 5 and 10 shillings a week. Leave was limited to public holidays and one week in the year.

Members of the
Women's Timber Corps,
probably trainees from
Sharnford Lodge, on
parade in Brechin in
c. 1943.

The women were not available to private estates at first, but efforts to get them were soon successful. The first squad went to the Dean estate near Kilmarnock where a forester called James Tait saw them at work and recorded

Snedding Scots pine with a 6-lb axe.

his impressions for the Scottish Forestry Journal: 'I espied thinning opera-tions in progress [while chancing to pass]. On closer investigations [*sic*] they appeared to be carried out by a squad of women without even the supervision of a man . . . The squad consisted of a forewoman and six assistants . . . From what I saw of the work done and how these girls set about their duties I am afraid I have to admit that men will have to take care . . . The woman in charge could lay-in a tree with the best of men and it is some considerable time since I have seen anyone so knacky in the handling of an axe'.[39] Tait found out that before the War four of them had been shop assistants, one a 'shoe operative', one a lithographer, and the forewoman a children's nurse.

Agnes Morrison was a hairdresser in Inverness in 1940 when she volun-teered to be a timber measurer with the WTC. A native of Lewiston beside Drumnadrochit, she was no stranger to working in the countryside. 'It was quite a good life,' she said in a newspaper interview in 2008,[40] 'The summer was fun. The winter wasn't so good but we felt that we were doing something anyway. It wasn't really hard work physically. We had gadgets for measuring the heights of the trees, but then you had to work out the volume, which wasn't always easy.'

Opposite.
Felling Scots pine.

Former lumberjills attend the unveiling of Malcolm Robertson's statue, which was commissioned by Forestry Commission Scotland in memory of the Women's Timber Corps, at Aberfoyle in October 2007.

After the war women were to continue in the forests, causing many of their male counterparts to reassess what they had considered to be men's work, but at the time it was a novelty and the wartime press naturally found the women ideal material for upbeat features. Take, for example, these almost-erotic lines from the *People's Journal* on 27 November 1943: 'Perched on the leather seat of a big caterpillar tractor another girl of the Timber Corps rough rides through a Scottish gulley [*sic*]. A log, measuring four feet through, is perilously tangled and precariously held on the steep slopes of the gulley. The tractor slams up, swift steel cable clinches the timber, and the log rips and roars down to the bottom.'

In Angus, John McEwen worked in a camp where both sexes were represented. He deigned to say nothing about the social side of this arrangement but was clearly impressed by the contribution made by the women: 'Practically all were from the towns with very little experience of country life of any kind, and none whatever of work in the woods. The great majority were decent, hard-working young women but, in my opinion, the work was far beyond their physical capacity . . . I do not recall one who would stand up indefinitely to the hard strain of what is, even to men, extremely arduous work. Many went at it very hard for a time but wear and tear ultimately got them down.'[41]

By late 1945, a war weariness settled on the lumberjills as on everyone else. In the Highlands they began to call themselves the 'forgotten women' and joined in the airing of grievances by the land girls, their 'sisters' who worked in agriculture.[42] They complained of long days, strenuous work, neglect and boredom: 'We don't mind the work if we were better treated' wrote one from somewhere in the Highlands, 'For instance, we have no entertainment in the camp, so we asked permission to run dances in our recreation hut. This was granted on condition that the dance finished at 1 am. We pleaded to be allowed to run it for another hour, but we were refused. We are 36 miles from the nearest picture hall . . . the nearest town is almost 100 miles away.' They protested that they were not highly paid – the basic wage of £5 per fortnight fell to £2 once tax, hut rent, food bills, insurance and uniform costs were deducted – and some could only go home twice a year with a free warrant. 'Sometimes we wonder if we have committed some crime or other and landed in prison overnight.'

One woman, identified only as MW from Kirkcaldy, poured her feelings into a poem called 'The Tale of a Forestry Lass', a lamentation that ends with:

> Now just another minute, please, for I would have you know
> When you are in the country and admire the trees that grow,
> Don't credit Mother Nature with all beauty that you see,
> Remember she depends somewhat on toilers such as me![43]

Much of the Forestry Commission woodland was not ready for felling by 1939. Although the decision was taken in 1940 to clear-fell trees between 20 and 35 years of age for use in the mining industry, a large proportion of the state forest was still too young, leaving private woodlands to bear the burden of supplying national needs. The Commission, however, continued with planting. In May 1941 some 700 acres on the Black Isle were being put under trees, but there was a problem finding accommodation for the workers who included many women. From his felling on the braes at Craig Phadrig, Hugh Morris moved to the Black Isle in late 1944 and worked there for the next two years in the forest nursery and at planting. He found himself staying in a bothy, the youngest of about ten residents. 'It was gey rough,' he recalled, 'not very sophisticated'. The food was not bad – 'we survived anyway' – and Hugh did a spell at the stove when the regular cook went on holiday: 'I was quite a good cook, my mother had taught me. Nobody fell ill anyway'. This meant rising at six o'clock to have the breakfast ready an hour later – just porridge, tea and toast, from supplies brought from Cromarty on a bicycle. There was a dance once a week for entertainment, and Hugh was able to cycle home to Inverness at the weekend.

Even early in the war, some foresters, such as Sir John Stirling-Maxwell, were thinking ahead to the day when hostilities would cease. The conveners of the various local authorities in the Highlands included afforestation as one of the measures for future development they listed in a memo sent to John Colville, the Scottish secretary of state, in April 1940.[44] In 1941 the Forestry Commission was considering the establishment of a new national forest park,

Scotland's second, in the Glen Affric–Glen Moriston area, where they already owned some 12,000 acres. Sutherland County Council debated reconstruction in October 1942 and called for more afforestation, and Sir Murdoch Macdonald, MP for Inverness-shire, was also of this view. In 1943 speculation was reported to be rife in the Highlands that over half a million acres were to be taken over for afforestation.[45] The Commission published its post-war forest policy in 1943, with its main proposal the ambition to expand the national forest to 5 million acres over the next 50 years.

By the end of the war, Caithness was reminding the rest of the country that trees could grow there. The Committee on Land Settlement, mindful of the land raids after the First World War, warned against a large back-to-the-land movement but called for a planned, coordinated programme of development that included afforestation along with hydro-electric schemes, fishing and other industries. A new Forestry Act became law in June 1945, reconstituting the Commission and establishing national committees in each of the home nations. In Scotland, Tom Johnston, who had been appointed secretary of state in 1941 by Winston Churchill, became in 1945 chairman of the Scottish National Forestry Commissioners in a reorganisation of the Commission. He visited Inverness early in May 1946 for the first meeting of the Highland Regional Advisory Committee on Afforestation and spoke to the press afterwards with an upbeat message that was typical of his driving spirit. 'We expect that in Scotland, directly and indirectly, at the end of fifty years we will have employed on afforestation about 125,000 workers; it will employ directly and indirectly more than agriculture or coal-mining; it will, in fact, be our largest source of employment.'[46] The people had to become afforestation-minded, he said. A dedication scheme was launched for private landowners, encouraging them to set land aside for planting by offering state grants of £7 10s per acre with further maintenance grants. The Committee hoped that this would persuade large landowners to come aboard. Johnston mentioned the large tracts of Rannoch Moor and Flanders Moss as areas that could be planted to produce valuable timber and constitute another step in the economic regeneration of the countryside, one activity alongside the exploitation of hydro-electric power and tourism. More immediately, the Scottish Home Department's programme for Highland development, issued in 1950, foresaw annual planting of 60,000 acres for the next four years, employing up to 3,000 workers, and costing around £5.5 million. 'Fundamentally the Highland problem is to encourage people to live in the Highlands,' it stated and, in this, forestry had a crucial role.[47]

CHAPTER 3
'AFFORESTATION HAS INJECTED NEW LIFE INTO THE COMMUNITY'
EXPANSION AFTER THE SECOND WORLD WAR

In August 1946, James Fraser, Conservator of Forests in the Inverness area, gave a talk in the Highland capital on forestry and its contribution to the war effort. Home-grown timber had met 75 per cent of the nation's demand, a vast improvement on the situation in 1914–18, but by the end of the war fully 66 per cent of the country's stock had been felled.[1] The extensive felling during the two world wars created what Lord Glentanar saw as 'a new and potentially dangerous situation', as he put it in a newspaper article in

A portable sawmill, the *Forresia* made by Wm Reid (Forres) Ltd., in action in Forres in the early 1950s.

February 1946.[2] There was time, however, to meet the problem with 'long-term measures faithfully carried out over a period of years'. Lord Glentanar distinguished between planting to produce timber as quickly as possible and reafforestation for 'embracing a biological purpose – to allow forests to function most effectively in their relation to the soil, the waters, the atmosphere, animal and man'. This was forestry as conservation, where biology, economics and aesthetics marched along together, and preserving the beauty of the countryside was paramount. The Commission's priority, however, was once again planting.

Between 1947 and 1949 a census was completed of all the woodland in Britain over 5 acres in extent. John McEwen worked on this in the counties of Angus, Kincardine, Perth, Fife and Kinross and wrote in his memoirs that he was not at all impressed by everything he found, considering the management on some private estates to be careless and wasting the land. The results of the census revealed the extent of woodland of different types throughout Scotland. The following table, from information published in *Scottish Forestry* in 1954, summarises the surveyors' findings:[3]

Species	*Acreage*
Scots pine	208,920
Sitka spruce	85,182
Norway spruce	70,785
European larch	48,069
Japanese larch	18,034
Corsican pine	3,494
Lodgepole pine	1,949
Beech	47,043
Oak	45,103
Sycamore	7,668
Birch	6,578
Elm	6,064
Ash	4,947

The total British acreage of forest was 3,640,000, of which 37 per cent grew in Scotland. It sounded a lot but it was in fact only 6.5 per cent of the total land area, the smallest woodland cover of any country in Europe, with the understandable exception of Iceland. An extensive planting programme began in 1946, with a target in Scotland of 36,000 acres per year by 1970.

In July 1947 the delegates to the British Empire Forestry Conference visited the Highlands. James Fraser showed them around the Black Isle where 10,651 acres had been designated for growing trees, and they also made trips to Culbin to view the new forest springing up on the dunes, and to see the ancient glades of Darnaway. Sir Roy Lister Robinson, the chairman of the Forestry Commission, said that he saw forestry as one of the three things that would revive the Highlands – the other two were hydro-electricity and tourism – but a great deal had to be done and that would require many more people. The Commission took over a redundant RAF facility at Blackstand on the Black Isle, creating a new village community, turning the hangar into a workshop and the landing strips into tree nurseries. Kenneth MacKenzie arrived there in 1949 and found 'up to one hundred workers attending to the needs of several million young trees'.[4] The Commission also benefited from the large number of war-surplus vehicles now available – lorries, vans, motor bikes, cars and bulldozers included. In Kenneth's own words, 'The Forestry Commission . . . which had operated for years with little more in the way of power assistance than bicycles and horses, had now . . . been mechanized.' Kenneth drove these lorries until they wore out in the 1950s. A government White Paper on Highland development in July 1950 set out a plan to plant over 750,000 acres of forest with eventual employment for 7,500 people; 60,000 acres were to be planted in the first four years, and this would be augmented to the tune of another 50,000 acres by the planting efforts of private landowners under a forest dedication scheme.[5] To encourage private planting the Commission also offered grants, during 1947–48 at the rate of £10 per acre.

In the words of one newspaper article, the Commission was seeking not only to grow trees but 'to repopulate the countryside with hardy, contented families'.[6] Apart from any other consideration, it needed labour in often remote countryside. Estates had cottages for their work force, but the Commission was thinking on a grander scale – the forestry village. The first one appeared at Ae, deep in the long, narrow valley of the Water of Ae, 10 miles north of Dumfries. The forest of Ae had grown up on eight hill farms brought into the Commission's ownership in stages from 1926. These extended to over 10,600 acres, roughly 17 square miles, of hilly ground with a high rainfall. By 1948 some 3,370 acres had been planted and the target was to afforest 8,000 acres, with the balance comprising the best land, set aside for agriculture, and the poorest, too high and too impoverished to be good for anything but rough pasture.[7] The forests provided work for 20 men and, although at times 50 German prisoners of war were drafted in, the demand for workers was growing. The proposal at Ae was to build around 80 houses, along with shops, a school, a church, a village hall and an inn. 'The combination of the forest and the village dependent on it is something new in Scotland,' wrote an anonymous contributor, possibly a Commission spokesman, to *Scottish Forestry*, 'and it represents an important stage in the process of resettling men and women in the country . . . Those who live in the village will feel that they are not isolated; they will be members of an active community, with all the advantages of living in a community, and without the disadvantages of urban life.' The first houses were completed in October 1949 and, although the original plan was never fully achieved, the village grew quickly in its early years around the farm of Glencorse. A village hall, initially an old army hut donated by the Commission, was put up in 1952 and a shop, to replace the mobile grocery vans, opened in 1956. Celebrations for the coronation of Queen Elizabeth in 1953 gave rise to an annual gala and, in

Ae village

Blocks of conifers of different ages spread over the hills of the Ae Forest.

The forestry village at Glenbranter.

1958, the village acquired a school. The roll in its first year stood at 49 pupils, a number that rose to its peak in the 1970s.

Thereafter the Commission put up houses for its labour force in many small villages and hamlets, at times in isolated pockets, and acquired existing properties. In the Loch Ard forest in the Trossachs, employees numbered 120 in 1951, including 23 women and 11 youngsters. When the Commission had started in the area in 1929 it had set out 15 holdings for staff, but the demand for labour rose when thinning of the plantings began in 1945 and new groups of houses were built at Braeval and Kinlochard. A small forestry village sprang up at Keip near Strathyre. There were also settlements at Aros on Mull, in Glentrool, at Wauchope and in several places in Argyllshire. Since the Commission had taken over the Inverliever forest, adjoining estates had been added, and by 1951 it had claims of being the biggest man-made forest in Britain. The majority of the men in the local villages worked in forestry at this time, and some of them had forest holdings. Don MacCaskill began his forestry career as a young forester in Ardgartan, 'a remote area which at the time [the late 1940s] was not easily reached by road and not greatly influenced by affairs outside the confines of its small village and huge forest . . . a community of true country folk, widely diverse in character and personal circumstance, self-reliant to an inventive degree and truly compassionate when a neighbour was in trouble. Nearly all of them, both men and women, worked in the forest . . . they taught me much and it was one of the best years of my life.'

The forestry villages of Achnamara, Dalavich and Eredine were finished in 1952. In the early 1950s, when Donald Fraser's father found work as a ranger with the Commission, with the job of reducing the roe deer numbers in Glen Errochty, the Fraser family was given a house 5 miles up the glen from Struan, 'one of six recently built semi-detached forestry cottages'. The most remote village was possibly the tiny settlement of Polloch, on the shore of Loch Shiel at the mouth of Glen Hurich. The Commission put up 12 timber houses here and the county council opened a school in one of the few stone cottages in the area. At first there was no shop and the only link with the outside world was by boat and train to Fort William; a road was later laid through to Strontian.

Between 1946 and 1958, the number of new houses constructed by the Commission reached a total of 574. Twice that number was built for forestry workers by local authorities or other bodies, so that by 1955 the Commission had at its disposal around 1,400.[8] This was a notable achievement, especially in the immediate post-war years when there were serious shortages, a problem solved by the importing of wooden houses from Sweden and Finland, which gave the forestry village a distinctive look. The two-storey, semi-detached dwellings themselves had an attractive appearance, but the wind and rain prevalent on the west coast presented maintenance problems not encountered in Baltic forests that had to be solved with shingling, recoating and window renewal. The cost of importing kit houses also became significant, and after a few years the Commission reverted to more traditional, indigenous designs. It also bought existing houses and provided bothies, hostels and caravans or found digs for unmarried staff and workers. At times these places fell far short of being comfortably in line with modern standards.

Some of the new residents loved the forestry villages; others could not wait to leave. It was often hardest on the women, many of whom moved to the countryside from urban streets and found the isolation and the lack of facilities too hard to bear. George Ivison, who liked Achnamara when he moved there and stayed on, recalled a new arrival in 1952 leaving on the same day he came.[9] The communities that fared best were probably those that were planned as extensions to existing villages. The forestry village is reminiscent of another optimistic post-war scheme, this time in the heads of the men in charge of the North of Scotland Hydro-Electric Board who saw their power stations leading to repopulation of the glens. Significantly it was Tom Johnston, the driving force behind the hydro-electricity schemes, who in April 1947 inaugurated the construction of Ae.

At Cannich the forestry workers moved in as the workers on the hydro-electric scheme moved out. Margaret West worked there in the Commission office as a clerkess and secretary in 1953. 'I was not the only woman,' she remembered, 'The wife of the chef who worked on the "ranch" also worked in the cookhouse. My office was just beside the "ranch" – that's what we called a big cedar building with dormitories, dining room and sitting room, originally put up for the engineers at the hydro scheme. The Commission took it over along with quite a few cedar houses where the married engineers had lived. The head forester at the time was Andrew Mackay and the foreman was Willie Cameron, who became forester, and then there were gangers. Jack Massie was the district officer. It was a big operation. I did the workers' pay. There were a lot of mobile workers, mobile squads who came in to do the forestry roads, they came and went, and I had to deal with their wages as well, and I did typing for the district officers.'

'It was busy. The forest was opening up at that time. They were purchasing pieces of land from the estates and taking over big parts of the hill ground. The roads had to be made and there was all the planting and what not. I think there must have been forty or fifty men there at one time, maybe more when the road squad came in. They had a better rate of pay than the ordinary forest worker, and they got subsistence if they came from outwith Cannich. The forestry workers did draining and planting but also had to attend to the existing forests, as at Guisachan, where they did brashing and so on.

'It was a very happy community. I was supposed to work nine to five but I

Opposite.
The Moffat hills from
Craigieburn.

lived at Erchless and it was difficult getting transport to Cannich. I cycled in the summer and in winter depended on lifts which sometimes used to land me a bit late but nobody said anything. A Mr Ward was the head of the road squad and he used to share my office. He was an ex-regimental sergeant major and looked like Joe Stalin with a big handlebar moustache. The workers included a Polish chap and one or two Englishmen. One chap he came as a worker but he was very interested in forestry and went on then to the college and became a forester. I think there were two or three who did that.'

In time the forestry villages came to resemble other country villages, as the Forestry Commission sold off properties and residents lived by occupations other than the forest. Lovat's dream enjoyed only a brief reality but it was hailed while it lasted. The author of the description of the Mull parish of Torosay for the Third Statistical Account of Argyllshire noted that in the early 1950s 'afforestation . . . has injected new life into the community', with the families of 30 Commission employees forming the core of a new settlement at Salen. People in the neighbouring parish of Kilfinichen and Kilvickeon were hoping that the Commission would extend operations to their area and reproduce 'successes achieved' in other parts of the island. Likewise, in Ardnamurchan, forestry was seen as 'an unquestionable boon' without which 'this district would be very badly off'.[10]

A dissenting view, but one written with the benefit of hindsight, was expressed by John N. Watson in *The Argyll Book* published in 2002. In his opinion, the purchase of farmland by the Commission at several times its market value had reduced the number of farms and therefore the population in the mid-Argyll–Cowal area from 120 in 1965 to fewer than 50 in 1990. Afforestation had meant that 'contractors carry timber as their main business . . . schools close, traveling shops stop coming, churches empty, buses are no longer viable, and the community spirit is undermined.' It is unfair to ascribe this decline in rural life to forestry and the counter-argument, that forestry delayed a decline already happening, can easily be made. Writing about Glentrool in 1966, G. Forrest showed how forestry there had reversed population decline in the parish and had caused a modest increase in the number of inhabitants between 1931 and 1961.[11]

The director of forestry in Scotland, Henry Beresford-Peirse, climbed on to a weathered stump in Glenmore on 8 June 1948, pointed to the Cairngorms with his crook and said that this land was now open for everyone to enjoy.[12] The Forestry Commission had acquired the estate in the 1920s but now had given part of it to the Central Council for Physical Education: this was the

A transformed
landscape of field and
forest, on Ballogie
estate near Aboyne.

beginning of the development of Aviemore and the surrounding land for
sports and outdoor recreation. The opening of Glenmore Forest Park was a
key moment in the recognition of forests as a social amenity. The 200 square
miles of Glentrool Forest Park had already opened in 1945, and Queen
Elizabeth Park in the Trossachs was to follow in 1953 and the Border park
linking to forests in the north of England. In 1946, the secretary of state also
set up a committee led by Sir J. Douglas Ramsay and Professor James Ritchie
to advise on national parks in Scotland: it recommended forming a
commission to develop a national parks system.

The lingering dispute between farmers and foresters continued around
the same focus that had existed in the 1920s – the loss of arable acres to timber
production. From many farmers, however, there was little protest, as Bill
Sutherland recalled, 'The reason for so much land being offered for planting
to the Forestry Commission in the 1940s was the severe infestation of sheep
tick, especially in the Border country. The tick-carried disease had disastrous
effects on sheep flocks so that farmers were forced to sell.' In January 1950
Captain Ian Campbell of Balblair, Invershin, a former president of the
National Farmers Union in Scotland, complained of the loss of farmland in
a public talk[13] and returned to the theme several times, for example saying at
an NFU dinner in Inverness in November 1952: '[The Forestry Commission
is] one of the greatest godsends we have had during our lifetime but the light
has now gone red and I think it is high time that a halt was called to the activities of a blind policy of acquiring land for afforestation purposes'.[14] The

Commission was in fact now committed to a policy of multiple land use – for example, Glentrool Forest Park had five forests spread over its 200 square miles on the land the Commission had been buying since 1921, but some 40 per cent of the area was still being used for sheep farming – but the farming sector was not wholly mollified. On Skye there was 'much controversy' over the afforestation of the hill pastures,[15] but the Advisory Panel on the Highlands and Islands, a forerunner of the Highlands and Islands Development Board, argued in 1964, in its report *Land Use in the Highlands and Islands*, in support of forestry, saying that agriculture had no 'inherent and special right in the land' and recognizing that it was at times very difficult to judge between the opposing claims of the Commission and agriculturists on the best use for an area.[16] A procedure had been in place for some time whereby the Commission referred its planting proposals to the Department of Agriculture and Fisheries for the nod to proceed – in the event of disagreement, the decision was passed upstairs to government ministers. In the Commission's defence, the Panel pointed out that it had hardly ever used its compulsory purchase powers, instead obtaining its properties by agreement. In the Highlands, by the end of September 1963, the Commission was giving full-time employment to 1,779 people, including nearly 200 crofters, and was a boon in remoter communities. The Panel concluded that the Highlands 'could stand a forestry programme substantially larger than the present one'.

Bill Sutherland continued to work in the forests in the south-west, around Lockerbie and Moffat, until he was transferred in 1958 to be district officer at Benmore, looking after the forests in the south of the Cowal peninsula and on Arran. In 1966 he moved to the Commission headquarters in Edinburgh, to the building known as the 'black banana' in St John's Road, where he worked as the acquisitions officer for the south of Scotland, including the southern Highlands. The job entailed keeping a close eye on the property market and assessing possible purchases for their suitability for forestry. When an estate or parcel of land came up for sale, Bill set off to inspect it, walking over the ground with a 6-inch Ordnance Survey map, examining the soil characteristics, the vegetation, the exposure to the elements and other factors likely to determine the yield class of any future plantations. 'Bracken was a sign of good land, better than grass,' he said, 'and birch was also a good sign, although at first it was got rid off and only later kept as nurse trees. Heather was a sign of acid, dry ground and it would keep trees in check. Norway spruce was bad for checking. I've seen them fifty years old and only three feet high, like bonsai.' Farmers, in Bill's experience, saw the sale of land to the Commission as a ready source of money, and many acquisitions were first proposed by their existing owners.

The post-war period was a time of high hopes and plans of utopian ambition. For a long time naturalists and ecologists had been examining the Highland environment and unravelling how it had been degraded by human activity, including forest destruction, the expansion of sheep farming in the nineteenth century and the later dedication of vast areas to field sports. Frank Fraser Darling was foremost in this field and explored the theme in detail in his classic work *The Highlands and Islands*, written with J. Morton Boyd. In his *West Highland Survey*, published in 1955, Fraser Darling wrote of the sharp increase in population in the Great Glen, up by over 8 per cent between 1931 and 1951 as a result partly of the extension of forestry, and also noted the increase in Cowal and South Knapdale again 'attributable to forestry.' The ecologist looked to forestry and collaboration between the Commission and the Nature Conservancy Council to rehabilitate the 'wet desert' of moorland prevalent across much of the Highlands.

In the summer of 1948, the secretary of state announced a scheme from the Highland Advisory Panel for an experiment in restoring a more mixed use of the land: around Lairg and Ardgay it was proposed to integrate 22,500 acres of forest with cattle and sheep rearing, the planting of shelter belts and a reorganization of crofting.[17] This ambitious plan involved 250,000 acres and by its very nature was a long-term experiment. By 1963, the Commission had planted 12,500 acres and was employing 66 men; 16 Commission houses had been built or modernized. In the same period of around 15 years, the numbers of beef cattle had risen considerably and the sheep population only slightly.

The training of foresters and forestry workers was a priority, especially when the demobilization of the armed forces was under way. Short courses began in 1946 at Darnaway and at Bowhill on the Duke of Buccleuch's lands for men with a few years' experience, offering applicants board and lodging and a wage of 15s a week. The Royal Scottish Forestry Society phased out its own diploma in favour of a new national qualification in forestry. Two-year courses were instituted at the Commission's own forestry training schools – there were two in Scotland at this time: at Benmore, which the Commission had acquired in 1929, and at Glentress near Peebles, which opened in 1947 – leading to a forester's certificate, although students could also leave after one year with a foreman's certificate. The first batch of trainees, 146 mainly

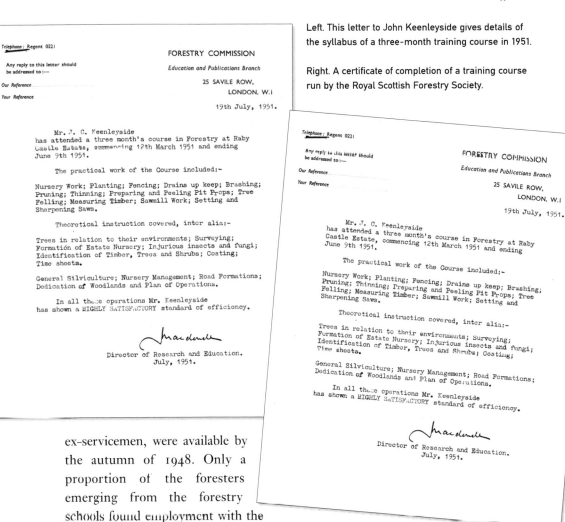

Left. This letter to John Keenleyside gives details of the syllabus of a three-month training course in 1951.

Right. A certificate of completion of a training course run by the Royal Scottish Forestry Society.

ex-servicemen, were available by the autumn of 1948. Only a proportion of the foresters emerging from the forestry schools found employment with the Commission; others went to work for private employers or found posts overseas. The number graduating from the forestry schools fell to around 110 in Scotland in 1949, a drop in recruitment that was ascribed to the low wages on offer in what was acknowledged as a healthy, interesting outdoor occupation. It was admitted that in the past, on private estates, 'wages have been miserable and accommodation in many instances . . . primitive . . . usually . . . a bothy'.[18] Commenting on the standard weekly wage of £4 in 1947, Douglas Brand from Aboyne wrote '[This was] as far as I know, the lowest wage paid to any worker in any industry which is of national importance'.[19] Brand had quite a lot more to say – forestry was losing 'first-rate, intelligent, diligent workers' because of the low wage. He thought the 'tied

Left.
The huts of the
Glentress forestry
school.

Right.
Benmore, the forestry
school near Dunoon.

cottage' system in operation on many estates, especially housing with dry lavatories, outside water and no bathroom, was also a deterrent but, more than this, the shortage of rural housing of any kind was keeping married couples away from estate employment. The basic wage was set at 90s a week ($£4$ 10s) from October 1947. But was it enough? At the end-of-course prize-giving at Glentress in 1951, Henry Beresford-Peirse appealed for more young men to choose forestry, as the number of applicants had fallen over the last two years and was 'now well below the danger level'.[20] Conditions for entry to the forestry training schools were eased in 1952 and those with only six months' experience were now accepted.

Finlay Macrae started his forestry career on Skye at the end of 1947 after service in the RAF during the war. That experience had eradicated his original ambition to do medicine: 'I felt that a course lasting six years would be a bit much and I wanted some sort of occupation where I would have an element of freedom, and that was why I chose forestry.' Before he could begin the forestry degree course at Aberdeen University, where he was to graduate in 1951, he spent a year gaining hands-on experience in Glenbrittle, one of the first Commission acquisitions to be planted on Skye. 'The forest hadn't grown to the stage where you were thinning it or anything like that,' he recalled. 'But we did all the draining and the planting and all that sort of thing, establishment work. Heavy work. We built roads with the pick and shovel. With the planting then, we had no ploughing. That was really before the day that ploughing became the right thing to do, or what was thought the right thing to do. What we did was draining and turfing, taking the turfs out and laying them at the right spacing and planting the trees in them. The trees were between six inches and one foot high. Sitka mostly. The move was on for Sitka then, Sitka was the in thing at that time. Really we were planting production forests, fast growing. Sitka was extremely fast growing, though I can't say it's one of my favourite trees. The main part of the forest was pretty well planted by the time I left there. Forestry on Skye started in 1932, mostly on the Loch Eynort side from Glenbrittle. That was good land, black, and they planted the Sitka directly into that and it grew like corn. Glenbrittle was peatier, certainly where we were planting, just on the foothills of the Cuillins. It was a big valley going right down to the sea.'

At the other end of the country, while coping with the tedium of dead-heading rhododendrons in the garden of Ford and Etal estate near Berwick-on-Tweed, the teenage John Keenleyside nursed a long-standing ambition to be a forester, an ambition planted in his mind at the age of ten when Bill Sutherland, then involved in the planting at Ae, had taken him to see forestry on Eskdalemuir: 'He showed me all this new fencing, new planting and

The last class of forestry students to complete their course at Benmore, in June 1965. Norman Davidson is on the right in the front row.

drainage work, and at the end of that day I said, right, I want to be a forester, and I never wavered from that.' When he told his estate employers of this desire, John was offered a five-year apprenticeship. 'That was fine. I spent the first year in the nursery, year two planting and tending trees, year three thinning, year four felling big trees, and the last year working in the estate sawmill, driven by a waterwheel.' His five years safely below his belt, John looked out the Forestry Commission brochure that Bill Sutherland had given him so long before and applied for a place at the Commission's forestry school.

'I went to the school at Glentress at Peebles in 1951,' he said. 'It was a two-year course. Glentress was set up for chaps returning from the war, and the intake was thirty students a year. It ran at full capacity until 1953 but by then there were five such schools in Britain and the Commission was getting over the hump, if you like, of training. The accommodation at Glentress was a corrugated iron building. One of the features of the Commission two-year course was one term spent in a location with a different climate and a different type of silviculture. There were four possibilities. They sent me to Benmore in Argyll. I was one of the last batch of students at Glentress.'

In 1953 the Commission had the opportunity to move the Glentress school up to Faskally, near Pitlochry, to the superior accommodation of an old mansion house that during the construction of the hydro-electric schemes of the North of Scotland Hydro-Electric Board had served as an engineers' school. The Benmore forestry school continued to train young men until July 1965. Faskally stayed open until the autumn of 1970, to the time when the Commission decided to hand over its training to the public education system. The other two forestry schools in Britain still in operation, at Parkend in the Forest of Dean and at Gwydyr in North Wales, also closed. The government announced at the end of 1969 that Inverness had been chosen as the place to have the new Scottish Forestry Education and Training Centre.[21] A forest industry training centre finally opened under the auspices of Inverness Technical College at Balloch in March 1975. Undergoing a series of further changes over the years, this is now the Scottish School of Forestry, offering courses up to degree level as part of the UHI.

A liking for the outdoors brought Glasgow-born Bryce Reynard into a career in forestry. He started his training with the Forestry Commission, a three-year period of apprenticeship, in 1962 when he was 18 years old. 'I was very typical of most of my contemporaries,' he said. 'In my first year there were twelve of us, and only one lad was from the country. The rest of us were all townies, but I had spent a lot of time in the Boy Scouts, camping and hiking.'

The apprenticeship began in Carradale in Kintyre, a fishing village Bryce already knew quite well from camping trips. After a year there, he spent a further 12 months in Knapdale, at Cairnbaan on the Crinan Canal, and his third year at Ardentinny on the east side of the Cowal peninsula. The three postings gave insights into the different aspects of forestry – nursery work, surveying and planting in Carradale, harvesting and felling in Knapdale, and various jobs in the established forest at Ardentinny where, in his time, there was no planting. 'The idea with the apprenticeship,' he explained, 'was that people, before they went to forestry school to study more on the management side, needed to have a flavour of what the men were doing so that in the future, whatever you asked the men to do, you would have done it yourself. We worked with hand tools and horses. The foresters in Knapdale and other places were supposed to give us a big variety of things to do. To me it was like paradise – working in the woods, chopping trees down, and getting paid for it, it seemed to me just magic. All my contemporaries were very keen on wildlife, and it was a super place to see wildlife. And we were in some lovely places. The remoteness wasn't a problem at all.' Bryce was one of four lads who started on the same day. For the first six months they stayed in lodgings, but then they managed to hire two caravans right by the seashore. They acquired a canoe and could paddle as far as Arran, two miles or so across the Kilbrannan Sound.

The apprenticeship over, the trainee foresters were sent to the classroom. 'The forestry school at Faskally was a super place to be,' said Bryce, 'I had a very happy time. There were twelve in my year, all males – the only women in forestry then were the clerkesses and some who worked in nurseries, but women foresters were just never heard of.'

Peter MacDonald went to Faskally in 1964. His father had worked in the Timber Supply Unit during the war and for the Commission in the late 1940s on the first plantings in Glenurquhart. Peter also found work with the Commission during his school holidays and enjoyed it sufficiently to decide on forestry as a career.

Norman Davidson's boyhood years were spent on a croft on the treeless Orkney island of Graemsay before the family flitted in 1960 to a farm near Turriff in Aberdeenshire. 'I had been interested in forestry before that,' said Norman. 'I was interested in timber as a material, the different types and so on, and I think I had heard about forestry on the radio. It appealed to me. I didn't fancy too much going into farming. Forestry caught my imagination and I intended to do that even when I was at school. After I saw an advert in the paper I joined the forestry department of Atholl estates in 1961. We were in the northern section in Calvine. The estate had three sections in those days – Argyll, Blair Atholl and Calvine. The Calvine section was managed by Bill Brand, the foreman forester, but the actual forestry manager was J.B. Hendry, a well-known forestry man in those days, well respected through the industry. He had been in the Forestry Commission at Drumtochty but had been with Atholl estates a long time.'

Norman and most of his young colleagues lived in a hostel, managed by the foreman and his wife, who did the cooking. 'I call it a hostel but it was a big stone house. There were six of us, six lads aged between 16 and 22. There were one or two other employees locally who worked there. We were, in those days, probably just fairly cheap labour while we learned the trade. I think our wage was something like £2 15s a week but £2 was taken off for board and lodging. We started work about half past seven and finished about five, but the winter hours were shorter. When I first went there, we used to work on Saturday mornings – normal at the time, but we didn't actually do very much on those mornings because some of the sites were three or four miles from the hostel. Sometimes we walked but mainly we cycled, so it took half an hour to get to some of the sites. The practice of working Saturday mornings died out quite quickly after we started. Calvine is on the main railway line, so we went down to Pitlochry quite a bit but we still had to keep our own rooms tidy, and do our washing and that type of thing, so that took up a little bit of time at the weekends. There was often a dance somewhere and we'd try to get down to that, in Blair Atholl or even in Calvine itself. Some of my colleagues had motor cycles and I got one as well latterly.'

The experience of estate forestry was excellent grounding for the career Norman wished to follow. After sitting the entrance exam for the Forestry Commission, he went to train on the two-year course at Benmore. 'The Royal Botanic Gardens looked after the grounds, the Commission had only the main building. Accommodation was in dormitory in the school for almost all the students, although married students had to find their own accommodation in the neighbouring villages. It was a big contrast with the estate. Life in Benmore was fairly regimented. For example, the students all had to take turns at being orderlies – sweeping the stairs, stoking the boiler, carrying the plates from the kitchen to the dining room, taking meteorological readings, and so on, but we had to learn the theory of forestry and the administrative systems the Commission used in those days. It was very much a Commission school. There were eleven of us in the class at the start, it later went down to ten – all men. I knew of no lady foresters at all.'

In his memoir, Don MacAskill remembers Benmore with great fondness: 'From the first reverential walk up its magnificent avenue of tall sequoias to the moment when I reluctantly had to leave, I enjoyed every minute.' His course ended prematurely when the Second World War broke out. Despite the regimentation and the rules, Norman Davidson also enjoyed his time there: 'It was a culture-widening experience. I met twenty-four students from all over the country, as far south as Cornwall, myself from the north, and all airts in between. I think almost all the students in my class ended up working for the Commission. The school was the entry card. We also did work in people's gardens and for contractors – cutting, thinning, snedding – and earned some money.' Norman decided to join Voluntary Service Overseas when his course finished in 1965 and it was two years later, after a stint as a forester in Sierra Leone, that he had his first Commission posting, to Leanachan forest near Fort William. As it happened, he was a member of the last group of students to complete their training at Benmore.

Hugh Morris was among the trainees who completed their course at Glentress in 1948. Taking advantage of the limited choice presented to him, he plumped for a posting to Farr, close to Inverness. This was a relatively new forest then, still being planted. 'I was put in charge of a group of displaced persons, mostly Yugoslavs. One of them spoke English and he relayed instructions. We had them for about a year before they went back home or elsewhere. They stayed in a hostel up at Erricht. Good workers. If you wanted a two-foot drain they would go down three feet, they kept on going.' After just over a year at Farr, Hugh was posted north to Rumster, a new forest being formed in Caithness. Here he and his wife stayed in a Commission caravan until a house was built at a nearby farm. 'I was there until 1956, for the planting of most of the original forest. It was mainly Sitka and lodgepole, with some Scots pine, highly experimental as we had no idea if the trees would survive. The wind was the biggest problem but at that time the winters were also very severe.' About eight men worked on the ploughing and planting. After the tractors had dragged their ploughs through the peaty soil, the ground was left until the following spring before being planted. Although the ploughing allowed much of the surface water to run away, further drainage was needed to prepare sections of the sodden, boggy moorland. It was a case of slow, steady advance across the bare, windswept ground: 'We did about a hundred acres a year.'

Hares presented an unexpected problem. 'It was completely over-run by hares. We used to drive them in the winter when it snowed. They could wipe out an area of planting by nipping the growing tips off the young trees.'

John Keenleyside's first posting was to Wykeham in Yorkshire, where he began his work in forestry research. This was followed by a year at the Bush nursery at Roslin near Edinburgh and, then, at the start of 1957 he was sent to the far north to continue research in the three counties of Ross and Cromarty, Sutherland and Caithness. John had a car but the A9 was blocked with snow and he had to travel by train. It was 3 January, and a blizzard was driving across the platform at Alness where he stepped off. There was no sign of anyone until from the obliterating white emerged a Land Rover with his new boss at the wheel. This was Geoff Bartlett – 'He had had some forestry training when the war started and, after his spell in the forces, came straight back into forestry at the end of the war. Those who had done a year's training were excused the second year and got a job when they came back because of the great expansion on at that time.' Bartlett drove John from the station up into the hills of Ardross to the Commission bothy called Dublin, beyond Ardross Castle. It was now 6 p.m. but the cook, called Wattie, had kept back some food for the new arrival – 'a plate of broth and some frizzled potato offerings,' recalled John in a series of articles he wrote for *FCA Today*, the magazine of the Forestry Commission Association.[22]

The Dublin bothy was built from rough-sawn timber, creosoted once a year and roofed with corrugated iron. The kitchen held a large ex-army cooking stove and there were ex-army folding tables in the dining area. The dormitory held 16 beds – single, narrow, uncomfortable and, along with the blankets, of military origin – but it also had lockable wardrobes and two stoves 'for which the Commission supplied low-grade, wet, pine firewood. The inmates had to light these stoves after returning from work in the hope that there would be some sign of heat by the time they had eaten their meal; which usually took a maximum of ten minutes.' Depending on the dryness of the fuel and whether or not the hopeful firelighter had added some creosote or, in the case of the road-building gang, cotton waste soaked in diesel, the dormitory filled with steam or noxious fumes. Lighting came from two Tilley lamps, and Wattie kept a careful eye on the meths used to start them. An ablution block with a washroom and toilet in a corrugated-iron lean-to without lining or insulation completed the arrangements.

The conditions were basic but, in the early 1950s, they were basic for most of the rural population. Porches and lean-tos with bathrooms or kitchens, frequently built with corrugated iron, were standard additions to the old, stone cottages that dotted the countryside, homes to shepherds, keepers and crofters. There was still a widespread absence of mains water and electricity, as the electrification of the countryside was waiting for the North of Scotland Hydro-Electric Board to complete its work, and local authorities had not yet installed comprehensive water supplies. Workers wore their own or cast-off military blouses and greatcoats, and used the war-vintage, canvas, gasmask bags to carry their piece and their flask to the field. Likewise, life in the bothy was reminiscent of the periods many of the men had spent in military camps.

John Keenleyside found that the catering in the Dublin bothy was, to say the least, eccentric. Wattie made no pudding but the inmates could make tea and toast for themselves if they liked, and cooked breakfasts, excluding porridge, were also missing until John, on his first day, bought some bacon and eggs for himself, only to find that his colleagues, who rose to start work half an hour before he did, got stuck into most of these supplies before him. A butcher's van came once a week, on a Saturday – mobile shops, always called 'vans', of various sorts were another feature of 1950s' rural Scotland – and Wattie was able to buy a lump of boiling beef that formed the basis of the main meals in different guises for the rest of the week. 'We once had a variation to this diet,' John wrote, 'An enterprising digger driver scooped up a salmon with the bucket while obtaining gravel from the river. On another occasion a deer which had been maimed in a traffic accident ended up in the cooking pot.'

Wattie was also in charge of the billing system. The bothy residents handed over 15 shillings a week for their accommodation but on top of that came a variable sum, a few shillings for the food, depending on the number of inmates, and another small sum for newspapers. The food bill was laid before the men on a Thursday evening – that was pay day. 'If he marched in smiling, that meant it was cheap; if he was dour, it meant costs had gone through the roof.' There was little entertainment, apart from what the men could devise for themselves. John liked to make marquetry pictures but the Tilley lamps did not throw enough light to ensure accuracy in cutting the veneers. There was reading material and a dart board – each man provided his own darts – and on Friday nights the Commission lorry roared down to Invergordon with a human cargo, keen to go to the pictures or a pub. The party continued in the bothy when the lorry came home at 10.30 p.m., often minus a few who had been unavoidably detained. At weekends, if the roads were not blocked by snow, the bothy tended to empty, except for those who were on duty of some kind. Times were changing, however, and the bothy at Dublin closed its doors before the 1950s were out, ironically as soon as it had been wired for the newly arrived electricity.

As he was involved in research in the far north, John found he was something of a mystery to the bothy inmates, who were all industrial workers and wondered why someone in the forester grades stayed among them. 'They tended to treat me as a potential industrial spy, fearing that I might convey some of their crack on piece work prices back to those in charge,' he recalled. As an assistant forester, John worked with Geoff Bartlett, the senior forester. They had no industrial workers and had to try to borrow labour from hard-pressed conservancy foresters or complete a task themselves. John also spent most of the week away from the bothy on trips in Caithness or Sutherland. 'I drove up on the Sunday night or the Monday morning and stayed [in the north] initially until Saturday at midday. Then we went on the five-day week

A group of research foresters at Ae in 1961. John Keenleyside is in the back row.

and we came home on Friday night. During the week we stayed in quite nice places – an obvious contrast with the bothy. We were paid subsistence so we stayed in hotels like the Royal or the Pentland in Thurso. Then we stayed in one down Strathnaver, at Garbhallt, near Ben Griam More, where dinner, bed and breakfast was £1 a night in the 1950s, in the middle of nowhere, and we stayed in Borgie quite a bit. Then as time went on we got a wee bit wiser, we built up a chain of crofters who did bed and breakfast, and we had ports of call in Watten, Strathy, and one or two places in Borgie and Strathnaver.'

The structure of the Forestry Commission itself reminded ex-servicemen of their army experience. The hierarchy of rank that had emerged in the service after the First World War persisted for many years. John McEwen's experience of it has already been noted. As Brian Denoon from Fort Augustus recalled in a series of articles in the *Inverness Courier*: '[The Commission] had a strong military feeling about it . . . its highest ranking officer was the remote and permanently invisible Conservator – equivalent to a General or Field Marshal. Then the high-ranking . . . Divisional Officers (Colonels or Majors); the District Officers (Lieutenants); the Forester (Regimental Sergeant Major); the Foreman (Sergeant); the Ganger (Corporal) and then down to the actual workers in the squads, the equivalent of the "poor bloody infantry".'[23]

There was definitely a hierarchy, with rankings,' remembered Bryce Reynard. 'There was the squad, the ganger, the forester, different grades of forester – assistant forester, forester, head forester, chief forester, the district officer, the DO, who worked in a distant place, you never saw him, and then you might get a grand tour from the headquarters when the chairman of the Commission might come round, and everything had to be spick and span and not at all normal.'

To complete the regimental impression created by this paramilitary structure, the foresters wore a uniform. Bryce Reynard described it: 'Green tweed suit, normal trousers or plus fours were optional. The plus fours gave you more material so folk would choose them, cut off the excess cloth and make it into a deerstalker hat. No shoes or wellies. The suit came from Hepworths, and because you lived in distant places you filled in your details on a postal form. Sometimes the suit wouldn't last a day – if you went into Sitka spruce, the tweed trousers could get ripped off. The jacket had a red collar with gold crowns, the same for all ranks. It was quite distinctive. Before my day the uniform had, I think, riding trousers [jodhpurs].' The old uniform had a khaki top with green collar flashes.

The uniform clothing did not mean the foresters were all cast from the same mould. Indeed many were characters. 'Hugh Mackay was the chief forester in Ratagan when I worked for him in Glenelg,' said Norman Davidson, 'His great strength was being anti-establishment, and he made it his life's work to get round the hierarchical structures of the Commission. As far as I was concerned, he gave you enough rope to hang yourself and, if you didn't hang yourself, you developed your own systems and techniques; if they worked he gave you due praise and if they didn't you got a bollocking at the end of the day, and that was fine by me. I got on well with him and learned a lot.'

Responsible for budgets, some foresters were stingy with equipment. 'They had some clout in the early days,' recalled Jimmy Henderson. 'I remember in Torrachility once with Adam Thom. There was a padlock on the tool box and he checked all the tools, he had a list. That was all right and, then, somehow, we went round the back of the tractor and he put the padlock down, and the two of us couldn't find it again, though we had about half an acre of heather torn out, looking for it. He used to give the trainee foresters rows too. They [the old foresters] had authority, they would have you shaking in your boots.' A visit from the district officer meant, in Jimmy Henderson's words, 'everything had to be spick and span, and we were cutting the bushes; when I started you [as a worker] couldn't talk to a district officer, it was a different attitude then.'

As a person involved in research, John Keenleyside admits he was 'an oddball', standing apart from the customary hierarchy, but he agreed that forestry was very militaristic in the past. 'Today you can start as a worker and end up as director general,' he said, 'In my day we were very much apart. I was very fortunate that I went through all the grades and ended up in Inverness as the forest district manager.'

The collection of good seed is a very important aspect of forestry. Foresters pay careful attention to the qualities of the parent trees, choosing seed likely to perpetuate desirable characteristics, in the same way as livestock breeders select among their animals. It is a natural way to improve the quality of a plantation and has been going on for a very long time, as long as forestry has been deliberately pursued in the countryside. Seed production on a commercial scale is probably less particular about parentage, but poor quality in any product from a commercial nursery would soon become common knowledge among foresters. When the Victorian planters bought Scots pine seed at 2s 6d a pound from Christie's Nurseries in Fochabers in 1854 they would have had a good idea of what to expect.[24] Christie's paid for cones gathered for their seed kilns at the rate of 9d per peck, the kind of job that may have attracted casual workers who collected from easily accessible trees without regard to quality.

Most young entrants into forestry began their training with a spell in the nursery, and it was not always to their liking. It demanded careful attention to small detail and the endless repetition of weeding. As many foremen discovered, women were often much better at it than men. Allan Macdonald recalled for me his experience of the two nurseries at Auchterawe beside Fort Augustus in the 1960s. About 50 people could be at work there, many of them

Lining out at the Ledmore nursery, 1952.

Lining out with a Talbot plough, Ledmore, 1953.

women. Once cones had been collected from the selected trees by climbing up on ladders, they were dried until the seed fell out. The seed was then sowed in beds and left under a cover of heavy laths of wood to keep the snow off until germination took place. Much time was spent weeding the beds, when the workers sat on the paths between them, carefully picking out the unwanted intruders, the tedium relieved a little by the good crack.

'We worked in pairs, with your partner sitting on the other side of the bed,' wrote Brian Denoon, 'From your position you were just able to reach to about half way across the bed with comfort. This meant that in theory the weeds would all be taken care of . . . The tree that we most loathed in the hills was the Sitka spruce . . . these beastly things were no less obnoxious in their infant state. While weeding them it was impossible to keep your wrists from being punctured over and over again by their needles. For whole days on end the insides of your wrists would be a blazing rash of raw pain.'

If the midgies became too bothersome old bags could be set on fire in the hope that the smoke would drive them away. When the seedlings had reached a height of about 4 inches they were grouped together according to their size and carefully lined out in nursery beds. A horse plough opened a small furrow before the seedlings were lined out along it so that their roots hung into the groove, a notched lath set down to ensure each was given the correct spacing from its neighbours. Another pass by the plough closed the furrow to bury the roots. Here the seedlings grew, once again under careful supervision and weeding, until at the age of two or three years they were deemed old enough for transplanting to the hill.

The Ledmore nursery, which, with the Newton nursery in Morayshire, supplied most of the young trees for planting in the east of Scotland, worked on a larger scale than the one at Fort Augustus. It took two growing seasons – 1950 and 1951 – to prepare the soil of what had been a farm before the Commission brought it into a state fit for raising seedlings. Various implements other than lining-out ploughs were hitched up to make the work as efficient as possible, and the staff were eventually able to line out 250,000 seedlings in a day, at a cost, as the ever-thrifty Commission calculated, of 4s per 1,000. In a season Ledmore turned out 8 million trees ready for transplanting.

Peter MacDonald described how sample forest plots with extremely good trees were set aside and left for seed, though one had to be careful not to gather too much from a rough old 'granny' tree, often more prolific than the finer growing specimens that might have the desired quality of timber. Seed collectors were paid by the weight of the bag for the cones they brought in.

Seed was not always collected by climbing trees. On the Atholl estates, where Norman Davidson had his first taste of forestry, an alternative approach was the common practice. 'Some thinning or felling was specifically done in certain localities actually to get seed, in September or October when the seed was ripe,' he said. 'I can remember it once. We were felling and women came up from the nursery. Nursery work was seasonal and it was very convenient for the women to work for a short time. I suspect that if a particular type of seed was required and the manager knew of a stand of good quality they would actually hold back the felling until the seed was ripe. Seed was always selected on the basis of the quality of the parent tree. Sometimes in Scots pine the viability is not that good and you will go along to collect a few cones before they are quite ripe. It is hardly worth bringing a ladder so some people used to take a light shotgun to bring down a few cones, and cut them with a knife to see how many seeds were viable. When the cone is green and soft, you slice it through with a sharp knife and if you can see more than three or four viable seed in that cut surface it would probably be worthwhile collecting seed from that tree or that locality. You can see the white, filled flesh of the seeds.'

'We scoured the country to find the finest trees and when we found them we actually went with a 12-bore gun and fired at the top and knocked off little shoots,' said John Keenleyside. 'We called these scions and grafted them on to ordinary tree root stocks we had grown in the nursery before we planted them out in seed orchards. Two things about that – they had the same genes as the good tree, and because their foliage came from the older, parent tree they started to flower very early in life and we were able to pick cones at ground level or very low down.'

Hugh Morris's posting to Rumster in Caithness happened as part of the Commission's ambition in the 1950s to establish forestry in the more exposed regions in the far north, on the mainland and on the traditionally treeless islands. 'No trees are to be seen in this region,' wrote the Reverend John Mill from Dunrossness in Shetland in the 1790s, 'excepting a few shrubby roan [rowan] trees and willows in the more sheltered valleys'.[25] George Barry in Orkney noted there were almost no trees in the islands 'except a few fruit trees in Kirkwall', but he knew that the remains of sizeable specimens were frequently dug from the mosses and opined that the few attempts to establish plantations had failed largely through lack of knowledge and care than through any other cause. In Caithness in the 1970s things were little better. A fir [Scots pine] plantation on the moor of the Warth Hill near John o'Groats failed after thriving for a short time: 'No charge ought to be brought against the soil and climate,' thought the minister, John Morison, 'as long as the exertions of industry are wanting . . .' Bare, windswept landscapes were also the norm in the Western Isles: 'There is not a single tree, or even any brushwood, to be seen in the whole parish,' lamented the minister of Barvas at the north end of Lewis, adding that the one attempt at establishing a plantation near Stornoway had also failed.

The Commission set up some experimental plots on Shetland in 1953 for the first time. Here the conditions proved too severe. On only one site, at Ward Hill in the south of the islands, Sitka spruce and mountain pine managed a survival rate against the wind and sea spray of more than 10 per cent. It took nine years for the tallest, surviving Sitka specimen to reach almost 3 feet in height, hardly a commercial prospect.[26] Only one variety of lodgepole pine, unsurprisingly having its provenance in Alaska, showed much promise, but Shetland has the honour of being the first place where tatter flags, stuck in the blast until they were shredded to ribbons, were set out to measure wind exposure.[27] Experiments on Hoy in Orkney had a similar outcome, few surviving into the 1960s from trees planted in 1954, except for slow-growing lodgepole, mountain pine and Sitka. Angus MacDonald, the chief forester reporting on these trials, ended his paper with the words '. . . the prospects of productive forestry are not encouraging'.[28] A review of the trial plantings in 1987 found the surviving trees to have little commercial value but they had provided biodiversity and were of conservation interest.[29] The first row of trees in the most northerly plantation, at Sullom Voe in Shetland, only reached a little above the height of the sheltering stone wall, although each row progressing inwards managed to struggle a little higher, resulting in a profile like the roof of a house.

The Commission began trial plantations at Balallan and Valtos on Lewis in the late 1940s, planting relatively sheltered areas with lodgepole pine and Sitka. The latter showed good growth and reached yield class 12, and more areas at Garynahine and Aline, planted in 1968–72, also supported Sitka. These experiments, and others by the Scottish College of Agriculture, proved that in the Western Isles woodlands given sufficient shelter could flourish and 'achieve quite respectable growth rates'.[30]

Caithness and Sutherland also offered some obvious possibilities for forestry. In 1947 the former had only 600 acres of productive woodland, while Sutherland fared considerably better with 9,000 acres. Both had larger acreages of scrub or felled plantation. The Commission acquired its first Caithness forest – at Rumster – in 1948 and began planting in the following year. Sutherland already had some large plantations and by 1953 had six state forests. These were almost all in the more sheltered south-east, with one exception, at Borgie on the northern coast. The Duke of Sutherland gifted this land to the Commission at its birth – the first area it acquired north of the Highland line – but planting begun in 1920 and kept up for several years had turned out to be largely a waste of resources. The techniques that worked in the south failed in this demanding environment, but now better methods of drainage and cultivation, coupled with improved machinery, held out hope.[31] Another area acquired in Caithness, the links and dunes of Dunnet Bay where fierce north-westerly gales in winter blasted growing plants with salt and sand, was tackled with the techniques worked out at Culbin in the 1920s. The wind dug into the dunes to scoop out unstable hollows, the sandy equivalent of corries, but this was countered by thatching the dunes with branches to trap the shifting substrate.

The research, conducted as replicated experiments in the field by John Keenleyside and his colleagues, was designed to locate new sites for planting and to find out what was required to make the trees grow. In the first year, progress was judged simply by the survival of the young trees, but from the third year the researchers resorted to height measurements. 'It was interesting work and we saw a lot of country. Some of it was hard. There was one place at Rimsdale in Strathnaver with a very tough type of peat. There was nobody there to help you so you had to plant the trees yourself, and this was tough peat to work on with the spade.

'At that time we reckoned the only possibilities were different provenances of lodgepole pine and the Sitka spruce. They could stand up to the wind. Japanese larch would do that to a certain extent but in such windy locations it became terribly bent and unproductive from the point of view of timber. The biggest advantage – and you can still see this in some places up there yet on the borders of plantations particularly where they border main roads – was that it is a fire-resistant species and was often planted in a chain-wide belt right round the edge of the forest. We used Japanese rather than European larch because in this country the latter has a bad history of die-back and canker. The Japanese larch was easily raised in the nursery and it didn't have this canker problem, so it was widely planted early on. Out of that came the cross between European and Japanese larch, and this hybrid larch was ideal because it had the benefit of the fitness of the European species and it didn't have the canker, but it was difficult to obtain seed of that.'

After his period in the north, John was posted to a silvicultural research out-station at Drumtochty, to the south-west of Stonehaven. He was to be there for ten years, the longest single posting he had in the Commission. Now he had married, and he and his wife settled into an old stone house that had been the head gardener's cottage on the Drumtochty Castle estate. The original wall garden and its surroundings proved a good place for seed orchards and tree-breeding research. 'If there was a down side to the house,' recalled John, 'it was that the office was in it and there was only one telephone and originally one toilet, and it wasn't very handy for staff. To reach the toilet I had to go through the dining room, up the stair, along the corridor. Eventually they put a toilet in the office and set up the phone so that it could be switched through to the house at night. And it was a party line – with the forester who ran the main block of forestry.'

'We were three staff – one forester, one worker and I was in charge. Sometimes we had help from students. The emphasis was different from in the north and the climate was different of course – in east Scotland it was much drier, it wasn't so exposed, but there was a big difference between the south end of the area, for instance near Forfar, where we were growing broadleaved trees, poplars, at a place called Halliburton on the road to Dundee, and the north end, on the hills above Huntly at Clashindarroch. Going up there was pretty tough. In those days we had long, hard winters up there. We tried to have all the measurements and work done by the end of October with the hope that we wouldn't have to go back until the first of April. Some times we had to go. The Clashindarroch forest stretched from Gartly right through to near the Cabrach, and that was pretty high. The road is often blocked in winter. Right at the north end some of the work was similar to Caithness. The Commission had been in there with research since the early 1920s and so there were things that were well established – provenance experiments, species difference, and so on – and they were at a stage where they required a different type of measurement, they required thinning out and assessment of the main crop and that type of thing. We had lots of sample plots.'

After the young trees have been reared in the nursery beds, they are planted out on the hill or wherever the new forest is desired. This is a necessarily time-consuming and labour intensive business, and always has been. When Sir Alexander Matheson planted 3,000 acres around Ardross Castle in the 1850s, he paid for 200 men to stay in barracks to complete the job. At the rate of 5,000 trees per acre, it took them six years – over 16 million trees, mostly Scots pine – and the total cost, including labour, was less than £3 an acre.[32] Various attempts have been made to try to speed planting up – by using, for example, a spade or mattock with a semi-circular blade – but it always comes down to a determined stravaig across the brae with regular digging, and in all weathers. Notch planting has been probably the most common technique, wielding the spade with one hand to cut a T-, L- or H-shaped notch and thrusting the young tree into the sliced soil with the other hand.

'I joined a squad of four, armed with a mattock, a Hessian sack, an enormous pack of sandwiches and two Thermos flasks of tea,' wrote Donald Fraser about his first taste of planting in the 1950s, in Perthshire. 'We climbed the winding track in the early morning sunshine to our place of work high on the steep, heather-clad hillside.' Donald recalled how he was surprised and

Planting on Nobseat in Fetteresso Forest in October 1952. Senior Commission staff on an official visit can be seen mingling with the workers.

horrified by the weight of the sack of young trees he was expected to carry as he struggled through the heather and rocks to keep up with the squad. Once they reached their scene of operations, they deployed in a line, adapted the sacks to act as planting bags and moved off, hacking a hole with the mattock and heeling in the small saplings. 'At first my hands almost seized up with the biting cold. The wearing of gloves was prohibited,' said Donald, adding how, after a week at the work, 'I marvelled at how I had toughened up.'

This was a common experience among young foresters. The newly trained Peter MacDonald was posted to Torrachilty Forest beside the River Conon in Ross-shire. The head forester was the lean and hardy Adam Thom, 'well known as an honest man who looked you in the eye and told you exactly what he thought'. A forester of the old school, Thom had a reputation for never asking a man to do a task he wouldn't do himself but he was not a boss to be trifled with. When Peter arrived he was instructed by Thom to take a squad of men to plant on new land on the lower slopes of Ben Wyvis. 'Right, there's the brae, lad,' said Thom, 'where you'll be planting.' The green flanks of the

Wyvis massif rise steeply towards the level summit ridge. How would they get the Sitka, lodgepole and larch seedlings up there? 'You'll be carrying them, lad,' said Thom. While the squad of some 20 men did the planting, Peter toiled up and down the braes, carrying the seedlings, tied with string in bundles of 100, in a canvas bag with a webbing strap to keep his workers supplied.

Norman Davidson found at Calvine that the foreman was always checking on what his workers were up to. 'He was never very far away and we knew ourselves the quality we had to keep. Depending on the conditions, direct notching – one cut – or making L- or T-notches – two cuts – to open the ground, you levered the spade sideways and twisted at the same time, and you put the tree in a vertical position. We tended to prefer the L-notch to the T-notch. The single notch was used in certain circumstances with another type

Planting trees on Skye.

Opposite.
Planting Sitka at Ae.

of spade on very steep, heathery ground, we called it a Schlich spade, for planting Scots pine, a robust, heavy spade with the blade coming to a point, heart-shaped, with a straight handle. You drove it into the ground and waggled it to open up the crack, put the tree in, and stamped it shut with your heel. For direct planting into uncultivated ground the trees we were planting were 12 to 18 inches high, probably three year olds.'

Glenelg was Norman's first experience of restocking, planting a new crop of trees on a site that has been clear-felled. 'It was too steep to plough. Tree roots would not have been a problem as the researchers had come up with a machine that could plough that type of terrain, although it looked a bit like a battlefield afterwards. On the hillsides in Glenelg where extraction had been by cable train there was a whole mess of branches and old broken stems where the men had to try and plant trees at regular spacing. They had to fight their way along while carrying the bundle of plants in the bag, with some protective gear against all the scratches. The top of the spade where you normally would put your foot was sloped off downwards so you could get it in amongst the branches and out again without trapping. Often you would be forcing your spade down through several inches of branches, trying to find the ground, and then you would lever the spade back and fore, insert the tree into the split as best you could – a slow and tiring business. We used lines of canes to guide the planters but it was a very difficult business and on top of that there was a problem with pine weevils, which were breeding in the stumps and attacking the planted trees. I would say on the best of flat ploughed ground you could plant between 1,000 and 2,000 trees in a day – 1,200 was expected – but on these steep conditions, 400 or 500 was sometimes pretty hard going. We had to offer some kind of piece work but it was a pretty hefty price.'

Willie Lindsay had no experience of forestry at all when he saw the newspaper advertisement in 1968 appealing for men. He had, however, a love of the countryside, honed by excursions during his boyhood in Ayrshire before he had found work in a mill making carpet fibres in Kilwinning. One strong attraction of forestry was the provision of a house; in Kilwinning Willie and his new wife would have had to spend around five years on the waiting list before they stood much chance of a council house.

'I had a fairly rough idea what to expect,' said Willie. 'I had an interview in Glasgow, at the head office of the Commission for the west coast, in charge of everything up the Argyll side. I canna mind what they asked me but I was used to wandering in woods, and I was quite good on plants at school. One of the science teachers knew I was good and would send me out into the woods. "I want such-and-such", he would say and he would rattle off on his fingers items for a nature study class, not my class but other classes. I would find him leaf galls on hawthorn bushes, or a sprig with berries on it, any of these kind of things.'

The Commission offered Willie a forestry worker's post on the island of Jura. 'They paid the fare and I think a portion of the flitting. The furniture went by a separate route but we and it all finished up at West Loch Tarbert. At that time they used to use the pier at Craighouse on Jura. They don't do that now – they haven't for donkeys' years – you have to go via Islay now, to Port Askaig and then the little ferry over at Feolin.'

Fewer than a hundred people lived on Jura in 1968, spread out over mainly the southern part of the island on estates or in the small villages. Another forestry worker arrived from Lanarkshire at the same time as the Lindsays and occupied the other half of the forestry house, two semi-detached dwellings of Dorran construction. It was a tied house, although the occupants were required to pay rent. The rest of the Commission staff comprised the forester, an older man called Jimmy Marshall, and an islander, Ian Cameron, who also did stalking to control deer in the forests.

'The first job was doing draining on a forest already established,' recalled Willie. 'The trees were about three feet high. You had to keep the drains clear or the trees got waterlogged. Then there would be the odd deer who got in and they broke the edges of the drills [furrows] and the earth would fall into the trenches and fill them in. We used to make a herring-bone pattern of drains – one big drain taking all the water away and small ones coming in from each side. A lot of spade work.'

Provided with waterproofs and rubber boots, Willie and his colleagues dug in sun and rain. 'There were some pretty wet days but we were outdoors in all kinds of weather. You'd be out on the hill praying for a good dry day. It didna matter if it was no warm, in the winter, as long as it was dry. It was the clammy wet cold when your fingers used to freeze. We used to wear mittens, your hand was warm but the tips of your fingers got very cold.'

'We started at eight in the morning and worked through until five. If we were away up at Lagg at the top end of the island, we'd maybe finish a wee teenie bit early, so as we could get back down just for about five. It would take nearly half an hour to get down the single-track road in a Land Rover.'

New forests were also being laid out on Jura and this meant plenty of planting, in the late winter, January right through to March, when the trees were dormant. 'We did lots of planting. They tried putting us on piece-work – you planted so many a day and got paid accordingly. But some days you had to struggle to do that because if the weather was inclement, the sleet coming sideways at you, you had to be like the horse and turn your backside to the wind, and walk down the furrows backwards, you couldn't face it, it was so wild. We were planting on the ridge turned over from the furrow. You carried a bag over your shoulder and you had a bunch [of saplings] in your hand. A bunch had about a hundred plants. You wouldn't be able to hold it, so we used to split the bunch, take the string off, hold half of it, and then put your hand back in the bag to get the other fifty. You had the spade in your other hand and you made two slashes in the ground, at right angles to each other, and lifted up the notch, put the tree in the notch, heeled the turf back, and that sunk it down a bit so the root reached the wettest bit of the ridge. Once you'd done your planting you went round with a phosphate bag and gave a wee circle of phosphate round your planted tree – just a couple of ounces in the palm of your hand, trickle it round. That was back-breaking because you were bending further down then than with the spade. Planting was all right for wee folk like me, but a big, tall, lanky fellow would have a much sorer back at night. Sometimes they got a helicopter to make stashes, piles of phosphate bags across the hillside, so it was just a matter of splitting one, taking some into your own bag on your shoulder. You still had to bend down, though, for if the phosphate dust hit the needles on the pine it would burn them.'

In the summer months the workers went back on drainage and the more pleasant task of checking the deer fences to make sure they were still animal-proof. 'In the south end of the forestry area, there had been a village away way back. The place was full of adders. You used to see them, lying, sunning themselves, and if they were groggy they didn't bother to hiss at you, just turned their heads slowly and looked at you.'

CHAPTER 4
'IT'LL NEVER TAKE OVER FROM THE HORSE'
WORKING IN THE FORESTS

Much of the success on peat came about through mechanisation. The tracked vehicle, with its wide steel tracks, and the development of special ploughs enabled bogs that had hitherto defied cultivation to be furrowed, drained and planted. The vehicles, often referred to generally as 'Caterpillar tractors' after one of the main manufacturers, were still liable to get stuck in the soft morass and even sink altogether out of sight. This was unsurprising once measurements found that bare peat could hold as much as ten kilograms of water for every kilogram of solid matter and that the amount in the sodden, anaerobic substrate often increased with depth.[1] These obstacles could, however, be overcome.

Ploughing trials with a Caterpillar 28 tractor at Clashindarroch in 1935.

Ploughing to prepare ground for planting trees had a long history stretching back to the early years of the nineteenth century.[2] It was recognised that it benefited drainage, aeration and the release of nutrients, as well as helping to suppress weeds, but the practice did not become common until the 1930s. Some earlier attempts involved more or less stationary steam traction engines dragging the plough on winch cables back and fore, but a two-horse plough was used on Lon Mor, near Inchnacardoch, in 1927, under the supervision of M.L. Anderson, the Commission's research officer in Scotland, producing results that were later useful in planting in Caithness and Sutherland. The Commission's first foray into ploughing had in fact taken place in South Wales in 1924 and over the succeeding years various experiments with different kinds of implement were tried, in Scotland for example at Teindland, Clashindarroch and, in 1939, at Borgie with a Caterpillar 20 tractor and a Unitrac plough making a 10–12 inch deep furrow.

Two traction engines ploughing by winch, East Lothian, possibly in the 1920s.

Above. Cuthbertson P and F type ploughs, Greskine, in the 1960s.

Right. Ford County ploughing tractor at Ardonald Moss near Huntly, c.1965. At the controls is Bert Legge, who came originally from Deer Lake, Newfoundland.

As early as 1912, Sir Charles Ross of Balnagowan had fitted an endless track on a wheeled tractor and experimented with it, gathering around him local men, including the Kildary blacksmith as well as some of his servants, to form an early research and development team. In his history of the forestry plough, S.A. Neustein suggested that a schoolboy from Biggar who came on holiday to Easter Ross probably joined in with this or at least had his curiosity stimulated by it. This youngster was James Cuthbertson who was to make a name for himself as an agricultural engineer; his significant innovations included the forestry plough named after him. Working with forester D.H. Ross and the Commission's engineer John Blane, Cuthbertson produced ploughs in the 1940s and also designed his own tractor, the Water Buffalo. Another engineer, J. Begg of Tarbolton, designed a plough that was widely used in the Borders in the 1940s and early 1950s but which proved unable to cope with heavy peat.

When Don MacCaskill worked in Knapdale in the late 1930s, drainage in preparation for planting was done by hand labour. 'We worked in groups, four in each, spaced across the hillside. Two men, each wielding a rutter . . . worked across the ground digging v-shaped wedges. Another man, with a cross-cutting spade, followed behind slicing across the V so that it was cut into sections. The fourth member of the team then dug out the turves with a three pronged fork called a hack and threw them into two rows on either side of the drain – thus forming four rows between each . . . It was winter, the weather often awful and the work backbreaking. The job took weeks to complete.'

The mechanical ploughing of the moors gouged out great drainage channels, up to 18 inches deep and varying in width up to 2 feet, encouraging water to flow out of the soaking ground. The result, leaving hillsides ribbed

November 1950, and an amphibious Cuthbertson Buffalo tractor drags a massive Cuthbertson double-mouldboard plough across deep peat at Strathy in Sutherland. The operation produces rows of turf five feet apart.

Cuthbertson double mould board plough in Strathy in 1950.

corduroy-fashion by lines of deep furrows, was not always pleasant to the eye, as many lovers of the wild landscape complained, but in time these scars would mostly disappear under a blanket of trees. A good tree cover helped to dry out the ground and long-term prospects, for further crops of Sitka and lodgepole pine, have been seen as better now for peatland forest than in the beginning. Double mouldboard ploughs were introduced in 1950–51, producing furrows 28 inches wide and 10 feet apart.

Ploughing became the speciality of roving bands of men who moved about the country to where their skills were required. Donald Fraser found them to be 'a cavalier bunch of easy-going characters . . . a pleasure and a privilege to work with.' One of them was Jimmy Henderson from Evanton. 'I was always interested in tractors before I joined the forestry in 1955,' he said about his first period with the Commission, in Clach Liath 'just up the back of Evanton'. 'I was there for a long time and you know how you get fed up. I couldn't see myself getting on. I didn't mind it but it was boring in the end, all the planting and draining.' After his spell of National Service with the Seaforth Highlanders, Jimmy took advantage of the agreement with the Commission to return to his former post. 'Through time I said to the forester,

can I get on to the ploughing? I used to see the boys ploughing in the forests. I fancied that, I always liked machines. Yes, that was all right, they said, but it took some time. Then this man, Johnny Banks, came and it was him who trained me. Ten weeks. In them days you had to walk behind the plough and you had to sit on the tractor until they showed you what to do. I hadn't driven a Caterpillar tractor before.' Jimmy learned his new skill in Clach Liath, becoming familiar with the Ross and Cuthbertson ploughs. He had to wait five years after his training before he became a permanent ploughman, though he did relief work throughout this period when other men went on holiday. This was valuable experience, giving him the opportunity to become familiar with different types of tractor. His favourite became the Fiat 60C.

Jimmy can recall with pleasure the names, characters and places of origin of all the colleagues with whom he worked, over 30 of them, and most older than he was. 'The ploughmen travelled around. I went as far as Lochaline in Ballachulish. You had to take your own car and you never got mileage on it. I was up at Helmsdale too but a lot of the boys in the north stayed up there. Shin was a big forest and there was a lot of ploughing done there. [Shin had five ploughing outfits at its peak, out of 27 in the whole North Scotland

Cross draining in Kintyre in 1966, with tractors in tandem towing a Cuthbertson plough.

conservancy.] Accommodation was usually in a caravan. The first one I got was shared with Jimmy Thompson at Inshriach, at Feshie Bridge. It was a wooden one with a double door, a top half and a bottom half, with a stove inside and bunks at the back. It was basic but it was all right. After that they got aluminium, long, green ones. I've seen the blankets and sheets stuck to the sides with frost in the morning. We got a bag of coal and that was supposed to last us a week. We were ploughing new ground and there was no wood to burn. The Calor gas cylinders used to be left outside and one morning they froze. They were held in only a little frame. Bob McBeath says, I'll soon sort that. He put the cylinder on top of the stove. I'm out of there like a rocket, I thought it was going to explode but it didn't. We did our own cooking. We had a good laugh.'

The ploughmen worked from seven or half past seven in the morning until six at night, but despite long hours on difficult terrain sleep was not always the priority in the evening. 'We were in Achnashellach,' said Jimmy. 'A road squad were there as well and this night they were shouting across the river to us. Donny Junor was with me, and Jimmy Paton. I didn't know the road squad that well but Junor of course knew them all. A lot of them were at Blackstand, the Commission's engineering depot on the Black Isle at that

A double mould board plough gouges out a trench on Deeside, September 1979.

time. They were shouting across — going for a drink? Yes! Junor had no car so I took my van. We landed up in Achnasheen. It was three o'clock in the morning when we got home, fell asleep, and up again at seven.'

The sleeping arrangements were not always as comfortable as a caravan. In Glen Hurich, Jimmy, Willie McBeath and Len Newman had to resort to an old hut. 'It had been left from when they had been building the roads, but it had been empty for years and the sheep had been in. We couldn't get digs and we had no caravan, and that's where we had to sleep. Just a shed. A mattress on the floor, that's what we had. The hut was high off the ground but the sheep were underneath and you couldn't sleep for the stink. I remember the district officer said, "Ach, you'll no be long in it, anyway, you'll be working all the time." We were there for three weeks.'

The ploughmen learned to read the ground and spot the soft areas and drier patches. 'If you were reversing up a hill you could go to the harder bits and go right up and keep a track for long enough, and come down the greasy bits. Once you were up high you could see. Bracken was slippy, too. Achnashellach, that was the worst place. Slimy. You'd have to leave the tractor just ticking over – the Fiat was good like that – so that you could pass over slippery surfaces. It was no use revving up, you'd be off like a rocket. The

The result: the pattern of turf ridges and furrows, and the relatively shallow rectangular drain created by the Cutherbertson double-mouldboard plough on the peat moorland at Strathy.

Ploughman Donny Junor looks on as a colleague excavates a drain in the first stage of recovery of a bogged Caterpillar D4D tractor and plough, in Benmore Forest, about 3 miles east of Ledmore Junction, Sutherland.

short grass and a slimy surface made it slippery. A patch of ground could stick below the tracks and you could sit on top of that and come waltzing down, skidding, I've seen us go about three or four hundred yards, just like a sledge. It was okay if you were going straight but sometimes it was sideways and if you hit a stump or a rock, over the tractor could go. Bits were quite dangerous but you got kinda used to it. It was common sense but it was always better if there were two of you together. Give you a bit of encouragement. A bit of competition. But Jimmy Paton told me, "Don't take chances. All you'll get in the paper is that much, a line or two" [of obituary].'

High on the western flank of Ben Wyvis there used to be, until it was felled in 2008, a lonely block of Sitka above the main body of the Garbat forest. It is reckoned to be the highest plot of planted ground in the country, reaching up to around 2,000 feet above sea level. Finlay Macrae mentioned this little wood as an example of good tree-growing soil high up. 'I just tried it to see how it would get on,' he said. 'The soil was good and it's growing, although I knew the exposure was enormous. It'll not grow to be anything but it was an interesting experiment. Seeking the limit. I spent sleepless nights over it because I had a fellow with a tractor up there ploughing. I was glad when he was out of there. I've learned since then.'

The fellow with the tractor was Jimmy Henderson. He ploughed Finlay's experimental patch in a Fiat 70 tractor, and admits it was more or less just to see if it could be done. On the steep gradient he ploughed downwards, the blade of the plough acting as a brake, reversing straight back up for each furrow. Usually the work was across more level moorland and, despite the reading of the surface, there was always a risk of becoming bogged down.

'Willie McBeath, poor Willie got bogged and all you could see was halfway up the exhaust. The back of the tractor was up, the head was down. It was a great big, slimy hole and Willie was shouting. We knew fine we could get him out, with two tractors and him sitting on and shouting, we pulled him right out through it. I've seen us in Corrour, six or seven of us, like a circus, all bogged in a circle in the same place. A fellow, Alec Thompson, he was sent for. He had a D6. Someone says what's the good of that? That wouldn't pull a fart out an eggcup. But it pulled us all out. We just anchored ourselves together and when he got one out he got the other out.'

The early tractors had no cabs and the ploughmen worked exposed to all weathers. 'I can safely say there were hard times but there was always a laugh. One time, I was on a pretty steep bit and it got steeper and steeper. The tractor took off. It was raining, a heavy shower. The Commission supplied a rain coat but normally we had our own. The Commission coat was that thin, paper

Bogged on Moss Mulloch, East Hookhead, near Strathaven in Lanarkshire.

thin, a black one, I remember. Thank God it was thin, because I bailed off, you see, and it caught in the clutch handle. Normally a rain coat would have held me back and I would have been caught in the tracks but this ripped right in two from top to bottom. It was like a bit of paper, man.'

Winter brought special problems. Except where long heather provided some kind of insulating cover to the ground, the moor could freeze and make the substrate too hard for the plough to break – once in the 1960s, Jimmy and his colleagues were sent home for six weeks until the weather softened. 'The rollers on the Fiat tracks had to be greased regularly but in winter with hard frost they used to seize up and we lit a big bonfire under them to loosen them,' said Jimmy. 'The diesel used to freeze too. One man used to have to drain the water every night [from the radiators] and there's no water out on the hill sometimes. You could spend the whole day just trying to get the tractor going. You had to be a bit of a mechanic as well as a driver, but if you did have a breakdown the mechanics used to come out.'

Then there were the odd situations that crop up in the countryside when the weather creates new problems. 'One Monday morning in Strontian, I was the first to go over this concrete bridge. There had been an awful lot of rain. You know, you're going and your head's down. I opened the gate and never looked across the bridge, and when I was driving over the bridge it was going down, down, down – the pillar in the middle underneath had collapsed and the two concrete slabs for the road had locked together in a V shape, and I went right down and shot right up the other side. I was across the bridge when

Trying to attach a winch rope to the drawbar of a bogged draining plough, at the head of Loch Shiel, Glenfinnan, in 1970.

the other fellow arrived. "Och," he says, "I'll chance it, you've done it." I didn't realise the state of the bridge until I was over.'

'The funny thing about these massive, noisy tractors was that you could get closer to deer on them than you could on foot,' said Bryce Reynard. 'There was one occasion when the ploughman, because he knew I was interested in wildlife, missed a furrow out because he saw a nest, and he showed me later where it was, and I went up to look at it. The tractor had gone on either side of this nest, and when I parted the heather to see it,

A D4 tractor ploughing with a single mouldboard plough, in the late 1970s.

up looked a short-eared owl. I put my hand under it, lifted it up and the chicks were hatching. I put her back down again and she kept still the whole time.'

Contour ploughing was adopted in an effort to minimise erosion on steep slopes. This brought problems of its own, such as a tendency for the upturned strip to break loose and roll downhill. 'If you weren't careful, the furrow would go over and over, roll down the hill away from you. I always remember Bob McBeath – he was going like a rocket and the furrows were down behind him, all that was open was a drain, the furrows were away down the brae, every one he did. The forester said there was nothing left to plant on.'

Norman Davidson remembered Jimmy Henderson ploughing in Sunart in the early 1970s. 'We never had severe boggings, as the moss was shallow and rocky. One block, Achnanellan on the side of Loch Shiel, was difficult to get into and we were working with mounted ploughs on tractors for the cultivation. Jimmy was a mounted plough operator. The plough was mounted directly onto the back of the tractor, with no linkage and no separate wheels. The beam of the plough can be lifted up, bringing the head with it of course, to lie 10–15 degrees off the vertical. The method was the tractor reversed up the steep slopes as far as it could go before it started to slip, dropped the beam and plough into the soil, just like the hook of an anchor, and dragged it down the slope. They could work on flat land too of course but they tended to have narrower tracks than the soft-ground tractors and be more manoeuvrable, and more robust in a way. Fencing was difficult too on the steep ground. I first used helicopters up there. All the fertilising was by helicopter as well.'

'We had an acquisition at Glen More at the western end of the Ardnamurchan peninsula, and there we used the trail ploughs, the softer ground machines. Sometimes we used a single furrow but in those days the double furrow ploughs were coming in and we were getting larger outputs, but the main concern with the single plough was the inherent instability created in the trees by the narrow flat formed between the furrows. They would be only about 5 feet 6 inches apart, and when the trees grew up the roots occupied only the little platform area so that in strong wind they would actually tip over the whole platform. To counteract this they were beginning double-furrow ploughing in the 1970s. The ridge and furrow pattern created by ploughing was inherently more unstable but it was a trade off between cultivation and stability, and there are ways around it – not thinning in the unstable areas, and felling quite early.'

'Ploughing in itself was a remarkable achievement, with the development of the ploughs, because the type of land that forestry was being increasingly assigned to was pretty cold, wet and miserable, and it was difficult to establish crops on some of those lands without the ploughing technique. This advanced the establishment of forestry by a very significant factor, not only on the wet, cold ground but also where there were iron pans below the surface. These were a severe restriction on tree rooting.' The iron pan was a hard layer in the soil caused by the leaching of minerals, and until it was broken it formed a barrier to root penetration.

Ploughing and the subsequent drainage were not sufficient in themselves to make trees grow on the boggy peatland. The research carried on by John Keenleyside and his colleagues had shown the necessity for fertiliser. 'Sitka needed nitrogen,' he explained. 'Through the 1960s and early '70s we spread nitrogen. We departed from the original procedure of treating trees individually to putting it on by helicopter, but that turned out to be unacceptable from a green point of view as some fell into the water courses. As time went on the application of nitrogen became banned. Fortunately the earlier work had come to fruition and we found we could get over that problem by planting the Sitka in mixture with other species, particularly where we were able to grow larch. We found out that if we got rid of the heather by mulching it they would grow away rapidly. Then we introduced what we called mulching free of charge by planting three rows of larch and three rows of Sitka, so the larch shed its needles every year and mulched for the Sitka. I'm talking about the difference between a Sitka spruce growing as little as ten centimetres a year and one growing at the absolute maximum of a metre in a year. In our vision we had it averaging on these poor sites at least thirty centimetres; if they were growing at all, they would produce a minimum of thirty centimetres.'

'The most beneficial, general fertiliser we used was called GNAP –

ground North African phosphate – and so we were attempting to be green, even that far back. GNAP was obtained from rocks with a depth of guano. An ounce and a half of this was enough to give a little tree a boost. The procedure was to plant through the winter and, then, when that was finished in April or May, go round and give them this. The concentrated stuff could be lethal in direct contact with roots, so it was spread on the ground around the tree. The most primitive way of doing it, with some of the old mannies, was to use a matchbox – that held an ounce and a half.'

A few foresters, among them Finlay Macrae, were never fans of ploughing on a massive scale and now ploughing is rarely if ever done. 'From the mid-1980s onwards, the ploughs started to disappear,' said Hamish Fraser, 'There was no programme for ploughing. With planting now, they do a lot of mounding with a digger. That's all they do – like moleheaps – they call it mounding. Put the tree in on top of the fresh ground. The digger is like a normal excavator.'

The advent of machines largely brought to an end the era of the horse. The forester with his Clydesdale horse dragging logs from the forest had become, and to some extent remains, the classic image of Scottish forestry, but now

Tree stumps are a major obstacle in ploughing and restocking. The technique of mounding has a number of advantages over ploughing on such sites, including less erosion, a more natural appearance, better drainage and warmer mounded soil for planting. In this picture, taken in March 1989 in the Borders, a mounder is being demonstrated.

A horse rigged with Swedish harness, South Strome, 1962.

this pastoral icon was set to be superseded by less romantic steel and oil. It was a fondness for horses that led Harry Obern, as a schoolboy in Kirkcudbrightshire in the late 1960s, to become involved in harvesting trees: 'I used to go after school at nights and through the holidays. That was down in the forests around Dalbeattie. It would have been in Dalbeattie Forest and Screel Forest. At the start we were just wee boys who could hardly reach the heads of the horses. They were mainly Clydesdales, but there were other breeds. The Clydesdale has a nice nature and it's an easy horse to work with.'

The squad with whom Harry had his first taste of forestry were extracting thinnings on piece rates, using horses to drag the felled and snedded logs to the loading area. 'Horses when you were on tonnage very seldom took one tree out,' he recalled. 'The men I knew, their horses were taking five or six big trees at a time, even eight or ten. The biggest trees would be cut in half – I think it was 18-foot lengths – but the horse would still take two or three of them at a time. The horse had a collar with a chain leading off on either side to a swingle bar on the back. I've seen wooden ones since but the ones I remember were steel. There was a cleek halfway across the bar and then another big long chain. When I did it, you would try to grab as many of the thinnings as you could, wrap the chain around them in such a way that they were always pulling against the hook. You would try to get all the logs to come together and put the chain around the whole lot in such a manner that it would tighten up as the horse pulled it.'

The horses worked for five days and at weekends were tended and allowed to rest in their stable in the middle of the forest, a shed with two stalls and an earth floor, and a waterhole nearby. 'The horses were definitely well looked after,' said Harry. 'You couldn't earn money without them. The horse did a day's work like everyone else but when the horseman stopped for his dinner the first thing he did was get the bag of corn. Quite often in the woods, he would just tip out the feed onto the ground for the horse.'

There was an attachment between man and beast, a fondness that could never be matched by the feeling between man and machine. Horses were individuals with distinct characters. 'I've seen horses standing on their back legs [as they pulled] just out of sheer guts,' recalled Harry. 'I remember one horse, a black and white thing, Murray it was called. This was an old, old horse – they'd had it a long time – but it was also very clever. A lot of the

Log extraction on a steep brae at South Laggan. The horse can go where a tractor would have difficulty.

horses that worked in the woods, you never had to lead them out. Once they'd done the drag a couple of times, you just put the rope over their back and put them on, and you would walk behind the trees they were pulling. The horse would get to the road and stop, and wait for you to come and take him. The men used the horses to walk logs over the bing when they were stacking them, sometimes using other trees or branches as guides and all this sort of thing. But this Murray was quite clever and if he thought he had the upper hand of his handler, which he often thought he had, he would be dragging the logs down and they might stop, stuck behind a rut or something, and Murray would immediately go onto his back legs – "I canna take all these, they're stuck" – that was the impression he was trying to put out. Quite often they would leave Murray in the stable in the afternoon because he was quite old, but he had obviously served them well.'

John McEwen remembered horses and horsemen labouring in wartime logging camps, working from seven in the morning until five o'clock, wading in deep mud, staying in poor shacks [the men], and found both were afforded 'quite despicable treatment'. He thought it 'not surprising that such a nausea

Hauling logs in Glen Orchy, in the 1950s.

against horse-labour has set in, that a horse is now seldom seen in the woods'.[3] McEwen published these views in 1963, but his grim picture of exploitation was not Harry Obern's experience: 'The horses were definitely well looked after. One man, I saw once, kicked a horse under its stomach. I can see the wee man doing it now but I can also see his boss turning round to him and saying "If you ever lay another finger on my horse I'll make sure you never work in the woods again. Out you go." He put him away. That was it, finished.

'The worst memory I have is of the day I saw a horse in a ditch upside down. The woods had drainage ditches. If the horse was dragging out and it got to a ditch, it should stop. The horseman would take the chain off, let the horse jump the ditch, and then put on a long chain to pull the logs across. I don't know what happened this day – I'm sure the horse was called Bobby, a big brown Clydesdale – but it seemed that when he got to the ditch he stopped, and maybe something frightened him, he decided to go before the chain was off, he just jumped. The trees held him, he came back over his quarters and down into the ditch. Nobody knew whether he was hurt, though he was awake. He was right on his back, and you were looking at his four hooves. One of the blokes was down in the ditch trying to keep him calm. The fellow that was with him, he sent me to get an old man who was part of the gang, "Away and get Uncle Jimmy". This was Jimmy Cowan from Lauriston and he'd worked in the woods all his life. I was in tears, feared the horse was dying. He came down and was calming me as much as the horse. He says, "We'll just dig", and they dug down to make a ledge for Bobby to roll on to. There was another horse in the stable, a useless thing that was on its way back to the man who'd tried to sell them it. They hooked the chains from Bobby's collar to this horse and pulled him over onto his feet. Bobby came out all right though he didn't like ditches for a long time.

'One of the last times I went to the woods, the men were trialling a winch and I can remember them saying "It'll never take over from the horse." This was a winch on a sledge, and you would use it to pull itself into the wood to a position, and anchor it to a big tree with a wrap-round chain, as basic as that. Then you had somebody – in our case, it was me – who went back and fore all day with a wire rope to pull in logs to a heap.'

The winch, possibly a Sepson, a radio-controlled machine developed in Scandinavia for farmer-foresters, was a glimpse of a future that had already arrived, although there was a long period of transition and the horse never completely disappeared. In 1960 R.E. Crowther published a study on the economics of extracting thinnings by horse – foresters seemed to be inordinately fond of calculating the comparative costs of everything – and concluded that the appropriate fee for the hire of a horseman and his beast was 30 shillings per day. He arrived at this figure by taking into account various sums – £80 for a horse with a five-year working life, shoes at £7 a year, harness £10, vet bills £3, and so on, all adding up to £276 for 12 months. He also noted that in May 1959 there were still 373 horses working in Commission woods in Scotland and predicted that their replacement by machines on thinning operations on difficult ground was 'many years ahead'.[4] Horse-drawn vehicles for extracting timber had been invented in Victorian times, if not earlier. One of these was the janker, a stoutly built cart-like object with high wheels, possibly 6 feet in diameter, a heavy bow-shaped axle between and a 10-foot pole leading to the horse; it carried heavy logs slung below the high axle.[5] In the south and east of Scotland, where gradients were kinder and the ground firmer, extraction by tractor and sulky, a stout wheeled chariot with chains to secure a log, could compete with the Clydesdale but, in the Highlands at least, the horse could go where wheels still could not.

In 1956 Allan Macdonald worked for a time for a local contractor, one of a small team felling and extracting timber by horse for a local sawmill at Fort Augustus. The wood was used in mining for what were termed 'crowns', the horizontal pieces held up by pit-props. 'It was on Commission property,' said Allan, 'Probably from the first plantings of Sitka, larch and Norway spruce in the early 1920s.' Sometimes they used a Caterpillar tractor where it could penetrate the dense stands but on the very steep ground above Loch Ness and at Laggan near Invermoriston the horse had the advantage.

'I was dragging timber with the horse for about a year,' said Norman Davidson of his early experience at Calvine. 'I enjoyed that but also found it frustrating, at the age of seventeen. The horse was guided by voice and not by rein. There was only a short rein that you threw over the horse's shoulder. It followed you up into the wood where you gathered several sticks together to form a load of several hundredweights, and the horse pulled it downhill to a site on the roadside. The first horse I had was very nervous and would often take off with the load, cantering downhill until suddenly the load would go behind a tree and jam or break all the chains or traces. The second horse was much more steady and more enjoyable to work with. But he was a crafty animal, once you loosened off the load he would move a few yards away and when you wanted him to come up in the wood with you he wasn't that keen sometimes and he would edge another few yards away as you moved towards him, and so on. So you ended up in a bit of a race with this horse before he was five miles down the road. Another thing with the horse was that, if you were starting at half past seven, you had to be up at half past six to feed him. On the whole it was a very enjoyable experience and, going home at night, the horse would be like a puppy, dancing behind you, a big Clydesdale.'

Not counting the equipment brought by the Canadians, the tractor, the winch and the power saw were among the first machines to put in an appearance, filling the advertisement pages in the forestry journals in the early 1950s. 'The "Tornado" does everything so much quicker' read the slogan for the Tornado power saw, a new one-man saw from the Danarm company already known for two-man petrol or electric saws. Alastair Macleod worked with these, when he was clear-felling in Glenelg in 1953 to make room for new roads into the forests: 'There was myself and another chap working with a crosscut saw. It was hard, hard going. We got a sort of two-man power saw – this was before the start of the power saws we have now – but it was very heavy and very awkward. It had a petrol engine on it, and a frame and the chain. It took two men to carry it. I used that for quite a while and then we got the ordinary chainsaw.'

Donald Fraser found that his first chainsaw was 'a cumbersome machine' as did Norman Davidson at Calvine: 'The first chainsaw – a Danarm, a 28-pound beast. Bill Brand, the foreman, worked with it initially, until he got fed up with it and handed it to me. We took turns at it. It was quite a heavy thing to handle and it was pretty frustrating, as in those days it wasn't that reliable and we didn't know much about the mechanics. The carburettor was prone to muck getting in. There was a bit of finesse to it that we didn't have but when it did work it was fine, you could nip along and cut a number of trees down in a short while.'

The advent of the chainsaw was a development that many older foresters remember. Bryce Reynard was learning forestry in Knapdale at the time: 'A lot of trees were still being cut with bushman saws and when the trees were felled axes were being used to sned them. Horses were still being used for extraction. The men using the chainsaws – heavy, temperamental things – were just doing it by themselves – there was no health and safety, no hard hats or ear muffs. You could listen and identify from the sounds of saws in the distance who it was. In the early days it never seemed to occur to anyone that you could sned with them; they were used for felling and the fallen trunks were left for an axeman to sned.'

The heaviness of the early chainsaws actually made it easier to do the job with the axe. Norman Davidson again: 'We worked with English-type axes

Felling trees to clear a rackway in Gartly Moor Forest in 1980.

more than the Scottish wedge. A Scottish axe head in elevation is almost like a rectangle but the English axe is much more shaped, with a waist, narrow at the top and expanding towards the cutting edge. I don't know any particular reason for that but we preferred the English axe and used them quite a bit. It was about four and a half pounds in weight. There were some heavier six-pound axes which we used on windblow in the big trees with heavy branches. We'd be at it all day, bent over, going with the axe. No problem at all, you could always handle the axe well in those days. They were taken home with you at night, you sharpened them in your own time, you had your own one with your initials on it. Your spade was your own spade as well. Each man had his own tools and looked after them. Even if we were planting three or four miles away the spade came home with you at night, strapped to your crossbar. At night you would sharpen it.'

The first forestry machinery exhibition took place in England in 1958 – Scotland did not have one until 1962. By then cableways and winches were being used to 'fly' cut logs to loading sites. The principle of these devices was simple – rig up a cable on pylons and use gravity to fly bundles of logs along it. The reality was more complex and fraught, requiring great care in positioning and security. Of these so-called 'sky cranes', the Wyssen Skyline was perhaps the best known at first, named for its designer, a Swiss engineer. It was first used in Scotland in Glenbranter in 1953–54. In the pages of *Scottish Forestry*, N. Deveria recalled his memories of these experiments, conducted under the nervous eyes of an expert team from the manufacturer: 'Some . . . are grim – we had two near disastrous accidents – but most are pleasant . . . Who would have believed it possible to select from a forest squad in the west of Scotland a team of men prepared to climb 60-foot poles with climbing irons only, to hang from crossed legs and safety belt while assembling support brackets at this height or to operate a winch by sixth sense which told them what was happening 1,000 yards away?'[6]

In the 1950s and 1960s forestry involved a great deal of manual labour.

Second-generation forest in Glenbranter.

Norman Davidson recalled being one of four or five young men, lifting 40-foot logs up to 12 inches in diameter at the butt to feed the estate's circular saw and produce fenceposts. 'We had to move in unison with that log into the saw blade and back out again, move sideways another 5 feet 6 inches, and move the log into the saw blade again, and so on. If you didn't do it in parallel and the man on the tail went off the line, you jammed the blades. Then the posts all had to be stacked for the tractor and trailer coming along to take them away. A lot of manual labour, we lifted some enormous loads to great heights. We became pretty fit and we never had any serious accidents.'

'Every log had to be loaded by hand,' wrote Kenneth MacKenzie about his lorry-driving days in Glen Affric, 'with the assistance of roadside banks, skids and ropes in the case of heavy timber, but it was really healthy and satisfying work. Maybe that was due to the fact that I was young and strong at the time, and enjoyed the challenge it presented.'

Elaborate, powerful machines were to appear in the coming years but the soul of the forester still resided in the axeman whose skill retained the ability

Brashing Sitka spruce.

to astonish. As Harry Obern recalled: 'On the big squads, where I helped as a schoolboy, there were six or eight blokes. Two of them, the bosses, would spend most of the morning cutting trees down with a chainsaw. On some they might take off the tops and some of the branches but the chainsaws were a lot heavier then. They didn't spend the whole day taking the branches off with the saws, that was done by three or four boys on axes. You would see them working their way up the tree and then stick the axe in the end and turn it over to do the other side. They had a bar with a chain and hook for turning logs but usually they just used the axe. Often you would see them sitting at their dinner time or their teatime and they would be sharpening their axes with a file. The blade of the axe was like chrome to look at. They were continually keeping the axe sharp. These guys started in the morn and they just didn't stop 'til teatime.' The axemen prided themselves on their abilities. 'A few were capable of splitting a standing match on a tree stump with one full swipe,' noted Donald Fraser. This display and rivalry was the lifeblood of the competitions already noted for the 1930s and which continue to the present day but where a key feature is chainsaw handling.

Another side of forestry in the 1950s was experienced by Charles Scott. He was studying engineering at Glasgow College of Technology on a sandwich course that allowed six months of work experience in the summer. 'Various people came and talked to us about opportunities, and the Forestry Commission was one of them. They were looking for people for the Dunoon area and the Inverness area. Well, my mother was from Inverness-shire and I thought it would be nice to go up there. The Forestry Commission office was in Church Street. This was in 1953. After the war they had done a lot of planting but not a lot of engineering, and some of the forests had no access roads, bridges or anything. After spending a day or two in the office in Church Street, I was immediately transported to Glen Affric with another student, John Imlah Neumeyer, from Aberdeen University. We were put up in the Tomich Hotel – that sounds very grand but it was an old-style hotel. There was no licence. Mrs Macdonald ran it and you got a knock at the door in the morning and a jug of water. There was a bowl in the room for washing. I think there was one toilet in the whole place. The cooking was excellent – we got our breakfast and evening meal, and a packed sandwich lunch to take with us.'

The two students had to map out reasonable routes for the building of roads into the forest. This involved much walking through the trees, paying attention to the gradients, cursing the burns and placing pegs in the ground to trace the centre line of the proposed roadway. Once that was done, a man with a bulldozer came to start the excavation and a senior engineer checked where bridges had to be laid.

'Some days we walked from Tomich Hotel into Glen Affric,' said Charles. 'On other days one of the foresters used to drive us up the glen to the far side of Loch Beneveian, and we used to steal a boat and row across and start the work from that side. The hydro–electric dam had just been finished. The first time we took the boat we were a hundred yards out before we realised that it leaked, so one of us was rowing and the other was bailing. It was all quite an adventure in a way.'

Glen Affric had then, as it does now, a reputation for being one of the most beautiful parts of the country, with a considerable acreage of natural Caledonian forest. After three months exploring its attractions, the students were given a new posting to a different environment, to Strome Ferry in Wester Ross. 'It had been planted very dense with Sitka spruce. There was no road then along the south side of the loch, the railway came along and you had to get the ferry across to the village. The trees hadn't been thinned. One day we went into the forest – it was pouring rain, we were wet through, we'd gone home and changed, and before we finished in the forest we were wet through again because of the trees. They were literally a metre or so apart and only 12 to 15 feet high, so we had to fight our way through the branches. You couldn't see a thing about the lie of the land. That was the smallest area we did but it had a very definitive slope, not a lot of room for manoeuvre. We had to chop down branches or the road-builders would never have found the pegs. You had to set off with a route you felt reasonable for the gradients and so on – we tended to work on the contour, knowing that that should be okay.'

Once routes had been pushed through the Strome Ferry forest, the students moved south again to tackle the same task in Glenurquhart. 'This was much bigger – in fact we got lost one day and this part was fairly flat, we couldn't tell if we were going up or down, and we had to climb a tall tree to see which way to go. They had actually built one road and it took us in a certain distance but the forest stretched over quite a big area there.'

Levelling a forestry road in the late 1970s – early 1980s.

Some 25 years after that summer, Charles Scott returned to Glen Affric and walked some of the roads he had pioneered, perhaps 10 or 15 miles, including the stretches along Loch Beneveian and from Guisachan over into the glen. He also bumped into the son of the bulldozer driver.

The road construction work was sometimes awarded to contractors but the Commission also had its own road squads. Allan Macdonald was for five years a member of one based in Fort Augustus in the Great Glen, whence it forayed out in the summer to stay in caravans or hostels and work in forests as far as Lochaline or Polloch in Glen Shiel. This mobile squad comprised a dozen men, equipped with a bulldozer, jackhammers and gelignite for blasting rock. Driving a road into hills where none had been before was a slow business – on the west coast a summer's work could accomplish 2 miles of roadway with drains and culverts – and the squad had to improvise, for example finding the needed gravel from a river bed if possible to save opening a quarry with all the attendant drilling and blasting. Once the basic route was dug, drainage had to be put in place and the surface spread with gravel to a depth of two feet on firm ground but 4 or 5 feet on the softer stretches. The road put through the deep peat of Torlundy near Fort William was virtually floating, and the ground used to shake for about 100 yards on each side when a lorry rumbled by.

After he graduated in 1951, Finlay Macrae was posted to Inverness. The main conservancy office in Church Street had a staff of 40 or 50 and looked after a large part of the Highlands as far south as Fort William and the march with Argyllshire. Finlay's destination was to be the Culloden office where he worked with the senior district officer, Alastair Mackay Fraser. 'There was just the two of us,' he said. 'We looked after everything down Loch Ness-side and out as far as Nairn and then to Speyside, that was my first beat. A big area, maybe 200,000 acres of forest. We didn't have a telephone. That was in the main house – Mr Fraser had his house nearby and when the telephone rang his wife would come and shout to us, "There's somebody on the phone for you". We had a forestry van.

'We did all the forestry work then ourselves, from the acquiring of the land, finding out who was likely to sell land to the Commission. You could buy an acre then for about £3. Very often land came to us because there were lairds who were only too glad to get shot of some. I spent most of my days there, as the assistant district officer, learning from this senior man. That was a very enjoyable time. He was an excellent man, outstanding in every respect. He was from Dornoch and he was a very religious man, very easy to work with. Our office was more or less an enlarged shed in Balloch. From there we did all our office work. There was no such thing as a typewriter, everything was by hand. It's most interesting now to see the big offices they have and all the computers, and it's astonishing to think we ran that district with pen and ink. We made all our own maps up as we went on — we worked five days in the field and half a day on the Saturday in the office, all our office work in a half day. No typist, no secretary, nothing.

'The work during the week was mostly supervising. There were foresters at all the beats, one at Strathmashie, down near Laggan, and one in the Queen's Forest at Rothiemurchus, another one at Inshriach, and as you came up the glen there was one at Culloden. We went to see what they were doing and how they were planning their work. We had outstandingly good staff. The foresters were excellent men – they had come into forestry to be foresters, and that's what they were. A place like Culloden would have twenty or thirty men working there, and forty or fifty in Speyside. Each place had its own gang, responsible to the head forester on the beat. And he was accountable to us. There wasn't really a lot of direction from the centre. The main planning was done there – you were told how much you were expected to plant each year, and so on. In our district there was very little thinning at that stage. We were in the process of creating forests, which I rather enjoyed. I've never liked cutting forests. I would rather create them than cut them down.'

The acquisition of land began with a careful inspection before a report was passed on to the Church Street headquarters for completion of the purchase. The district office and the forester on the spot considered how it could best be used, what species were to be planted and so on, before the forester was left to put the plan into action. 'We would have a programme each year for each forest,' said Finlay. 'Some would be doing twenty acres of planting, some fifty, and a very big forest would be doing sixty a year. It would be reasonable to expect a squad of ten men to plant an acre in a morning, maybe two or three acres in a day, depending on how easy it was, the steepness of the terrain, whether they had ploughing to attend to or turfing to do.'

Land the foresters acquired at this time between Dores and Inverfarigaig on the east side of Loch Ness was covered by birch, a tree then considered to be a weed. 'We had to thin the birch first and then we went in and underplanted it with Norway spruce,' said Finlay. 'When it came to looking after the trees, we had rabbits and deer to contend with. Usually we fertilised the trees, with a small handful of NPK – nitrogen, phosphorus and potassium fertiliser – scattered around the plant. We weeded the plantings every year until the trees were out of that stage. Spruce especially, which was fast growing, would be out of the weeding stage in three or four years. Then it was a case of just watching it grow.'

In April 1953, Finlay left Inverness to take charge of his own district at Fort William. 'I did the whole of Lochaber, right down to Fiunary, and Mull. An enormous district, a lovely district, but of course constantly wet – 100 inches a year was quite common, and I'd come from maybe 35 in Inverness. But it didn't bother me because I was from the west, I was used to rainfall. We were largely into spruce – the west is very much spruce-growing country. We were also responsible for looking after the growing of trees in private woodlands. Private forestry was emerging in the 1950s and it grew quite rapidly. Our programmes were larger but I must say some of the small programmes were interesting. I went as far east as Corrour, where Sir John Stirling-Maxwell, a real pioneer, had started planting in 1927. We were advisers to the private fellows but very often they had factors on the estates and we would liaise with them and decide on a common route ahead. Nearly all were forestry graduates or at least had been to the forestry school.'

While the foresters at Culloden were nurturing the new plantations by Loch Ness, over on the west coast in Glenelg, Alastair Macleod was hard at work felling. Born on Rona and long resident on Raasay, Alastair moved to a new croft on the mainland in 1953. 'I met the forester chap who was in charge of Glenelg and I asked him if there was any chance of part-time work,' he recalled. 'Och aye, he says, so I started then. It was part-time. I was taking days off for hay and so on. It fitted in quite well with the crofting.

'The woods in Glenelg were more or less mature. They were starting putting roads in, so we had to clear fell for that. We had one Clydesdale horse for taking the trunks to the roadsides. The trees were planted too thick, about six feet apart, and you didn't have so much space. They were 27 years old, I think, when we started cutting. They usually got stuck [against other trees] but you stuck the axe in the bottom and you pulled the tree along until it was clear. Once it was on the ground you had to sned it, trim off all the branches.

You needed quite a bit of practice to make a good job of snedding with a four-and-a-half-pound handaxe. On an average, two of us would cut eighty trees in a day. But you had to keep the saw sharp, with a file to keep the teeth at a certain angle. You had to have the saw set as well, you had to have the teeth one one way and one the other. Then you'd cut a wider groove, otherwise it would jam. I was very good at setting the saws.

'We started at about a quarter to eight in the morning, I think. You had half an hour for your lunchtime, and you worked until five o'clock. You could have a tea-break but sometimes we were on contracts. They used to send an officer round to offer you a contract – you felled a tree here and there as a sample tree and it was snedded down. Girth at breast height – that was the sample – and that was for maybe ten trees in the plot and they made an average of that, the cubic measurement of that, and you got a contract. At that time the ordinary pay would be about £5 a week for a labourer. Being on contract, if you worked hard, sometimes you could double that.

'You had to provide your own clothes. You weren't equipped with anything. We had good fun. It depended on the people working with you, and the people in Glenelg were great. There would be about ten of us at the felling. All local men, except one or two. There was one Englishman – he was the horseman for a while.'

Experienced fellers could work very fast. By Loch Awe, in the late 1940s and 1950s, Tommy Stewart and his father were so experienced. 'We could cowp a hundred trees an hour,' he says in the book from the Touchwood oral history project for mid-Argyll.[7] Tommy says his father learned in turn from his father. This was an instance of forestry skill being passed from generation to generation, and there must have been only a few places in Scotland at that time where that kind of knowledge existed to be handed down.

It was the practice in this country to fell a tree as close to the ground as possible. John Keenleyside remembers the old forester in charge of his squad saying 'Keep the stumps low, laddie, it doesna matter if you skin your knuckles. Remember, a foot at the bottom o the tree is worth ten foot at the top.' 'There was none of this high stuff that the Newfoundlanders do,' said Bryce Reynard. During the two world wars, the high stumps left by the Canadians and Newfoundlanders raised many a disapproving eyebrow on this side of the Atlantic. The Canadians had, however, brought with them a cable system for flying logs from the felling site, a system called the Blondin after the famous tightrope walker.

The technique of felling was straightforward, but it took skill and fitness to put it into consistent practice with hand tools. Bryce Reynard explained, 'You started with a cut, either with the crosscut or a bushman saw, in the side to which you wanted the tree to fall. This was called the mouth, and then with your felling axe you'd take a throat out of it. Then you came in from the other side, slightly higher up, with the saw. Unlike what you might think, this crashing of timber, very seldom did they fall down, you had to push them over, because in the forest they would just lean against the next tree, and you had to drag them to the side and so on. [Nobody shouted "timber" except perhaps at first because they thought they were expected to.] There were various tools you could use to move them but when you're young the challenge was to see if you could get them out yourself. Over your shoulder and drag them out. The horseman came along. We didn't use the horses. They were with people who had been on the go for a long time, not just students like us. Some were on contract but certainly in Knapdale a lot of horsemen had Forestry Commission holdings. I remember Bud Gillies, he used the expression "If you sang Annie Laurie, it would make the rain come on". It was one of those things – if you were fed up or bored, you'd be desperate for a wet day so you could have a rest.'

'It was mainly Sitka spruce and Norway spruce we were felling and in those days it was going away mainly for pit props. Thirty-foot lengths on the back of a lorry, to mills to be cut into pit prop sizes rather than cutting them to size in the wood. They were thinnings and the ones to be felled were marked beforehand by teams of two or three men who left a blaze on the chosen trees, an axe mark about chest height on two sides of the trunk. Racks were marked as well for extraction where the horse would come out. A rack in this context means a track. Generally speaking if you were to stand in the middle you wouldn't be able to touch a tree on either side, that kind of width, about six feet. These would extend for considerable distances. In the horse days they could have curves but when winches came in they had to be dead straight.'

Thinning allowed the maintenance of tree cover and at the same time encouraged the growth of good trees. The alternative, the clear felling of stretches of woodland, has become common for economic reasons but it has drawbacks. 'I don't like to see clear felling,' said Finlay Macrae, 'The days of thinning are over, really, continual thinning. We used to have the first thinning at 30–35 years of age, and then at 40 years, and maybe 50 years – trees were allowed to grow on until they were a hundred years old. Thinning was a skill that we were taught – how to get the right spacing. We were looking for trees with a straight stem and a good head on it, a healthy tree, and if we got a runt beside it we would remove that. But you took about six foot spacing when you planted and by the time you were at the first thinning you were out maybe 15 or 20 feet.'

The Blondin tackles were succeeded by new systems for extracting logs. By 1964, one model of winch system, the Isachsen Mark III, was in use in the north-west Highlands, hauling logs from a maximum distance of 170 metres, although 140 metres was usually a more effective range.[8] In the Leanachan forest near Fort William in the late 1960s, Norman Davidson led a team of six fellers and two winchmen working with this relatively new equipment. 'Cable cranes were just starting in those days,' he said, 'and I enjoyed their development. There was a lot of experimentation with them. We worked with short lengths, what we called high lead systems, only going to about 100 metres, maybe only 50 in certain circumstances. Then the skyline was beginning to come in which was a slightly different cable crane system, whereby a carriage is supported on a taut skyline and it can go up over hill and down dale, supported by trees along its length so that you can go up to 300 metres. In those days communication between the man at the bottom and the choker man at the top was by hand signals and shouting, before we began to use radios – pocket sets with earpieces that filled up with water and didn't work – and so on. Then we were working with different anchoring systems.'

The installation of a cable crane needed preparation. The forester began by choosing a suitable strip of forest and marking the trees to be felled to make room for a rackway, which had to be 12 feet wide and separated from the next rackway by about 20 yards. 'When you were marking the rack, you would have identified a suitable spar tree, an anchor tree, at the top and a few trees as anchoring trees at the bottom,' said Norman. 'The spar tree holds the cables above the ground, with cables going down to several trees behind it as stays. The skyline comes down under tension to the tower at the winch, which is stayed back as well. Basically the logs are hauled up to the skyline and then hauled down on the skyline. There's a lot of tension on that 19 mm steel cable. It's a disaster if the spar tree breaks.

'It was heavy equipment to manhandle, you usually carried on your back all the pulleys and anchor ropes to the top spar tree, and also ropes and metal supports to hold the skyline above the ground. To pull up the skyline itself you used a light polypropylene rope, walked up the rackway with it and brought it back down, and used that to haul up the main cable. The double-drum winch was at the bottom, fixed to a tractor. The maximum distance was

Windblown timber being extracted by an Isachsen winch at Coirintee in Ben More Forest, Argyll, in 1969.

300 metres for the skyline but it was difficult working at that. It could take two men the best part of a day to set up the initial rack – heavy work and you needed ladders to climb the trees – but once that was done you just had to carry the pieces across to the next rack, to the left or the right.'

A point at the higher end of the rack and to the left of the spar tree was probably the most dangerous place to stand. Here the haul-back line, which pulled the carriage back up the skyline, came out to the side and down another rack back to the winch. 'You had to be careful standing in the bight of that because if a pulley broke you could get a nasty accident. The other dangerous point was down at the winch itself where the cables were running. If the haul-back line broke, the carriage – it probably weighed nearly one hundredweight – would just come rattling down the skyline at 30, 50 mph. The carriage hung

An Isachsen double
drum winch on a
Ferguson tractor
hauling out spruce in
Inverliever Forest in
1966.

from two wheels that ran on the fixed skyline cable. I never saw an accident to a man but certainly to machinery. Spar trees often broke, cable broke, skylines broke, and all had to be fixed. We were all taught how to splice cables, and a skyline needed something like a 60-foot splice.'

Swinging out the felled logs needed attention to detail and keeping to a sequence of moves. 'We were felling in pulp mill lengths, about 3 m or 10 feet. Everything was converted into 10 foot lengths. The fellers stacked their produce in little stacks, possibly 4, 5 or 6 hundredweights [200–300 kilograms] on a bearer so the choker man could put his cable around the head of the bundle of logs. Once the carriage came up, it was anchored at the right spot so that you could drag the cable sideways to the stack and then haul the bundle in. It was a question of applying the brake on the haul-back line and hauling in on the haul-in line until the load came up to the carriage, and then once the load was at the carriage you eased off the brake on the haul-back line and the whole lot, the carriage and the load, moved down towards the winch. It is quite difficult to perform because you have to balance the force on the hauling-in winch with a certain weight on the brakes on the haul-back line so that you keep the load semi-suspended. You don't want it jammed against the carriage too hard because it puts a lot of strain on the winch.

'The winchman couldn't see the load for much of the time so he depended on the engine responses on the cable crane itself and the sound of the wires. It was quite a skill to get that load down without dragging it too much on the ground or jamming too hard against the carriage. The choker man gave him as much instruction as he could in the limited communication system they had. It was a skilful art in those days. When it was well done, it was nice to see, a joy to behold, as they say. They still do it now but it's pretty expensive. They have what are called locking carriages, meaning that the load is brought to a point, however close the choker man thinks it should be, and it is locked at that point, a certain distance from the carriage. All you have to do then is haul it down and ease off on the haul-back line. It is simpler and far less stress on the whole mechanism. The locking carriage is heavier but simpler to work.'

One of the fitters who travelled around the Highlands to keep the machinery working was Hamish Fraser, now in charge of the Commission's engineering depot in Inverness. After serving his time as an agricultural engineer in Inverness, he joined the Forestry Commission in 1970 and, after some general work, spent a year, in his words, 'doing nothing but welding plough heads and all those things.' The work involved adapting or modifying the heads to make

better furrows. One idea, originating with the manager Mr Logan, was to make an L shaped sock to cut a step in the side of the furrow into which a tree could be planted so that it would have a little shelter in its early period of growth in the peat bogs in the north.

Hamish grew tired of the welding and, when he challenged what he was always doing, 'I was shoved the following Monday to the west coast, where I had a van and became a mobile fitter.' This meant staying in the west in digs during the week and coming home only at weekends. 'We kept in touch with walkie-talkie radios. The area I covered at that time was from Slattadale in the Gairloch area right down the west to Invermoriston and Skye.'

The Commission had begun to use winches in felling operations, first Igland and then Isachsen models. 'Keeping the winches in operation was the most important part of the job. The biggest problem we had was probably clutch bearings. They just weren't quite heavy enough for the long hauls. But

Dragging timber with a skyline crane.

the winchmen were good because if, say, they broke down two o'clock one day, by the time you got there the next morning, they had it all stripped ready for you, to get the bearings in and set the whole lot up. I recall we had eighteen of them working, two in Slattadale, two in North Strome and two in South Strome, and six in Moye in the Ratagan area, and another six in Glen Eynort on Skye. There weren't so many Commission employees on Skye, it was contractors, they had a camp but they worked on the Commission's own machines. In those days it was mostly wood for pulp in Glen Eynort, but then they finished the pulp and got on to logs. All the pulp then went to Fort William, to the mill at Corpach, and the logs to the sawmill there.'

Another fitter covered the far north, where the work was nearly all to do with ploughing, but Hamish occasionally gave him help or relieved him. This meant dealing with bogged tractors. 'We did a lot of debogging in our time. There would hardly be a week going past but somebody was stuck in a hole somewhere. I've seen them well out of sight. In those days – in the '70s and '80s – we had twenty-four ploughing outfits, from Argyllshire right to Caithness. Once we got them out of the hole – if they had been out of sight completely – the engines were full of water. We had to take them in here and clean them all out, strip down the injectors and clean out all the foreign matter and peat, and wash them all down, change all the oils. The glass in the cabs would be all pushed out. Hose them all down with fire pumps. Most of it was done on site with our own mobile fire pumps. That took the worst of it off before they came in here.'

The memorial – a granite boulder with a metal plaque – can be found beside a minor road that cuts over the crest of the Black Isle in Ross-shire. The text reads 'In tribute to James Fraser, Conservator of Forests, Forestry Commission, who between the years 1924–1956 established many of the forests viewed from this point and others far beyond.' 'He was a very, very able man,' recalled Finlay Macrae, 'the son of a Dingwall family who were saddlers by trade.' His obituary in *Scottish Forestry* highlighted his 'energy and dour determination, brightened by a sense of humour so strong . . . that his own laughter sometimes prevented a story's point from reaching the audience. He was quite unconventional . . . and penetratingly critical'.[9] After graduating in forestry from Edinburgh University in 1912, Fraser taught at the West of Scotland College of Agriculture and, surviving military service in the First World War with the Argyll and Sutherland Highlanders, joined the Interim Forest Authority, the forerunner of the Commission. Lovat

Fixing the chain around a bundle of logs for the skyline crane.

Opposite. Dragging
bundles of timber
towards the skyline
crane.

appointed him as head of the forestry school at Beaufort. In 1931 he became the divisional officer in charge of the north, later rising to the rank of conservator. Fraser died in January 1959, at the end of a life spent in forestry, a life that spanned many of the early developments in his chosen profession.

By this time the activities of the Commission had wrought far-reaching changes across the country. 'It is no exaggeration to say that these new plantations have changed the entire landscape,' commented William McNeill of Aberdeen University's department of forestry in 1963.[10] 'Much of the planting has been done on bare heather-clad hillsides . . . Deep ploughing and heavy equipment . . . with the use of chemical fertilisers, have made possible the successful afforestation of sites previously considered unplantable.' He was speaking particularly of the north-eastern counties but the remark applied equally to most of rural Scotland. In May 1961 the Forestry Commission celebrated the planting of its 100,000th acre of new woodland in Argyll.[11] It could look back on other achievements: several hundred houses built, several hundred miles of road laid, employment – both direct and in 'downstream' industries in sawmills and so on – running into the thousands.

A young plantation on
the Dalmeny estate with
the Forth bridges in the
background, in 1972.

By the mid 1960s, the Commission forests were producing over 100,000 tons of timber worth £2 million each year – all of it destined for use as pit-props, poles, fenceposts and wood pulp – and private forests were increasing this output by another million tons. The Commission had over 200 forests, covering a total of 1.6 million acres, of which 754,000 had been planted. The

The Dalmeny estate today.

Opposite.
This tree, at Ardkinglass, was considered to be the largest one in Scotland in 1953. It is a species of the noble fir (*Abies*) genus (*John Keenleyside*).

three largest were Loch Ard, Inverliever and Culbin. There were tree nurseries at Newton (Elgin), Kirroughtree (Newton Stewart), Ledmore (Perth) and Tulliallan (Alloa). With about six staff employed for every 1,000 planted acres, the work force reached to over 4,550, about half of whom could be found in the six counties of Bute, Argyll, Inverness, Ross and Cromarty, Caithness and Sutherland. In September 1973, when Queen Elizabeth the Queen Mother unveiled a boulder in the Queen Elizabeth Forest Park at Aberfoyle to commemorate the planting of the Commission's millionth acre in Scotland, the Commission chairman, Lord Taylor of Gryfe, said its woods had produced over 600,000 tons of timber in the previous year, worth £3 million.[12] This was progress but Britain was still reliant on imported timber, able to meet only 8 per cent of its needs from domestic sources, said Lord Dalkeith in a presentation to the Royal Highland Show in November 1970.[13] The industry was still dealing with other issues that had come to the fore in 1919 when the Commission had been founded, mainly those of land use. Dalkeith argued that afforestation was better use of the land, providing more work and higher profit, than hill farming but not everyone was convinced.

Voices were still being raised on the now familiar topic of the afforestation of agricultural land and the best use of resources. Sheep farmers in the Borders were reported to be alarmed at the spread of the plantations.[14] Fearful for part of their common grazing, crofters protested to the Scottish Land Court over the Commission's wish to plant around 200 acres a year on the estates of Glenspean and Inverroy. James Shaw Grant, the chairman of the Crofters Commission, referred to the 'explosive subject of forestry' in a

talk in Drumnadrochit in February 1966 and tried to take a balanced view; he acknowledged the benefits to farming from, for example, shelter belts, but argued that 'the effective planning of land should come from below or with the knowledge of those who worked the land'.[15]

The Commission was rapidly becoming the largest landowner in the Highlands. By the end of the 1970s the North Conservancy held 670,000 acres, employed about 750 workers, and spent some £2 million a year. The Conservancy's planting programme – around 16,000 acres a year – represented almost one quarter of the planting in the whole of Britain. The Commission could argue that it kept many villages viable and provided more work than hill farming in rural areas, although the amount of employment was falling as mechanisation increased.

The continuing afforestation, however, was coming under attack from another direction. Campbell Steven summed it up in 1970 in writing about the Argyllshire glens: '. . . the armies of conifers have invaded the glen in crushing strength, serried, black and altogether displeasing'.[16] The Sitka spruce and the lodgepole pine were becoming commonly seen as alien invading species and a blight on the landscape. Writers often resorted to military metaphors to convey their indignation. Indeed there was something forbidding about a dense conifer plantation, the branches clustered so thickly that no light could penetrate to the ground, where nothing grew and everything was buried in a layer of shed needles. The way ploughing and planting ignored contours and cut across gradients, resulting in rigid, unnatural geometric blocks of forest, also offended the eye. On Arran, 'Many residents had objected to afforestation quite vehemently on the grounds that it would spoil those aspects of the island which most attracted tourists'.[17] In the hills around Moffat, on the watershed between the catchments of the Annan and the Tweed, as elsewhere in Scotland, the contrast between forest and open moor can be seen to striking effect in the late summer when the dark conifers give way to the views of green bracken and purple heather. Steve Tompkins worked for the Commission and in private forestry before he began to question the policy in favour of conifers and to the neglect of broad-leaved trees and summed up his argument in his book whose title says it all, *The Theft of the Hills*, published by the Ramblers Association in 1986.[18] By this time, he wrote, 90 per cent of the afforestation in Britain was taking place in Scotland, much of it by private landowners supported by generous public subsidy. There was, he said, a 'forestry lobby . . . which benefits greatly from public funds without troubling too much about public consultation.'

To answer such criticisms, the Commission appointed in 1964 its first landscape architect, Sylvia Crowe. A prize-winning garden and landscape designer, she made her reputation on a series of commissions across the country before she was charged with making the state forests appear better to the beholder. She summarised her views in a book, *Forestry in the Landscape*, which proved to be very influential. She was not the first to consider the appearance of forests; for example, the fourth and fifth dukes of Buccleuch were reputed to lay out woodland on their large estates in the Border hills to match the cloud shadows. Crowe laid down some basic principles advising when planning a forest to take into account the scale of the landscape. In open, rolling countryside large blocks of conifers would appear less intrusive than they would in a more rugged area of small glens and steep hills. It was also advisable to consider the contrast between open and planted areas, the proportion of broadleaves to conifers, and the colours of the foliage. 'A hillside planted solidly with conifers may often be linked very acceptably to an agricultural valley with its broadleaved hedgerow trees,' she wrote, 'if broadleaves also feather up the gullies on the hillside.' Lines should follow and break in sympathy with the contours, and such principles should also be followed in clear felling.[19]

Although most of the state forests were in the Southern Uplands and the Highlands, some forestry also took place in the central lowlands. Donald Fraser's first posting when he joined the Commission in 1961 was to Blairadam Forest close to the Fife village of Kelty. 'The presence of woodland at first appeared slightly alien to me midst a hostile landscape of thrusting black pit bings,' he recalled. In 1968 E.J.M. Davies described Cumbernauld Forest as the only Commission forest entirely within the industrial belt. It was planted in the years between 1965 and 1967, and here was one place where the foresters had to concern themselves with problems of pollution, theft, arson and vandalism.[20] Davies may have been mistaken in his claim – it probably depends on how one defines the central belt – as the Commission had planted trees in 1953 at Selm Muir near Livingston.[21] More planting followed until by the mid 1980s over 3,500 hectares had been placed under mainly conifers by the Commission and a further 2,690 hectares by private owners, an increase of forest cover from less than 4 per cent of the land to over 10. The rise and decline of heavy industry left scars across the landscape – it was estimated in 1975 that waste bings covered some 7,000 hectares, with an equal amount of land left derelict from other causes. The soil at a former coal washing plant near the village of Forth had pH values less than 2. The foresters experimented with planting on such highly acidic or degraded soils with considerable success, and the forests probably have a proportionally greater benefit in encouraging wildlife, providing recreational facilities and generally enhancing the landscape than they can have in the rural parts of Scotland that have known little large-scale industry.

The Forestry Commission offered a satisfying career for men and women with a keen interest in the outdoors and many employees speak fondly of the camaraderie and the friendly spirit prevailing in the service. 'The forestry has always been a kind of family firm,' said Bryce Reynard. 'Mention a forester and the chances are I know them. It's that size of organisation where you tend to know folk. In my year at the forestry school we were all individuals but we all got on very well in a group.' Nevertheless, from time to time the Commission experienced some difficulty in retaining staff. Dissatisfaction with wages accounted for some of this, especially when coupled with staying in remote locations. The indefatigable John McEwen incurred the displeasure of his masters on this point in the early years of the Commission, as he described in his book *Who Owns Scotland*: 'Between 1920 and 1924 the FC was paying its workers around 45 shillings per week. This "high" wage did not suit the finances of the private estate owner and great pressure was brought on the FC to reduce it . . . I was told to pay something under 40 shillings. I just refused to do so . . .'[22] Generally wages for forestry workers were kept more or less on a par with the rates prevailing in agriculture while, retaining the distinction between officers and other ranks that ruled at the time, foresters had a salary. In the 1950s the basic wage was around £6 a week and by 1971 this had risen to £13–14 per week, while a head forester earned around £1,800 per year. In 1977, the worker's wage reached the range of £23–28 per week, slightly above the basic wage of the agricultural labourer.

A system of piece-rate working was often brought into play with benefits to both parties, as Norman Davidson explained: 'Very often we were on day work for one-off type jobs but if there was a sizeable job like a month's or two-month's planting you got piece work then, so much per bundle of plants and the rate is for example a shilling a bundle, as the foreman would say. We worked hard whether we were on piece work or not but on piece work at least we were getting another pound or two. It was an advantage to both parties, the estate got higher output, though not necessarily a better quality, and we got an increased pay packet at the end of the week. We were all fairly fit and able to make over the day wage on piece work without any great problem. Another thing the piece work rate didn't vary from the youngest to the oldest, like the day wage, so if you were young and fit you had the capacity to get up towards the wage of the older age bands.'

'The men on piece work got so much a tree when felling and so much a hundred when planting,' said Bryce Reynard. 'It was based on the expectation of a feller cutting down a reasonable number of trees in a day so that he would end up better off than he would be on time work. He had the choice. There was and probably still is a kind of hierarchy. Those who are cutting timber, working in the wood, get more salary and higher status than the ones on the hill, doing the planting, ploughing, draining, those kinds of jobs.'

The piecework rates varied according to the difficulty of the task in hand. Restocking, or planting on clear-felled ground, was often more difficult than planting for the first time on open moor and the rate set by the forester had to take this into account. Allan Macdonald saw piecework as a 'wee incentive and said the forester was always being pestered by his squad to raise the rate, although of course he had to answer to the district officer and had his own motive for keeping the rate down.' On his first experience of planting, in Glen Errochty in the 1950s, Donald Fraser was paid 3s 6d for every bundle of 100 trees planted, 'which, after a back-breaking week's work (the best workers planting 900 plants per day) earned £7 to £8 per 5½-day week; providing it didn't rain.' This was the big drawback with piece rates – nothing was earned when work stopped through bad weather 'unless the period lost on a given day was over two hours.' The result was that whenever possible Donald and his companions bent their shoulders to the rain and carried on.

If the rain became too heavy, the squad on time-work took shelter. Bryce Reynard again: 'You didn't go home, you just waited in case the rain would stop. It had to be pretty wet before you were stood down, not just a drizzle. In those days, too, people went out on the hill at the start of the day, whether planting or felling or whatever, and you came back at the end of the day. The shelter was a hap, a wooden framework with tarpaulin that went in the back of the lorry that took the squad out and was abandoned at the last place where the men were dropped off to work. There was no wet-weather clothing, you just had to take your own stuff. In those days, too, the outdoor clothing people wore was just their good clothes down-graded. They were there in dungarees and suits. The ganger decided when wet time started and he would try to push it to get more work done.'

Retired foresters are fond of remembering the comradeship and crack during their days working in the woods. Peter MacDonald recalled how the midday break allowed time for a haircut. 'There was one worker, Jock Lee, in Glenurquhart who carried his hair clippers in his piece bag and sat his customers on a stump. Among the squad there was an old-timer who was never seen without his bonnet and would keep it on even when subjecting himself to Jock's tonsorial attention. He was reputed to have a splendid mane of black hair. On pay day the head forester would turn up to dish out the paypackets at the roadside. The old-timer borrowed a pair of specs from a colleague to see to the formalities. These turned out to have no legs as their owner was in the habit of attaching them with an elastic band around the back of his head. The old-timer stuck to his principles and refused to remove his bonnet to don the specs, saying "If you've got to take off half your clothes, the glasses are no use".'

The much-vaunted military-like structure of the Commission did not extend all the way down the ranks. 'The military analogy failed completely as far as discipline was concerned,' recalled Brian Denoon, 'It was really the lack of discipline that was one of the attractions of working in the Forestry [in the early 1950s]. It wasn't so much slackness more the fact that the workforce had come to an accord with the management over certain contentious areas.' One of these was the definition of 'wet time' and when it was reasonable to down tools and seek shelter. It depended on the work: 'If . . . we were at the hated weeding in the nurseries, with their endless beds of bristling baby trees, we headed for the sheds at the first spit of rain, and out came the fags and the packs of cards'.[23]

'Wet time sitting in the hap?' remembered Bryce Reynard, 'In the first forests I was in, in Carradale, the men in the squads were mostly from Glasgow, with a few local fishermen, and they could spend all day non-stop cracking jokes. There was no gambling but I remember one occasion in Carradale where with my first pay I had bought a pair of binoculars. The men were on time work and in the middle of the morning they all stopped and gathered around this one fellow who sat on a stump with a sheet around him, and he proceeded to get a haircut. My job with my binoculars was to spot the forester coming in the distance in his van and warn the others.

'The men from Glasgow brought lots of dodges with them, inevitably. Simple things. As a forester you would have to measure bings of timber where the logs were end on. Sometimes you would do a sample measure, put a tape round to get the diameter, and one of their tricks was to put a finger under the tape to make it a bit bigger, and enlarge the average. You can imagine the bing with the thick ends of the logs at the roadside. Another trick was to go round and cut off some of the ends from the other side, take them round the front and hammer in the short lengths so that the bing would appear bigger than it was.'

Winter blizzards meant working indoors at odd jobs such as tools maintenance or making fire brooms from birch twigs, said Allan Macdonald in Fort Augustus, but in the average winter days were lost only when it was very wet or when the snow lay deep enough on the ground to obscure the lying timber and make safety a problem. Hours were shortened to take account of the early sunset and it would be necessary to come off the hill at four o'clock to travel back to base by the end of the working day. In the summer, especially in the West Highlands, the midgie brought torment. The Commission supplied an anti-midgie cream which 'seemed to do all right', in Allan's words, but had a tendency to seep into one's eyes in sweat. Many workers chose instead to equip themselves with their own anti-midgie protection and, in this regard, in recent years, a spray-on cosmetic has won a considerable reputation for efficacy.

Disillusionment with low wages led some to seek other employment, but for others the disincentive was poor housing in remote places. This did not deter all, and many foresters look back with a certain fondness on the pioneering aspect of their accommodation in their first postings. Rural housing in general could be quite basic in the inter-war years and even into later decades. In Sunart in the early 1970s Norman Davidson's home was a caravan – 'The only running water was cold water from a burn and there was no toilet and no electricity' – until his marriage and the construction of a new office at Strontian brought him permission to convert the old office into a house – 'It was a palace compared to what I had before because it had a shower and a toilet.'

The Commission provided tied houses for married staff but single men were on their own. A caravan was a frequent recourse if an old cottage to rent could not be found and there was no bothy or hostel. Bryce and Elizabeth Reynard married while Bryce was working in Glenbranter Forest and were given a house near Strachur – 'An old house, a typical Highland house, two rooms up and two down, white walls and a black door,' said Elizabeth, 'Previously it had had an outside toilet but a small kitchen and bathroom had been built on, and we had a Rayburn stove.'

Rent had to be paid of course and the Commission could prove to be a stingy landlord. When the Reynards prepared to do some decorating, the clerk of works measured out the paint he thought they would need and poured it into a coffee jar – 'That's all you need for that room' – and they had to battle for a larger wallpaper allowance. The Strachur house was not too remote although the nearest bus stop was a mile down a track, a daunting prospect for someone on foot in bad weather. 'Bryce took the car to work and that was me, stuck,' said Elizabeth. They made weekly or fortnightly trips to Dunoon and between these excursions the twice-weekly butcher's van also brought groceries. Freezers and many other domestic appliances were not yet readily available but there was a garden, plenty of firewood and generally a pleasant rural environment. The Reynards kept goats and poultry and even a fox at various times.

From Strachur and Glenbranter the Reynards moved to Glenmore, but after three and half years the time came for another move – to their most remote posting. 'This was how the Commission worked in those days,' said Elizabeth. 'We came home from a day out and there was a little envelope under the back door. "Staff – in confidence" and it said you will go to take up the position of forester at Pennyghael, Isle of Mull, in six weeks' time. We had to get the map out to see where it was. And as for staff in confidence, on Monday morning, when Bryce went to see his squad, the first they asked was "How are ye goin' tae like livin' on Mull?"'

It was different from his earlier experience, Bryce found. The Commission owned a fifth of the island then and half of that was afforested. It was large-scale work with much preparation – deer fencing, ploughing, fertilising and planting with Sitka, lodgepole pine and hybrid larch. Helicopters used the Reynards' garden as a landing pad, giving Elizabeth her first opportunity to view her home from high above: 'It was a big glass bubble. I was scared but once I was up I felt it was wonderful.' Bryce enjoyed being the forester on the Ross of Mull although it was a posting dreaded by many because of its remoteness.

The initial impression, however, had been less than encouraging. 'We arrived there on a cold October day. We went into this house and there was not a light bulb in sight. There was a Rayburn and a fire, and the grates in both were broken. Sewage was flowing down the driveway to meet us from the septic tank. I had a wee child of four and one of six,' said Elizabeth. She admitted that the first thing she did when Bryce went off to work was cry. 'I was reluctant to go to Mull because in Glenmore I had been about to get a job. It's not that Mull wasn't nice but, where we were, it was a long way to anywhere. There was a wee hamlet, maybe half a dozen houses and a hotel and the school. There was a post office when we arrived but it closed. In fact the school shut when we left because it was no longer viable. We were there from 1976 until 1981. But there were good things about it, in the sense that the school was like a community school and they had Hallowe'en and Christmas parties and everybody in the whole area went, from the grannies to the babies.'

With no reception for television and only a bad incoming radio signal, the Reynards and two other families formed a film club. The Friday night showings became the weekly highlight in the small community. Bryce became adept at switching from reel to reel on the two projectors and Elizabeth made the screen with sheeting she had got from Ireland. 'The big treat of the week was to have a Sweetheart stout and a Mars bar at the film.' Elizabeth also ran a bed and breakfast, worked in the hotel sometimes, and collected winkles. The scenery was magnificent with a fine view of Iona and Ben More.

'When I was on Mull there must have been over fifty employed by the Commission,' said Bryce. 'On Thursday, pay day, I had to go up to Salen to collect the money and on the way back pay the squads as I passed. I remember one occasion. Because Mull was full of deer, every plantation had fences and if you went through a gate you had to shut it after you. On one day, when we had a lot of ploughmen in as well, and they were up different roads, I had to open and close gates thirty-two times by the time I got round everybody. The pay was counted and sorted by the girls in the office, and I had to hand it out and get it signed for. The rules said that you had to vary your time and route when you did the pay run but on Mull there was only one road. In a place like that you do favours for folk, you might take somebody's hen food from a dealer to a farm, and drop off the *Oban Times*. Say you were doing a fence and you ran out of wire netting or stobs, you just had to knock on the door at the nearest farm and somebody would give you what would keep you going. If your car broke down, somebody would give you help.'

The news broke in 1960 that plans were afoot to build a major wood pulp mill at Annat Point beside the village of Corpach, four miles from Fort William.[24]

A helicopter takes part in a fire-fighting training exercise in Inverness-shire. The Bambi buckets are filled with water from a nearby reservoir or river.

Loading timber for sea transport at Loch Melfort, possibly in the 1960s.

The viability of the project seemed assured. The Commission said there was plenty of timber, especially as large stocks of thinnings were now being harvested from forests planted since the 1920s. At the time, most of the pulp and paper came from overseas – only something like 4 per cent of British paper came from British pulp in 1962 – and this was a market the Corpach mill and the Scottish forests would be ideally placed to exploit. There was also much optimism over the prospects for timber-based industries in general. Construction of the Corpach mill and of houses for the new work force went ahead in 1963. Fort William braced itself. The *Highland News* summed up the promise of the new industry on the eve of its opening: 'The new wood pulp mill . . . could well be one of the answers to the problem of Highland depopulation . . . this enormous £20,000,000 project . . . has already persuaded Scots from all corners of the world to write asking for jobs . . . there have been about 2000 applications . . . There is no doubt whatsoever that the mill will turn Fort William into the boom town of the Highlands . . .'[25]

In a ceremony at Inchnacardoch on 3 June 1965 the director general of the Commission, Sir Henry Beresford-Peirse, attended the felling of the first tree to feed the new mill. The mill would need half a million tons of wood per year from the West Highland forests. It was a dream come true, he said, and it was

fitting that Sir John Stirling of Fairburn should have initiated the felling as he was the most distinguished and best-loved forester in the Highlands. Mindful of the controversies over afforestation, Sir Henry spoke of woodland being important for recreation and nature as well as for industry, and of careful management so that the hills would not disappear under a blanket of conifers. The mill itself was officially opened in September 1965 by HRH Princess Margaret. The first delivery of pulpwood from a private estate followed in October. Dr T.H. Frankel, the managing director of the Corpach operation, sounded Cassandra-like a year later when he told the Aberdeen branch of the Institute of Directors that it was still cheaper to produce a ton of wood pulp in Canada and ship it 3,000 miles to Britain than to make it from home-grown timber, such were the costs of felling and extraction. It was hardly surprising, therefore, that the mill lost money in its early years.

It was a brave experiment that did not really prove successful and, while it ran, it affected forestry across the Highlands, as much effort was put into felling to keep it supplied. 'It had to close because Scottish forests were not able to supply enough timber from within an economical range,' said Norman Davidson, 'Bear in mind that in Scandinavia and Canada they plonk a pulp mill in the middle of a forest, so within fifty or one hundred kilometres they

A Bedford lorry hauls out 12 tons of pulpwood from South Strome, 1963.

have an endless supply. Some forests were many hundreds of kilometres away from the mill at Fort William, and there were difficult sea crossings as well, from Mull and Skye. The intention was good but road systems were extremely poor on the west coast. Only light lorry loads – eight tons – and long journeys.

'A lot of good timber went into Corpach and it was actually the saviour of forestry, it revitalised it. Without the mill at that particular time forestry on the west coast would have stagnated. Timber was growing there but there were no markets for it, there wasn't the critical mass or volume of big stuff to attract a sawmill to develop in a big way. The pulp mill took the small diameter timber and a lot of the big timber as well, as there was no market for saw logs, so it was only shortly after the pulp mill got going that the infrastructure came in, forestry roads and so on. As the need to supply the pulp mill increased so the infrastructures were created to give access. The whole thing expanded enormously.'

Peter MacDonald was posted to Mull in the late 1970s, where the Commission office at Aros served the whole island. This was a forestry village then, with Swedish timber houses and almost all the households deriving their livelihoods from forestry. Indeed, by 1970, the Commission had become the biggest landowner on the island, with some 38,000 acres and over one quarter of them under forest. The forestry operations provided around 70 full-time jobs. Two sawmills on the island took some of the felled timber but puffers left from the pier at Craignure with cargoes for Corpach.

Wiggins Teape closed its mill at Corpach in 1981 and began to export the timber it had contracted to buy to pulp mills in Sweden. The economics of the industry were now dictating that it was better to ship timber abroad than process it into pulp at home. Other downstream industries were, however, continuing. In November 1985, George Younger, secretary of state, opened a £12.5 million factory at Dalcross near Inverness to produce timber sheeting for construction, and there were several large sawmills in the country. By the mid 1990s, there were around 14 large mills in Scotland and many more smaller operations. The modern sawmill is a far cry from the circular saw and bench set-up where men heaved and held logs in position against the blade. Computerised cutting programs control the machinery and even the sawdust and bark are recycled into construction board, garden mulch and other products. These developments have had a feedback effect on the forests, as John Keenleyside explained: 'Nowadays they're harvesting Sitka about 35 years old. I never envisaged that I would see cut down the trees I saw planted in 1972 when I was in the Ardgartan Forest. We used to think that a crop rotation would be at least fifty years and for pines much more, about eighty years, but of course the demand has changed. The old sawmills handled dead trees and the modern sawmills are looking for a big run of even-sized logs which will go through automatically. In the old days it was a couple of men shoving them up to the bench, you know, and if they cut a couple of these big sticks on a water-wheel sawmill in a day they thought they were doing well. In the days of the water-wheel sawmill, we were transporting trees into the sawmill by horse and pole wagon. About a ton of timber, and that might be only three or five logs.'

Paper making continues today at Irvine in a large plant drawing timber from Argyll and Dumfries and Galloway. The multinational Arjo Wiggins resumed paper-making at Corpach but the manufacture closed again in 2005, and the premises were sold to BSW Timber, one of the largest sawmill companies in Britain. The downstream industries dependent on Scotland's forests continue to expand, subject to the fortunes of the market place.

The morning of 31 January 1953 began in the Highlands with a north-westerly gale. The wind veered to the north, battering the country with sleet and snow, borne on gusts that rose to hover between 80 and 90 miles per hour and reach well over 100 miles per hour at times. The fierce storm peaked in the early afternoon but by then, in the space of some three hours, swathes of forest had been toppled in a belt stretching from Easter Ross to Forfar, a total of some 5 million trees.[26] In the 'great gale', as it came to be known, trees more than 40 years old suffered the most, those below a height of 30 feet usually escaping harm. People who saw the havoc wreaked by the blast spoke of trunks bent right over by gust after gust, of woods falling like a pack of cards, stem by stem, of trunks breaking or being uprooted. In some places the wind cut out a clearing and proceeded to enlarge it, in other woods it completed what the forester might call heavy thinning and in the worst instances blew down everything. In some places the trees fell in neat lines and in others came down every which way to leave a mass of tangled limbs and foliage. 'Woods lying in the lee of the storm with a southerly aspect generally escaped damage,' reported A. Whayman, 'but some in the lee . . . were flattened by a kind of "bouncing" of the wind'.[27]

As most of the Commission woodlands were still below the critical height of 50 feet – almost all trees over that height came down – they suffered much less damage than private forests. In the North Conservancy, the Commission

Left. Windblown Sitka at Inverliever.

Right. The wind can blow over individual trees within a woodland, such as this Scots pine in Strathspey, April 1989.

lost an estimated 0.6 million cubic feet of timber, the private woodlands 7.1 million cubic feet. The equivalent figures for the East Conservancy were 3.3 and 39.8 million cubic feet. Around seven estates in Aberdeenshire and Angus lost over 1 million cubic feet. It took more than two years to clear away all the felled timber, an enterprise assisted by government grants. The final estimate of the losses was 51 million cubic feet, the bulk of which was sold for pit-props, railway sleepers and boxes.

Another instance of strong winds, on 14–15 January 1968, brought down an estimated 38 million cubic feet of timber, this time mainly in the south-west Highlands. Over 700 acres of mostly Sitka fell in the Inverliever forest. Bryce Reynard was living in a caravan on his first Commission posting at Barcaldine, north of Oban: 'Trees were cracking all around me. The caravan was shaking and I was thinking which way to jump if it cowped, but the only thing that happened during the night was that the door blew open and the window blew out. For the next few weeks our job was to check folks' houses that had lost roofs and so on, get roads open, make sure people and property were all right. Roads were blocked everywhere. I remember a rowing boat was found on telegraph wires after it had been blown from the shore. In a hotel in Oban a wave had hurled a stone from the beach, through a window to knock a tap on and cause a flood. Sheep were sheltering under a tree when it was blown over and one of the animals had its leg pinioned in the ground by a branch. Because of the storm I was transferred to Glenbranter where they had much more in the way of windblow. It took four years to clear it up. A huge job. There were even fellers from Cornwall coming up to clear the fallen timber. That storm affected a swathe right through the centre of the country, through Argyll and Glasgow and the central belt, right through there.'

Records of wind damage in past centuries include the occasion in January 1791 when the parish minister in Kiltearn, Ross-shire, noted 'a remarkable event, greatly to be regretted . . . the high wind broke down, and tore up by the roots, about 6,000 fine fir in the different plantations upon the estate of Fowlis'.[28]

Dealing with windblown timber was one of the challenges John Keenleyside faced when he was posted to Ardgartan Forest in 1972. 'It had been badly hit by the 1968 windblow when over 100,000 tons of timber were blown down over 269 hectares of forest in difficult terrain,' he said. 'All the timber had to be extracted by skyline winches and there was inadequate roading in the forest to let lorries in for it. We had to embark on a programme of roading and train people in the use of skyline winches. Power saws were pretty much in then but they were very heavy and noisy, and the windblow was difficult and that resulted in a lot of health problems – "white finger" [Reynaud's Phenomenon] for the operators, and a lot of bad backs from humping the timber out to the skyline rackways to be brought down. The other challenge was getting the windblown area replanted, and there was still a little bit of the original afforestation to be completed, on smaller lots on more difficult sites with poor access and poor soils and very exposed.'

Because trees fall in different directions in a windblow and can end up tangled and under tension, clearing them has dangers, as Norman Davidson learned on one occasion on the Calvine section of the Atholl estate: 'I was cutting a large silver fir, and we were using the crosscut, mainly because we could hear what was happening with the big trees. I wasn't quick enough one day and fortunately the tree was very slow but the big butt came off the stump under tension, and it went sideways and upwards and it caught me in the stomach and threw me about six to eight feet to one side. Fortunately it was a very slow motion. I was winded a bit but otherwise unhurt. You bloody, stupid fool, was the safety lecture I got afterwards.'

After his spell on Mull, Bryce Reynard moved into research based at the Bush estate in Edinburgh. 'My main job there was to study wind effects to see where you could plant in exposed places and to learn what caused trees to blow over. One of the nice things about it was that I travelled throughout the whole of Britain. I had a line of tatter flags at Aonach Mor before the ski tows were set up. The flags were invented in Orkney by a farmer who wanted to know where to site his house. They were like big hankies tied to posts and the wind shredded them to varying degrees according to the exposure. They looked cheap and nasty but they were made from aerodynamic-quality cotton used to cover gliders. After two months you could compare them – within and between sites – and see how the wind had affected them. This was repeated for at least two years. The line of flags at Aonach Mor was the longest line in Britain at the time and the results showed a beautiful curve with the most tatter at the top and the least at the bottom. It's a far cheaper method than using anemometers, though I had these up as well on masts in various parts of the country. We had one near Moffat, at Rivox, in a commercial forest. We had a tower up to tree height, about 50 feet, and a mast another 50 feet above that so that it reached effectively 100 feet from the ground with various anemometers on it. It was quite exciting climbing to the top. That was okay on a day that was completely cloudy or completely blue sky but on a day with fluffy clouds you could swear the whole thing was falling over when you looked up.'

Most winters see some trees brought low by the wind and there is little the forester can do against such a natural force. Fire is another matter. The smell of smoke or the sight of a puff above the trees is enough to make 'a forester's heart bound'.[29] Although lightning can ignite a fire in a dry season, in Scotland most forest fires spring from some human action. The cause can be an unlikely one: in May 1960 a diesel lorry with a red-hot deposit falling from its silencer started eight fires in a distance of 6 miles through Glencoe. The impact of fire was summarised by Tom Johnston in a speech in Inverness in May 1946.[30] Between 1919 and 1939, he said there had been 6,200 incidents causing the destruction of 13,500 acres of planting worth £185,000. Half of the damage had been started by sparks flying from the engines of passing locomotives. He foresaw the expected increase in numbers of hikers and holidaymakers in the countryside as adding to the risks and hoped for a 'great development of afforestation-mindedness'.

The back files of local newspapers are filled with reports of fire. For example, a young plantation burned for about a week on Fyrish Hill by the Cromarty Firth in September 1919 and sailors from the naval base at Invergordon joined the attempts to control the blaze. Two hundred acres of forest and moor near Blairgowrie caught fire in the same summer and Dundee fire brigade found that 'So rapid was the spread of the flames at times that the motor engine itself [was] threatened . . . and the intense heat . . . turned the water from the hose into steam'; the same reporter found the noise of the fire 'like a rushing, mighty wind'.[31] Ross-shire was beset by several fires in the dry summer of 1920.[32] Every spring the press carried warnings of the risk and called for vigilance on the part of the public. A carelessly discarded cigarette butt was suspected to be the cause of an outbreak in Glen Nevis in May 1946 that destroyed 150 acres of young trees, an occasion when the north-east wind sent the flames 'roaring from tree to tree'; 100 soldiers joined the fire brigade and foresters in the fight to control the blaze and 2 miles of hose were laid to suck water from the River Nevis.[33]

A familiar sign from Commission forests in the 1960s and 1970s.

Fighting a forest fire at Culloden, 1946.

Fire in a Caledonian
pinewood.

Another hazard in the past was the common rural practice of burning off dry grass, heather or whins in the spring. The papers of the Commissioners of the Forfeited Estates noted, for example, in March 1776 how a certain Isobel Cameron had saved the firs of Rannoch in 1763 by running several miles to raise the alarm after some boys and herds had allowed a moor fire to burn out of control.[34] In the right circumstances, in a dry season, fire could dig itself into peat and smoulder unseen for over a week until a freshening wind could urge it once more into an open blaze. If a fire could not be extinguished by the rows of beaters, efforts focused on preventing its spread. Beating out flames, soaking the ground, clearing firebreaks and hoping that the wind would not rise enough to make the sparks and flames leap the gap.

'When I started you daren't go on leave from February until May–June,' said Hugh Morris. 'Many a night I spent sitting outside on the Black Isle, after extinguishing a fire, in case it flared up again.' 'Fire was very serious,' agreed Bryce Reynard, 'I think now because of mobile phones, radios and so on, you can get messages back much quicker but in the old days it could take some time to get a message about a fire. I remember one in 1976, the year I left Glenmore, at Carrbridge. It wasn't on Commission ground but all the surrounding forestry operations and estates were asked to supply labour, and it went on for three days.'

An outbreak put pressure on the foresters to react quickly to try to contain the flames. Bryce Reynard again: 'When we talk about fires it was often not a forest fire but fire on moorland threatening a forest. On one occasion on Mull a lot of molinia, the purple moor grass, went up. It was very dry and in the spring of the year it is just like tinder. I think it was started by teenagers from Glasgow, who were on holiday in the area and were maybe smoking a cigarette. It was maybe a mile from the forest but the wind was blowing it towards us. Until the reinforcements came, we didn't have many men. I went ahead with the ranger and the rest of the squad was coming behind with more equipment. We made a decision – for me, for the first time. This fire was coming towards us and we started another fire, back burning, although it was a big risk. We went to a burn, a kind of boundary, and lit a fire just at the head of it and burnt a strip maybe a metre or two wide, putting it out as it burned. We lit a clump of molinia, set fire to it and trailed it along the ground. When the uncontrolled fire came it stopped just like that. You have to make the deliberately burnt strip longer than the front of the fire coming towards you and in this instance it was some hundreds of metres. It was a race. We could see the fire coming and we just kept moving ahead, firing and putting out the vegetation on the bank. This area, the Beitheach [as in birch], was very prone to adders. The ranger when he was gathering molinia for his burning clump felt something wriggle inside it; it turned out to be a frog but he got a fright.'

'I had one of the biggest fires the north has ever seen,' recalled Finlay Macrae. 'That was at Fort William one February. February and March are the bad months, as once April comes in the molinia has a bit of green in it and it's not quite so dangerous. The train, leaving Fort William and pulling out to Spean Bridge, had quite a haul and on that stretch the fireman had to be busy stoking. The hot cinders would pop out on to the vegetation. One day in the course of about eight hours we lost 800 acres of young trees, all about three feet high. It was spreading at about 200 feet a minute. We used to stick a stake in the ground and time it. The molinia in the spring time, it's deadly. We didn't stop the fire, we let it burn out. There were hundreds of men beating it but it had no effect. Forest fires now seem to be small. When I was in forestry, you wouldn't ask for leave during the fire season, you wouldn't get it – that's from about October to April. Easter was a very bad time. Now you have the advantage of helicopters dropping water from the air. I think that is effective – it takes the sting out of a fire, you know.'

In the early 1980s, Fountain Forestry and PLM Helicopters at Dalcross developed a technique of scooping up water in buckets holding 100 gallons and flying them to the location of a fire, where a team on the ground could deploy a portable pump to quench the flames. Flying buckets in rotation allowed this effort to go on without interruption.[35] Another aerial technique, developed in Europe, is known as water-bombing, emptying the bucket in one shot over the blaze, the accuracy and the impact velocity of the deluge able to extinguish flames at once.

'I've never seen a fire in a fully grown woodland,' said Finlay Macrae. 'It's more resistant. There is no low vegetation. To get into the crowns of the trees, the fire has to get up through vegetation, the wind drives it up. A fire can sweep through a mature wood and do very little damage to the trees. It's just the main stems that are affected, and if it's a rapid fire there's hardly any effect.'

CHAPTER 5
'A CENTRAL PART OF OUR CULTURE, ECONOMY AND ENVIRONMENT'
FORESTRY NOW

After his two years in research at Lairg, John Keenleyside was promoted to chief forester and posted to Ardgartan Forest. The date – the first day of April 1972 – was a significant one in the life of the Commission. 'It was the day the Commission changed to metric measurements, and it was also the day we got our first computer. Now I had never worked in an ordinary Commission forest in my life, so I was a bit lost and a wee bit confused, but my colleagues, my staff, were equally confused. It was a very sharp learning curve for all of us. In actual fact it helped me. Against the experienced people I had there with the old paper system of producing accounts and everything else, I could have been very inefficient but going on to the computer meant it was easy. My predecessor, before he retired, gave me only two bits of advice – never to employ anybody from Glasgow, and the news that the clerkess was getting married on Friday, so I wouldn't have one next Monday but if "you take my advice you will poach the girl we had here before, she has raised her family, they're getting up a bit now. If she would come back, that would be fine". So I went to see her and got her back. She was the queen bee in the office and it worked out.'

'So, we had the kingpin, Mary, in the office. I was the chief forester. We had a head forester   his main function was the harvesting operations. We had three foresters – one on forest management, which was planting, one assistant to the head forester, and one who had more general duties and was in an outpost at Lochgoilhead. We had twenty-six forestry workers but we also had sub-contractors. For example, we might tell them about a section with windblown trees and say we would pay them £2 a ton to get it out. If they observed the rules we would keep them on. The rules in my time were about safety measures – hard hats, safety boots – and some days you might go round and see them with no hard hats on and only trainers on their feet. We could

Opposite.
Silka forest 60 years after planting, Inverliever.

John Keenleyside stands beside a plot of larch he planted with seed chosen from the ten best larch trees he could find in Scotland. The larch in the picture are now 50 years old.

not tolerate that. The good ones got further contracts. The bigger merchants came in on what we called standing sale. The timber on the point of the peninsula was completely blown and the company who took on the clearing up on this very difficult terrain had a three-year contract. The normal skyline is 300 metres but they had brought in one that was capable of bringing in timber from 600 metres away. When they had finished the windblown parts they were awarded the first big standing sale. This coincided with the start of clear fell after the windblow. It was an area planted in 1926 with Douglas fir, which had grown very well, though one or two had died, so the operation was known as "beat up" – it was beaten up with our friend, Sitka spruce. When it came to the cutting in 1972 the average Douglas fir was one cubic metre and the average Sitka was 0.75 cubic metres. But one or two Sitka excelled themselves – we found one that had five saw logs in it and contained 5.68 cubic metres of timber, and in a subsequent felling we came up with an even bigger one that had 6.2 cubic metres, after forty-seven years growing. They were big trees. That was the start of the clear felling of the forest.'

'There was a follow on from the clearance of the original windblow. The windblow wasn't fussy of course about boundaries and initially we just had to get rid of the timber but when we had time to breathe we went back to those areas and landscaped them, fitted them into the landscape, so that the original area of 269 hectares became well over 300 by the time we adjusted the boundaries to fit the landscape and tidy it all off.'

The forester has to contend with pests, any plant or animal that threatens to reduce significantly the well-being or growth of the trees, although what was considered a pest in the earlier years of the Commission, when the overall aim was to maximise timber production, is now a cause of surprise. For example, take this statement from the report of a visit to Skibo in Sutherland by the Royal Scottish Forestry Society in 1951: 'Throughout the whole of Sutherland the forester's worst enemies are bracken and birch'.[1] Bryce Reynard remembers being shown at the forestry school how to eradicate birch by ring barking. 'When I came into forestry, birch was considered to be a weed,' said Finlay Macrae. 'We were cutting it down as fast as we could. That has all changed, and I'm glad about that.' Bracken is a problem for a young plantation in that the quick-growing fronds can shade saplings. The only way of dealing with it on rough ground was to keep cutting it back – expensive in labour and time – until the trees became established and tall enough to escape from its smothering. On more accessible terrain, machinery was available, such as the Holt Tractor Bracken Breaker, demonstrated at Amat, near Ardgay, in June 1949. This was reported in *Scottish Forestry* as the first crushing of 1948, over an area previously crushed twice in 1946 and again in 1947, altogether a cheaper method, at around 10 shillings an acre, especially with 50 per cent grants from government, than any other, though also a clear tribute to the enduring toughness of the plant.

Any animal that threatened to damage a tree could be, and was, labelled a pest species. Deer and grazing sheep are obvious suspects but in the past the squirrel, the hare and the rabbit have also been subject to control measures. Hugh Morris found that the hares in the Rumster area in Caithness could wipe out a newly planted patch of forest by nipping the growing tips off the young trees. The best way to deal with this threat was to mount a hare drive in the winter months and shoot them. Fencing was the obvious resort to keep animals out but sterner methods also had to be adopted. The Commission employed trappers – the job title was later changed to ranger – who spent their time culling the then undesirable. As late as the 1970s capercailzie were seen as pests and were marked down to be killed.

Squirrel and rabbit clubs were common before the Second World War, formed specifically with the aim of hunting. The results were often published, presumably with a sense of achievement, and the hunting was encouraged by the payment of bounties. The Commission offered hunters 1 shilling per tail for grey squirrel in 1953, and in the ensuing 12 months 4,066 fell to the gun and the trap. Dreys were also destroyed wherever they were found.[2] Foresters were convinced of the destructiveness of the squirrel: 'There is not a Scots pine wood in upper Deeside, between the ages of 30 and 60, that is not completely spoilt by squirrel damage,' declared Johnston Edwards in 1933.[3]

Deer have always been a problem, as Finlay Macrae explained: 'They can do an enormous amount of damage – four or five red deer can wipe out an acre in a night. We were fencing all the time, everything we did was enclosed. We would fence 60 acres in one patch and maybe 40 in another, depending on how the land was required. We controlled the deer by shooting. I was deeply involved in shooting because I had a great personal interest in stalking. Not only did we cull deer [in the 1950s] but we culled things that are absolutely forbidden now, such as capercailzie. Anything that interfered with forestry was not thought to be a good thing.'

A significant step in preventing damage by deer, rabbits and other animals to young trees came about in the late 1970s. Graham Tuley, a graduate in forestry from Aberdeen University who had moved on to research at the Commission's establishment at Alice Holt Lodge in Hampshire, conceived of placing a translucent tube around sapling oak initially to provide the young trees with a mini-greenhouse environment to promote their growth and discourage competition from weeds. The results from trials in Graham's back garden were very encouraging and led to formal experiments from 1979 onwards. Very soon, this innovation intended as a hedgerow or copse technique was picked up for large-scale planting, and now the translucent tubes, officially termed tree shelters, can be seen on newly planted land across the country. Some foresters felt it would encourage trees that were 'all shoot and no root' but this proved not to be a major problem, while the advantage in protecting the saplings from animal damage was obvious at once and reduced any need for heavy fencing.

A plantation of Sitka, lodgepole pine or any other tree is of course potentially a paradise for any insect that happens to feed on that species and a

Young oak yet to leaf protected by an array of tree shelters, Drumtochty, May 1986.

considerable research effort has been put in over many decades to find methods of control. Viruses, bacteria and fungi also can be a problem, and it is not always clear what is happening. Johnston Edwards, forester on the Birkhall estate in 1928, noticed something odd in larch plantations on the opposite side of the Dee on the Glenmuick estate: for a mile or more the crowns of the trees were bright red in colour. 'I must confess . . . I was absolutely puzzled . . . for I could not find the least sign of either insect or fungus present.' A careful search did pinpoint the culprit as a moth identified as *Grapholitha diniana*, not known in Scotland before but common in parts of Austria. In two years all the larch were stripped 'just as if every tree had been thoroughly scorched by fire'. The damage was done by the caterpillars feeding on foliage.

Monitoring for insect outbreaks is a regular task for the forester, who now has a larger battery of weapons with which to combat pests. 'For two or three weeks in the year I was doing a lot of sampling for pine beauty moth,' said Norman Davidson about his experience in the Lairg area in Sutherland around 1980. 'We were susceptible to pine beauty. That was the major pest among insects. The pine beauty tended to specialise on areas where there was lots of lodgepole and where the peat was of a certain depth, probably over 6–8 inches deep. The pupae drop onto the ground and burrow into the peat to escape the winter frosts. The adults lay their eggs all over the place, the caterpillars eat the needles. The researchers developed a system of monitoring the number of pupae in the peat through randomly selected plots. If we found over 30 pupae per square metre we had to start to prepare for a possible infestation, possibly spraying with chemicals. This was done mainly by fixed-wing aircraft but helicopters were also used. They devised a system for ultra-low volume spraying, dispersing the insecticide by a spinning disc into an aerosol of very tiny, charged droplets that stuck to the needles. Every three or four years an infestation seemed to happen. The caterpillars, otherwise, could devastate 40 or more hectares in fairly short order. They eat themselves out of a home but they do not expand massively outside the infested area. The caterpillars would also attack Sitka in a heavy outbreak. The more serious Sitka pest from our point of view is a fungus that rots the core of the stem. The old name is *Fommes annosus* – it's called *Heterobasidium annosum* nowadays.'

In his memoir *Highland Reflections* Donald Fraser remarked that in the early days of the Forestry Commission some old-time foresters did not like the public coming into their woods. They may have thought that, at best, people would simply get in the road and be a danger to themselves and others, at worst they might start a fire, carve their initials in valuable timber or do other damage. There may also have been lingering suspicions from the days of gamekeepers, poachers and privilege. The Commission's attitude to the public, and the latter included of course the taxpayers who funded state forestry, began to change very early in its history. The 1930s saw an increasing interest in the countryside as a place for recreation. Walkers, ramblers and climbers were resorting to the open hills with great enthusiasm at weekends, and a demand grew for national parks or open spaces where people could roam without worrying about private property and trespass. The Commission recognized this and began to accommodate it. All of the forest parks include moors and mountains unfit for planting but ideal for hillwalking, mountaineering and other more robust outdoor pursuits.

The pace of change quickened from the 1970s onward until it became almost a revolution. The countryside was still a place where people lived and worked but it was becoming increasingly, to use the 1950s' term, an amenity for town dwellers. Two generations before, escape to the country at the weekend had been confined to the wealthy, but now it was within everyone's grasp. In a sense, therefore, Lovat's dream of repopulating the glens through forestry was coming true but in a way he had not foreseen, as a migratory population appearing in waves during weekends and holidays and retreating again as quickly.

In the Countryside Acts in 1967 and 1968, the Commission was granted the power to develop the forests as a social and public resource. John Keenleyside, then chief forester at Ardgartan, remembered the impact. 'Recreation was becoming the in thing,' he said. 'There was an upsurge in 1970 as people were becoming better off and were more on the go. More demand for pitches for caravans and tents. We had a site that accommodated 240 caravans and tents. Then the Caravan Club site took another sixty caravans adjacent to ours. We called them the green wellie brigade. They didn't have toilets in those days but they were usually spotted using our facilities because of the green or yellow wellies. Further along there was a youth hostel and beyond that a camping site for youth groups and another for the Camping Club of Great Britain and Northern Ireland, with eighty pitches. So, there was a honeypot of concentration of tourists there. All these people arriving were after something to do. They wanted to spend some time in the forest environment. We set up forest walks of varying lengths. This was the first time it was done on such a scale. We had 4-, 6-, 8- and 12-mile walks in

the forest. We had a contact with ANWB, the Royal Dutch Tourism Association, and they came over in large groups and stayed sometimes for a week with us, and we felt the need to provide separate entertainment for them – we got on well with them. More specialised were the orienteering groups, army groups for training or to help us with bridge building and that type of thing, and fishing groups who could fish on the river beside the campsite or on the river Goil on the other side of the forest. Then we had day-permit shooting for those who wished to shoot roebuck – in May – they came from Denmark and Germany, and later on they came for stag shooting in July – mainly Germans but a number of Scandinavians – and then in October we had hind shooting but they weren't really interested in that, it was cheaper, the clients tended to be English, Dutch or Belgian. Only a percentage stayed on the campsite – they tended to be better-off people and mostly stayed in hotels, but they went out with our rangers.'

Visitor centres opened in many places and became standard features of Commission woodland. A few were estasblished as modest affairs, signboards with mapped-out paths and leaflets with information, but now the centres can include franchised tea rooms and shops handling thousands of visitors. The Murray Forest Centre at Fleet Forest near Gatehouse of Fleet, a log cabin

The caravan and camping site run by the Forestry Commission beside Loch Long in the 1970s.

dispensing information for the visitors, opened on 30 September 1969 as the forerunner of a new type of forest gateway for the public. Five large ones existed in 1990 – Glenmore, the David Marshall Lodge in the Trossachs, the Queen's View, Clatteringshaws Deer Museum and Kirroughtree.

Like most of the Commission's forests, Culbin Forest is promoted as 'a wonderful place to walk, cycle and ride' and has graded trails for visitors to follow with explanatory maps to show the way. A tall viewing tower, dubbed Hill 99 after a name probably given by the early foresters, pokes up from the largest sand dune in the middle of the forest to provide what the publicity people call a squirrel's eye view of the Moray Firth and the surrounding landscape. Leaflets summarise the history of the forest and explain how the shifting dunes were tamed. The exploring visitor can still find the evidence of that process, desiccated trunks protruding like ribs from the ground to show where thatching was laid to trap the sand. An excavated pit by one of the roads, where some 10 feet of living pine trunk has been exposed, is a dramatic demonstration of how the growing trees were in a race against the sand that threatened to overwhelm them. Near the Welhill car park, one of the forest access points, a small grove of beech has a plaque commemorating their planting in 1969 by the prime minister Harold Wilson and Willie Ross, secretary of state for Scotland, to mark the Commission's jubilee year.

In the 1970s, private estates were also realising the potential offered by public access, and they too began to open visitor centres with attendant attractions, often the enticement of viewing a mansion that hitherto had been guarded by signs declaring 'Private'. The seat of the dukes of Buccleuch at Drumlanrig invites the public to see not only the contents of the rooms in the castle but also to learn about the estate's forestry operations on the 241,000 acres in its ownership – 'one of the best managed estates in the world,' in the opinion of botanist David Bellamy on the audio-visual presentation, producing 50,000 tons of timber each year.[4] On the edge of Aberfoyle, the David Marshall Lodge, named after the chairman of the Carnegie Trust who gifted it to the Forestry Commission in 1960, is extremely busy in the holiday months and lays on many activities, among them trails, footpaths and adventure pursuits.

The increasing use of the forests by the public – the Queen Elizabeth Forest Park attracts over a million visitors each year – has had the inevitable consequence of raising the awareness of forestry and its part in rural life. It has also provided willing recruits to the conservation movement and at the beginning the increasingly vociferous clamour against the planting of conifers in rigid blocks across the landscape. Sir John Stirling-Maxwell's old lament about the absence of a 'forest sense' from the Scottish psyche was being addressed in new ways.

The Conservative government elected in 1979 wrought some far-reaching changes on state forestry. The Commission, whose headquarters had been shifted to Edinburgh in 1975, had its functions split between the so-called Forest Authority and Forest Enterprise, the former charged with research, pest control, training, tree felling control, and advice and grant aid for the private sector, and the latter taking care of the national forest estate. The government wanted the forests to continue to expand but called for a shift of effort to the private sector and the sale of Commission forests into private hands to reduce public spending. In a speech to the Royal Scottish Forestry Society on 25 March 1981, Lord Mansfield described how the government expected the 'greater share' of forestry to be undertaken by private enterprise and tried to reassure the many people who feared the Commission would be privatised that this was 'not in any way to denigrate the Forestry Commission or all that it has achieved during the past 60 years'.[5] The legislation to implement these changes was enshrined in the 1981 Forestry Act.

The decades since the Second World War have also seen the rise of the forestry contractors, private firms that have taken over much of the management of forests. Of course there have always been private entrepreneurs engaged in forestry, but now a number of large firms were to rise to prominence, reflections of the Commission often seen in their structure. One of these was Fountain Forestry Ltd, which, established in England in 1956, expanded into Scotland in 1967, with a headquarters in Perth, and soon became a familiar name in the countryside. In 1975 the company used helicopters to carry half a million young trees to planting sites in Perthshire.

Other companies included Scottish Woodland Owners Association (later renamed Scottish Woodlands Ltd), UPM Tilhill and the Economic Forestry Group. The contractors offered a complete service to the private landowner. Over the years the fortunes of forestry on private estates had fluctuated in response to economic conditions. Captain Derick Forbes of the Scottish Woodland Owners Association complained in 1975 that the tax system had been behind the drop in planting from 14,690 hectares in 1973–74 to 7,970 hectares in 1974–75. To emphasise the importance of the private sector, he pointed out that private forestry employed around 4,000 people with another 1,600 in downstream transport and processing.[6] In Scotland as a whole, productive private woodland made up almost one third of the woodland area by the 1970s, and planting – throughout the years between 1919 and 1969, usually well below the levels achieved by the Commission – had been encouraged by various government initiatives, offering grants and other incentives. From 1983, private sector planting, boosted by tax breaks, overtook Commission planting.

In November 1969 at a meeting of the Royal Scottish Forestry Society in Inverness, K.N. Rankin of the London-based Economic Forestry Group complained that forestry in Scotland was suffering from a lack of planning. If this were to be rectified, he argued, a national forest of 3 million acres, some 16 per cent of the land area, could be produced in 30 years, with employment prospects of two men for every 100 acres. In fact, the figure of 16 per cent was to be exceeded by 2009. The effects of the privatisation of much forestry employment, the reorganisation of the Commission and increasing mechanisation went against one of the hopes that were born in 1919. In a study of the effects of forestry in the parish of Strathdon published in *Scottish Forestry* in 1987, A. Evans described how it had failed to stem rural depopulation. The Commission took over three estates – Auchernach, Rhinstock and most of Tornashean in the upper strath – in the 1950s, and in the 1961 census most of the population of 656 people were engaged in farming, forestry and gamekeeping. The number of residents halved in the following 20 years, despite the expansion of forestry and the growth in the popularity of field sports. By 1987 only one resident Commission worker was still in the parish. The administration was being done from offices in other places, and the work of thinning, felling and so on was left to contractors. The Commission houses had been sold, and some had become holiday homes. A similar pattern of decline in the resident population had occurred on the private estate of Candacraig in the same parish. In the space of 30 years, employment in forestry and keepering had dropped by 93 per cent although the area of forest had increased by the same amount.[7] It seemed the end of Lord Lovat's dream of a viable rural population wedded to the forest and the field.

The Commission sold 7,300 hectares of land in Glen Affric in 1985 back to the son of the landowner from whom they had acquired it in the first place in 1951. The new owner paid £50,000 but six years later sold the estate off in two lots for £1.8 million. A profit could hardly have been more handsome and the Commission was attacked for having allowed the original transaction. Dr Ian Richardson of Laggan wrote to *The Scotsman* to denounce what he saw as serious damage to the community and the betrayal of two reasons for the

Commission's existence – to provide employment in the countryside and to arrest rural depopulation.[8] Dr Jim Hunter also warned against the wholesale disposal of forest land to a new generation of landowners, often remote figures with little interest in the glens, when an opportunity was being missed to create a cadre of 'small foresters' and forest-farmers, a policy that would have been in keeping with the original social role of forestry.[9] Brian Denoon wrote of the 'rage and disbelief' he felt when he heard being questioned the need for a Forestry Commission and the 'very notion that there should be any social responsibility for small rural communities'.[10]

In the mid 1980s Fountain Forestry became involved in the controversial planting of the 'Flow Country' in the heart of Caithness and Sutherland. The name of this region of lochans, bog and moor that sprawls across some 1,500 square miles of high ground in the centre of the northern counties used to be current only among a handful of keepers, shepherds and naturalists, but it soon became much more widely known as conservation bodies mounted a campaign against afforestation encouraged by tax incentives for private investors. In May 1988, during an excursion by the Royal Scottish Forestry Society to see for itself what was going on, the district manager of Fountain Forestry said in Lairg that, although their operations in the Flow Country had started in 1979 with the support of the Department of Agriculture and Fisheries and the Nature Conservancy Council, it had taken until 1985 for the Royal Society for the Protection of Birds to warn of the effects on breeding bird populations. Only some 12 per cent of the Flow Country was affected by afforestation.

Finlay Macrae was involved as a consultant with the planting in the Flow Country. 'The heart of the matter was that the government was offering grants for forestry,' he said. 'I was responsible for design work on the forestry there. It wasn't an easy thing to do but I had in mind deer getting shelter, even if it wasn't within the woodland, the breaking up of the land would shelter it, but I recall being there with a fellow one day, and we went out by helicopter to the heart of this Flow Country. We got out of the helicopter and I said to this chap, now, if you could just go for a hundred paces and I'll stay here. At one hundred paces, when he jumped on the ground, I could feel it shaking. It had ten to fifteen feet of peat. Trees were never meant to grow there. Environmentally, the planting of the Flow Country was a silvicultural error.'

John Keenleyside, who was based in Lairg in the early 1970s, has a balanced view of what happened. 'My feeling is that there is a place for both forestry and conservation provided you fit it in properly. There are masses of areas in Sutherland in particular that will never be suitable for afforestation, so they can be left as wild land. Perhaps the mistake was made because that kind of land was cheap but, as pioneers, perhaps they worked on too big a scale. We were working on a bigger and bigger scale to make it economical but once the companies came in they were doing it bigger still. Strathy Forest stretches more than twenty miles down from the north road to Forsinard. The sad thing about it now is that where the trees have grown quite well it has turned out that the roads are not fit to carry the weight of timber.'

The region is now recognised as one of the largest surviving areas of blanket bog in Europe, an environment that has persisted since the end of glaciation some 10,000 years ago. The tax-incentive scheme that had encouraged the drainage and planting of conifers on areas of the bog was discontinued in 1988 and a conservation effort, mounted by various organisations, has set about restoring the flows to their original state. The RSPB, which has bought 17,600 acres of the bog, opened a visitor centre in a former railway station at Forsinard in Strath Halladale to explain the importance of the habitat.

Forestry in general underwent some other far-reaching changes during the 1980s. A drive for efficiency saw the introduction of more mechanisation, and the appearance in the forests of the harvester and the forwarder. Developed in Sweden and Finland, the harvesters are large, complex pieces of equipment that have been evolved from excavators and are capable of performing several tasks in sequence. Hamish Fraser explained how they work: 'They clear off the brash a bit at the bottom, clamp the tree, the saw automatically comes down – just like a power saw, the same blade but bigger – and cuts the trunk, and as it cuts it lifts the trunk and automatically tilts it over to the horizontal and then, on two big feed rollers, runs the trunk through knives that delimb the tree. The normal-size big tree can be felled, sned and cut into lengths in between 10 and 15 seconds. One man does the whole job that in the old days would take maybe two men half an hour to an hour. I don't think there's anybody employed now in the Commission who fells trees in the traditional way except for a special purpose such as a road line. It's all harvesters now. In a clear fell you can do maybe 20–25 ton an hour.'

The cutting mechanism can be programmed to produce timber of a required size. 'You can set the sizes of the logs that you want – ten feet long, or whatever – and it's all based on the diameter,' explained Hamish, 'The machine recognises the diameter of the stick and it'll go to the certain length you want that diameter for. The logs are sorted according to size and when the

A Valmet harvester felling at Kindrogan, in around 2001.

forwarder comes along he knows exactly the sizes and the order to take them out in. You'll see stacks of different sizes of timber at the roadside. The harvester is a very sophisticated machine and it has done away with a lot of labour. They are very expensive to run and you have to keep on top of the maintenance. In the early days, the biggest problems were with the electrics. To buy one you're talking about well over a quarter of a million now; I would say the top of the range is now well over £300,000. A lot of boys can keep them for up to six or seven years and they can go on for maybe twelve years, depending on how hard they're worked.'

Just as the harvester has replaced the worker with the axe and the chain saw, the forwarder has on all but the steepest slopes taken over from the

A harvester at work.

skyline and winch to bring timber from the felling site to the roadside. It is also a one-man operation. With its own crane and grab, the driver can pick up logs, load them on the bogey towed behind and bring them to the access road for lorries to pick up. Allan Macdonald spent three weeks at Ae to learn how to handle these newcomers to the forest. 'I found it very interesting,' he said, 'I enjoyed it. I like machines. It was amazing the slopes it could go up, although you had to take care on slippery ground and drive straight up and down if possible.' Jimmy Henderson also began to operate forwarders in the 1980s. Driving the machine, with its mounted crane and bogey, took considerable skill over rough ground and in the narrow space of the rackways. Jimmy was praised for his maintenance, something he tends to explain by

Extracting spruce, Ae.

saying he was brought up that way, to look after everything, and when he retired he had been using his forwarder for over six years. 'The bogey took about six ton of timber,' he said, 'The most I ever took out was 100 ton in a day but usually it was much less. That was on the Black Isle and it depended on the rack, and how the timber was scattered, the ground and the distance.'

The changes in state forestry during the 1980s caused some distress among older hands. In a powerful piece written for *Scottish Forestry* in 1999, John Davies, retired from his position as conservator in South Scotland, put these feelings into black and white, deploring the shift in forestry policy that caused a drop in the skilled labour force, the amalgamation of individual forests into districts, a decrease in new planting, the selling of forest land, and such changes in forest management as the cessation of thinning. The old objective of the Commission to counter the rundown in the rural population

Opposite.
A Bruunett forwarder at work in the Ae forest.

Loading timber at the roadside in Strathyre.

was abandoned. 'I look back over the last 20 years with deep sorrow,' concluded Davies, 'The old idealism . . . has gone and we now have an organisation which tries to be all things to everyone. No stable employment. No permanent local foresters. Neglected forests run on very basic cost-cutting lines. Very, very sad'.[11]

While some senior staff in the highest grades had been isolated to an extent from the practical hands-on work of forestry, their subordinates were more sanguine about the changes and took them in their stride. 'I wouldn't say there was a lot of opposition to the reform of grades,' said John Keenleyside. 'Some of them didn't know too much about the nitty-gritty, getting the big forest schemes done. Cost was always a big item, we were always being hammered down in costs. We had a tough bunch of workers and contractors and we were the guys who had to face up to them, but when we got the change

of grades and some of the senior staff became district managers a lot of them didn't make it very well because they were now faced with the reality of life. Some took early retirement and some were luckier and were promoted into specialist jobs.'

Norman Davidson had been posted to Lairg by the time the changes were implemented, working once again with Hugh Mackay mostly on large-scale ploughing and planting. 'When I first went, we were doing not far short of a thousand hectares a year,' he said, 'Hill land, around Ledmore Junction and up that way, and the Crask, Dalchork and all those places. We had two tractor drivers permanently stationed there, Innes Macleod and Alastair Matheson, and other tractor drivers would be brought in for specialist roles. That was where I learned to do extensive forestry. At the height the squads were up to over fifty men, and there were six or seven keepers. Five men worked in the

Extracting thinnings with an Isachsen double-drum winch and a Hiab hoist on a Bedford articulated lorry, Durris Forest, Aberdeenshire, 1963.

woods but all the rest were concerned mainly with establishment planting and drainage. Then the management system was changed and forests were amalgamated into districts. There had always been a district officer looking after several forests but this change was the amalgamation of several forests into a district forest run by a management team. I went to Dornoch then, to the main office for Sutherland and Caithness. Ian Michie was the district manager to start with, and then Arkle Fraser came in. I was the assistant, as it were, and I covered all the planting in Caithness and Sutherland, probably about four thousand hectares a year in those days but dropping to two or three thousand latterly.'

The Commission began more and more to look for efficiency in its operation, weighing up the costs of salaries and the advantages of having contractors. Some experienced hands felt the results were not always desirable, inevitable though some of the changes may have been. The reduction in manpower was done mainly through 'natural wastage', an oddly poignant phrase in the context of forestry, but some thought there was a loss of too much accumulated and inherited skill, although increasing levels of skill could be seen in the private and contract sectors.

Norman Davidson was posted to Aberdeenshire in 1989, one district where the Commission did retain many of its employees and continued to innovate. 'This district was one of the first to experiment with thinning machines, and now there are thinning machines all over the place. Part of the role of the state forest service is to innovate, take the early risks and show the way. The private sector is also more innovative now, depending on the market conditions. There's a solid base of forestry expertise out there now, especially for harvesting, but it's always difficult to get hold of planting contractors. There are machines that can do it, although the plant size is limited, hardly big enough to withstand the insect pests we do have, but they are working at this right enough. Harvested sites can now be cultivated with tracked diggers, and there are special machines for quite steep slopes, but I've done enough heavy cultivation to recognise it's not the answer everywhere.'

Other changes were, however, afoot. Things were stirring down in the forests and among those who had an interest in their future.

In 1956, the Forestry Commission bought Achilty wood, west of Contin in Ross-shire, some 82 hectares with one of the most northerly oak woods in Britain. The acquisition of such properties conferred on pockets of native woodland a degree of protection that they might otherwise have lost. The

Commission has a crucial role in conservation and its statutory duties were amended in 1985 to recognise this. At the same time a new policy to increase the planting of broad-leaved trees was adopted, and Dr J. Morton Boyd was taken on board as a consultant. Apart from its concern for the natural well-being of all its forests, the Commission has some 340 Sites of Special Scientific Interest within its purview and cooperates with conservation bodies. The forests also shelter a number of sites of archaeological importance. In a few places conservation now became the main aim of the foresters, something that was to the liking of many, as they have always shown an interest in the natural world, combining a serious enthusiasm for conservation and wildlife with their 'day job'. Indeed, it was a love of nature and the outdoors that brought several into forestry in the first place. In his account of his first year as a forester, in Ardgartan, Don MacCaskill made it plain that he was both a forester and a naturalist but first and foremost the latter.

In 1963, Finlay Macrae was transferred to the Dingwall office of the Commission. 'I spent a lot of my time in Glen Affric,' he said. 'I was fascinated by the pinewoods and it swung my thinking a bittie towards native woodland and conservation. I was terribly lucky to get Glen Affric in my beat and in 1963 I started on the regeneration of some of the pinewoods. It was expected that we would stick to the native species, even to the collection of seed. You never took seed from another source. We collected seed in Glen Affric, took it to the Black Isle nursery and raised it there. We weren't entirely successful in planting to start with, because of the ravages of deer and other difficulties, but eventually – I think it was about six years – we started to do very elaborate fencing and we reduced the size of the areas we expected to regenerate, and they are there now for everybody to go and see. The bit I concentrated on was to the south side of Loch Beneveian.'

'We used to raise about eight million transplants a year in the Black Isle to go back to Glen Affric. We collected pine cones, took them to the kilnhouse, heated the cones and the seed fell out, and sowed seed beds. After about ten years we gave that up because we were starting to get natural regeneration. After we fenced the place off in three sections it came more readily then. We planted out the young trees over a period of years. Eight million is not an awful lot when you think of 4,000 or 5,000 trees per acre. The survival rate was surprisingly low at times. I've seen areas planted towards the end of the autumn and I'd go back in the springtime and half of it would be devoured. Until we got on top of the deer problem by intense shooting there was no hope of success. Now Glen Affric is almost at the stage when you could take

Exposed bog pine roots in Glenmuillie, Glenlivet.

Opposite top.
Two mature and several young cones on a Scots pine in Strathspey.

Opposite below.
Spruce has been clear felled from this area of Glenmore to leave old, dead or dying native Scots pine behind.

all the fences down. Once the trees are 30 feet high they're out of that danger and you've got everything on the ground you could wish for, and enough regeneration that a lot of trees will survive. In fact you're reproducing the ideal situation for deer. I would advocate letting deer back into the woods that are out of the danger stage, perhaps in lower numbers. Certainly, if you get a Scots pine and birch woodland growing well, and allow deer into it, you won't get the damage . . . it's natural, all their food and their shelter is there. Glen Affric today – the sight you see is very different from when I came. There's far more birch wood, and aspen and rowan. The whole ambience of Glen Affric is different. I was sorry to leave. To be truthful I spent too much time there, for I would be off to Glen Affric at the least excuse.'

In June 1999 the press marked the planting of the 250,000th tree in the restoration of the forest in Glen Affric.[12] For Finlay, Glen Strathfarrar, roughly parallel to Glen Affric and around 4 miles to the north, is the most beautiful glen in the country. 'It's pretty well unchanged,' he said, 'Plenty of woodland and more so now, though when you get to the top [west] end, nearer Kintail, it peters out – poorer soil, harsher conditions. Now I would say I am

very largely orientated to native woods, environmentally sensitive woods, and, in fact, spiritual woods.'

Conservation has naturally led to a growing interest in native species and the restoration of woodland, and there are now a number of organisations dedicated to this aim. The notion of restoration immediately raises the issue of restoration to what, and the almost universal answer has been to create – or to re-create – the original forest cover of the landscape, original here meaning what scientific investigation has revealed about the nature of the natural forest, the forest that would have continued to exist if it had not been destroyed by human activity.

When the last of the glaciers retreated or melted away at the end of the most recent period of glaciation, a date most geologists would put at around 12,000 years ago, the landscape was left bare and open. Colonisation by plants resulted first in a tundra-like environment with dwarf birch the predominant tree, as suggested by the pollen remains in cores from loch sediments and peat bogs. By 10,000 BC the climate had warmed sufficiently to permit birch and juniper scrub to flourish. This gave way to more diverse woodland, with birch, hazel, oak and elm in sheltered glens, and then from about 8,000 BC an expansion of pine forest took place. It is this last ecological phase that has caught the imagination of the restorers and a number of bodies now involve large numbers of volunteers in regeneration and expansion.

Research by H.M. Steven and A. Carlisle, published in 1959 as *The Native Pinewoods of Scotland*, has been extremely influential in this regard. In the early 1950s, the two authors identified some 35 pockets of native Scots pine surviving in various parts of the Highlands, from the shores of Loch Assynt in the north to Glen Falloch in the south and, in the east, Ballochbuie on Deeside. Their total has since been increased, although it has not always been possible to fix with certainty which are genuine relic populations and which may have been planted later. More recent studies on genetics have produced surprising insights, among them the discovery that the Scots pine in the far north-west are distinct enough from other populations to suggest they survived the Ice Ages in some offshore Atlantic refuge.

Some environmentalists have become puritanical and accept only species that can be proved to have grown here naturally without human agency and therefore constitute the chosen flora to be considered in restoration projects. Even the worthy and hardy sycamore, often the only tree to grow in some exposed parts of the country, until very recently ruled out of court, as it seems

it was brought here within the last 2,000 years, a period of residence not long enough to cancel out its foreign provenance. Similarly, in this continuing debate on restoration, the few voices who have queried the extent of the prehistoric pine forest and the view of what is 'natural' have tended to be disregarded.[13]

A surviving patch of native Scots pine forest at Easan Dorcha, Wester Ross, in 1992.

The Forestry Commission maintains the aim of creating semi-natural forest in many places, with a mixture of broad-leaved trees and open spaces, conscious primarily of conservation and landscape, with timber production and recreation as of secondary importance. A consequence of these ideas has been the rehabilitation of the birch, the tree once regarded as a weed. The organisation, Highland Birchwoods, formed in 1992, promotes the use of indigenous hardwoods and supports many projects on biodiversity, forest management, conservation and sustainable development. In collaboration with several other bodies, Highland Birchwoods is also interested in developing Scots pine as a resource.

'Originally there was little or no hope of growing broadleaves up there in the north, but perhaps a combination of global warming with better understanding of cultivation and fertiliser needs now makes it more possible to grow them as amenity species but not as timber species,' said John Keenleyside. 'The most likely species is birch but birch is not natural every-where in Sutherland. We did some experimental work on that and we found out that to get the birch to do well up there we had to collect the seed, grow it and plant it back near where it originated. There are varieties adapted to local conditions. Birch is quite a difficult species to transplant. You can grow it quickly in the nursery but there are big failures after planting. Another thing that has helped in that respect is planting things in shelter tubes. We also experimented with Scots pine. Again I would say there are better sources of seeds available now and, as with the birch, if you want to plant trees at, say, Loch Maree, you want the seed or material from there.'

In the course of my interview with Finlay Macrae in his home in Dingwall, he said at one point, 'I am astonished at people. Say you have a farmer with a hundred acres, and twenty acres may be very poor. I can't understand why they don't plant the twenty acres with birch or something and use it as a fuel.' Earlier in this book, we have seen how the farmers and crofters have long harboured suspicions and even resentment towards the foresters, as if they represented two incompatible ways of using the land. Various schemes to encourage private planting of trees on farmland have not had much success, noted W.E.S. Mutch and A.R. Hutchison in a study of this contentious relationship in 1980.[14] 'In this respect,' they wrote, 'British farmers differ notably from their Scandinavian and West European counterparts, many of whom own woodland, manage it effectively and regard it as a normal income-earning asset on the farm.' It seemed that the only time our farmers showed an interest in forestry was when they were offered a good price for some acres from a would-be forester. Mutch and Hutchison detected, however, a shift in the old attitudes and a growing awareness of the potential of so-called agro-forestry.

The suitability of combining crofting with forestry has long been recog-nised in a few quarters. We have seen how Lord Lovat considered them to be eminently suited to each other. It was being spoken of again in the 1930s when the Commission began its planting programmes on Skye, and in the mid-1950s a report on crofting for the secretary of state saw forestry as an ancillary activity for the crofter. An early attempt to combine the two came to an end in the 1960s because of complications involving crofting law and because research had opened the way to planting on exposed peatland previously considered unviable for forestry. In the late 1980s, the Scottish Crofters Union took up the challenge again and argued for reform to crofting law to allow crofters to plant and manage their own woodlands. In 1991 the passage of the Crofter Forestry (Scotland) Act gave crofters new opportunities to afforest parts of common grazings and made grants available. After five years or so, eleven townships had taken advantage of the project and another five had earmarked some 210 hectares for natural regeneration.[15] Perhaps surprisingly, most interest was shown in Lewis. Crofters saw woodland as providing shelter for their livestock and enhancement of the landscape and biodiversity as more important than timber production. On the other hand, it was impossible to convince all that planting was a good move, as it involved loss of grazing and probably would provide havens for foxes and deer.

We now have the concept of the woodland croft which can range from a holding that is mainly woodland to one that is mainly agricultural with a woodland element. The idea was introduced in 2006 by a steering group that included representatives from Forestry Commission Scotland, crofting bodies and development agencies. The group saw woodland crofts as tackling in one sweep problems associated with housing, rural livelihoods and woodland management. There would emerge new business opportunities for the crofter and development could take place in a sustainable way, with innovative housing and energy conservation, with a deliberate nod in the direction of the way things are done in rural Scandinavia and other parts of northern Europe.

These developments have coincided with the re-assessment of native species such as birch and research into how livestock and forestry can be integrated. At Achany near Lairg it was found that cattle with calves could over-winter in woods of Scots pine and larch without undue damage to the trees, provided the soil and the drainage conditions were right.[16] Research into what is now termed silvi-pastoralism or agro-forestry has gathered momentum in recent years and, at the same time, attention has been paid to the history of how woodlands have been used as pasture. A recent, large-scale Forestry Commission Scotland scheme has introduced sixty Highland cattle to some 4,500 hectares of land on the hills around Loch Katrine in the Trossachs. In time it is hoped to build up this herd and have it live in a kind of symbiosis with broadleaved woodland, some of which will be planted and some of which will be left to regenerate naturally, aided by the grazing behaviour of the cattle. This is the biggest project of its type in Europe.

Another development has been the growth in community-owned woodland. In an echo of Scottish forestry in the Victorian years, the Countryside Commission looked in 1990 to Germany to see how community woodlands worked and to find out how they could be introduced here. The Central Scotland Woodlands Initiative and the Central Scotland Woodlands Countryside Trust published their aim in 1993 to plant one million trees on marginal farmland between Glasgow and Edinburgh. This plan envisaged mixed stands of broadleaves and conifers enhancing the open country, often high and bleak, across the waist of Scotland. Community woodlands now can be found across Scotland. The first was formed in 1995 in Laggan when the community took over the management of the local Forest Enterprise plantation. What is possibly the most northerly is at Dunnet in Caithness and looks after the forests first planted as an experiment by the Commission in the 1950s. Now the National Forest Land Scheme extends this approach to allow not only community organisations but appropriate public bodies and housing organisations the opportunity to buy or lease national forest land where this can provide increased public benefits.

The Scottish Executive published its long-term forest strategy in 2006 setting out its policy aims and laying down the framework that will guide Forestry Commission Scotland – forestry is a devolved responsibility – over the next fifty years. It identifies our forests as 'a central part of our culture, economy and environment' and the range of policies now implemented by the Commission certainly bears out this approach. For example, it has turned to social science to explore how forestry can be of benefit to society, and phrases such as 'Social issues are a fundamental part of sustainable forest management', which would have mystified older generations of woodsmen, now appear in FCS publications. 'Different individuals, groups and organisations have diverse needs and expectations of trees and woodlands,' reads one part of the FCS website, 'People expect to have the opportunity to contribute to sustainable forestry decisions, and different kinds of knowledge feed into those decisions. Furthermore, as the environment changes, society and institutions adapt and form new relationships around the resources that they use and manage.'[7] The role woodlands can play in promoting public health has also been recognised; the role of forests in recreation is an obvious part of this strategy but it has been rendered more formal with the issue of a publication called *Woods for Health* which highlights not only physical exercise but the more subtle benefits woodland offers, for example, for the relief of stress. The WIAT programme – the acronym stands for 'woods in and around towns' – aims to create new woodland, bring neglected woodland into active management and encourage people to make better use of woods in their vicinity. This is particularly aimed at the more populated parts of the country and focuses on urban woodlands. For WIAT, the woods in question are defined as lying within a kilometre of settlements with more than 2,000 people; in Scotland this comprises some 18,000 hectares, most of which are found in the Central Belt though the northern cities of Aberdeen and Inverness and even Stornoway, Thurso and other small towns are also included. The Glasgow and Clyde Valley Green Network is an example of a long-term initiative under this policy.

FCS would like to see the amount of woodland in Scotland rise by 2050 from the present 17 per cent of the land area (1.3 million hectares) to 25 per cent. It hopes that downstream processing industries will deal with 8.5 million cubic metres of timber each year instead of the present 7 million. The

A cyclist tackles Seven Stanes Trail around Ae. Several forests now provide venues and challenging trails for mountain biking.

woodlands will help in flood control and increase biodiversity, they will provide fuel and sustainable construction materials, they will play a major part in recreation and enhance the quality of life for residents and tourists alike. Forest tourism is estimated at the present time to be worth £160 million annually. Woodland festivals are now held and initiatives like the 7 Stanes project in South Scotland have extended the portfolio of woodland activities to include a world-renowned venue for mountain biking. In 2050 native tree species will make up 35 per cent of the forests – it is only 29 per cent now – and ancient woodlands will be kept in good condition. Most of the woodland – perhaps some 70 per cent – will remain in private hands, or at least not be part of the 'national forest estate', the proportion looked after by the Commission.

At the present time, Scotland is divided into five conservancies – Highlands and Islands, Grampian, Perth and Argyll, Central, and South Scotland. Each is charged with the promotion of sustainable forestry, balancing timber production with the need to conserve landscapes and biodiversity. They also advise and give grant aid to the private sector. The management of the national forests is the responsibility of ten forest districts from North Highland to Galloway in the south.

'As time goes on the goalposts shift but in forestry it's hard to make a quick change,' said Bryce Reynard. 'In the old days we acquired an area of ground that nobody else wanted and planted it from end to end with Sitka spruce, making a big square on the landscape. Nobody complained because it reflected the forestry policies of the time and usually all the local folk were employed but now there are different ideas of what a good landscape should look like. Programmes of planting and felling now are done very sympathetically to the landscape but we can't change everything immediately.'

The forester has to take the long-term view. 'If you think you're just passing through you won't do the right things. You have to do what's right for the land. I'm a very patient man. I used to wonder why we were rushing to answer the phone at the first ring. We were dealing with trees. When a tree is felled in fifty years' time no one will say, if only he'd answered the phone a bit quicker … What's the rush? Inevitably nowadays foresters as a breed are viewed as pen pushers or are sitting in front of a computer screen. A lot of forests now are covering huge areas and there's no way you can know the local folk. In the past it was a more tight-knit community. I would even say that foresters now have less hands-on experience and are more administrative. We were always trained as naturalists. You read the ground, you had to study the soil and the plants growing in it. When we did forestry at first you got on and did the job, you didn't have to ask if you could do it. Now there are umpteen meetings to see if it's okay to do anything. The approach is certainly more thorough.'

Some of the issues raised in the forest strategy such as climate change and renewable energy generation would have puzzled the Commissioners back in 1919 but they might readily have understood others such as the need for integrated land use. Forestry has gone through many changes since the Commission's birth when its main aim was simply to ensure the country had a strategic reserve of timber. The original Commissioners would certainly appreciate the fact that forestry sustains some 7,600 direct jobs and another 3,100 in the primary wood-processing industries. The UK-wide organisation, the Confederation of Forest Industries, which also represents private forestry, has stated that forestry supports 19,000 direct jobs. The recognition by the government that 'forestry can bring much needed economic activity and employment to fragile and remote rural areas' would have them nodding in full agreement. If Sir John Stirling-Maxwell could see the present extent and diversity of activity he might conclude that there is at last a growing forest sense in Scotland. Over the past nine decades the men and women of the Forestry Commission and of the private estates have built on the efforts of earlier centuries to change the face of the country. We have all benefited from their work, and I hope this book has presented an outline of that. They have left a legacy that is in our hands and, in a sense, we are all foresters now.

Two solitary Scots pine on the moors near Achnasheen.

NOTES

The following abbreviations are used:
FC   Forestry Commission
HN   *Highland News*
IC   *Inverness Courier*
NSA New Statistical Account of Scotland
OSA *Statistical Account of Scotland*
PJ   *People's Journal*
TSAS, TRSAS, SFJ, SF: Several references are to papers published in the journal of the Royal Scottish Forestry Society which has changed its name over the years as the name of the society itself has changed, as follows: until 1889, *Transactions of the Scottish Arboricultural Society* (*TSAS*); from 1890 until 1926, *Transactions of the Royal Scottish Arboricultural Society* (*TRSAS*); from 1927 until 1947, *Scottish Forestry Journal* (*SFJ*); and since 1947 *Scottish Forestry* (*SF*).

CHAPTER 1:
'all but a lost art'

1. The planting of the first tree was not seen as a significant event. The local papers, the *Northern Scot* and the *Elgin Courant and Courier*, made no mention of it. I am grateful to Joanne Clark, Diana McGowan and Alan Stevenson of Forestry Commission Scotland for their help in pinning down the details but the main record seems to be in Pringle (1994).
2. J.B. Dent, 'Scotland's untapped potential for forestry', *SF* 43: 1989.
3. 'The development of state afforestation in the Highlands', *Transactions of Inverness Scientific Society and Field Club*, Vol. 9, 1918–25.
4. Blackie, 1882.
5. Royal Commission, 1895.
6. Napier Commission evidence, vol. 4, p. 2952.
7. Napier Commission evidence, vol. 4, p. 2964.
8. A. MacCallum Scott, 'Afforestation and the Highlands', *Scots Magazine* 4(5): 1926.
9. S. Johnson, *A Journey to the Western Isles of Scotland in 1773*. Boswell's own account bears out what Johnson wrote. There are many editions of both Johnson's and Boswell's accounts. I have used the 1906 edition, published by Alexander Gardner, Paisley.

10. *OSA* VIII, Creich, Sutherland.

11. *OSA* V, Urquhart and Loggy Wester, Ross and Cromarty.

12. Sinclair, 1795.

13. Quoted in T.C. Smout, 'Some problems of timber supply in later 17th century Scotland', *SF* 14(1): 1960.

14. W.B. Walker, 'The history of forestry at Eskdalemuir, Dumfries-shire', *SF* 29(1): 1975.

15. *OSA* XII, Coldingham, Berwickshire.

16. *OSA* I, Jedburgh, Berwickshire.

17. Cregeen, 1964.

18. Millar, 1909.

19. R.M. Tittensor, 'History of the Loch Lomond oakwoods', *SF* 24(2): 1970.

20. *OSA* III, Torosay, Mull.

21. *OSA* VI, Kilchrenan and Dalavich, Argyllshire.

22. *OSA* XIV, Speymouth, Banffshire.

23. Grant, 1898.

24. *OSA* XIII, Abernethy and Kinchardine.

25. Rampini, 1897.

26. Letters D1042/1/280–288, Highland Archives, Inverness.

27. J.T. Smith, 'Scottish home grown timber trade 1854–1953', *SF* 8(2): 1954.

28. Highland Folk Museum Oral History Tape, HF7/24/cb 068/B.

29. Mitchell, 1884.

30. *NSA*, Speymouth, Morayshire.

31. Rampini, 1897.

32. A. MacCallum Scott, 'Afforestation and the Highlands', *Scots Magazine* 4(5): 1926.

33. Sir John Stirling-Maxwell, 'A decade of state forestry and its lessons', *SFJ* 44(1): 1930.

34. *NSA*, Cromdale, Inverness-shire.

35. J.H. Alexander, 'The forest nursery trade in Scotland 1854–1953', *SF* 8(2): 1954.

36. There is some brief information on John Reid in M. Hadfield et al., *British Gardeners: A Biographical Dictionary*, London: Zwemmer, 1980; and J. Mills et al., *Rosehaugh: A House of Its Time*, Avoch: Avoch Heritage Association, 1996. The edition of Reid's book to which I referred is the one edited by A.H. Hyatt (1907).

37. The history of Perth burgh wood can be found in A.R. MacDonald, 'That valuable branch of the common good: the forestry plantation of eighteenth century Perth', *SF* 51(1): 1997.

38. *OSA* VIII, Edenkillie, Morayshire; and the Earl of Moray, 'Darnaway Forest: an example of afforestation in the eighteenth century', *TRSAS* 38 (1): 1924.

39. *OSA* XVIII, Fossaway and Tullibole, Perthshire.

40. *OSA* III, Dalziel, Lanarkshire.

41. The Gordon letter of 1762. In: M.T.T. Phillips, 'The origin of the old Scots pine planted by Gordon Castle estate', *SF* 50(3): 1996.

42. Millar, 1909.

43. *SF* 17(3): 1963.

44. Fraser, 2004.

45. Grigor, 1868.

46. *OSA* XX, Dunkeld, Perthshire.

47. C.Y. Michil, 'On the best means of increasing the comforts and of improving the

social and moral condition of under-foresters and apprentices on large estates',
TSAS 5(1): 1870.

48. W.M. Gilbert, 'The late Mr Malcolm Dunn, Dalkeith', *TRSAS* 16(1): 1901.

49. L. Boppe and E. Reuss, 'The forests of Great Britain', *SF* 14(1): 1960.

50. F. Story, 'A visit to German forests', *TRSAS* 16(3): 1901.

51. *PJ*, 27 Nov 1926.

52. Lindley, 1935.

53. A. MacCallum Scott, 'The forester', *Scots Magazine* 1(1): 1924.

54. Lord Lovat, 'Afforestation', *TRSAS* 22(2): 1909.

55. *IC*, 26 Oct 1909.

56. *IC*, 12 Nov 1909.

57. *IC*, 28 Dec 1909.

58. *IC*, 28 Nov 1909.

59. *IC*, 24 Dec 1909.

60. *IC*, 14 March 1911.

61. *IC*, 6 June 1911.

62. Lord Lovat and Captain Stirling. 'Afforestation in Scotland: forest survey of Glen Mor and a consideration of certain problems arising therefrom', *TRSAS* 25(1): 1911.

63. *IC*, 18 July 1911.

64. Sir John Stirling-Maxwell, 'The place of forestry in the economic development of Scotland', *TRSAS* 27(2): 1913.

65. Wonders, 1991.

66. *PJ*, 19 Sept 1916.

67. *Transactions of the Inverness Scientific Society and Field Club*, vol. 9, 1918–25.

68. *PJ*, 16 Aug 1919.

69. *PJ*, 27 Dec 1919.

70. *PJ*, 22 Mar 1919.

71. M. Sutherland, 'Women's labour in forestry', *TRSAS* 32(1): 1918.

CHAPTER 2:
'the creation of a forest sense'

1. Sir William Schlich was born in Germany and studied forestry at the University of Giessen. After losing his post with the Hesse state forestry service he joined the forest service in India and eventually was appointed professor at the Royal Indian Engineering College in England in 1885. When the college closed he transferred to the University of Oxford and became a prominent teacher and advocate of state forestry in Britain before his death in 1925.

2. McEwen, 1977.

3. McEwen, 1998.

4. J.A. Johnson, 'John McEwen OBE – an appreciation', *SF* 47: 1993.

5. *PJ*, 26 Oct 1918.

6. *Perthshire Advertiser*, 11 Oct 1919.

7. A.M. Scott, 'The forester', *Scots Magazine* 1(1): 1924.

8. *IC*, 11 Feb 1921

9. Ryle, 1969.

10. *Ross-shire Journal*, 14 Feb 1919.

11. *PJ*, 30 May 1920.

12. *PJ*, 21 May 1921.

13. *PJ*, 22 Dec 1923.

14. *PJ*, 21 July 1923.

15. *PJ*, 15 Sept 1928.

16. Lord Lovat, 'Land acquisition and forest workers' holdings', *TRSAS* 40(1): 1926.

17. *PJ*, 18 Aug 1928.

18. Davies, 1979.

19. *PJ*, 4 May 1929.

20. *IC*, 2 Aug 1929.

21. *Ross-shire Journal*, 7 Sept 1928.

22. Sir Arthur Mitchell (ed.), *Macfarlane's Geographical Collections*, vol. 2, Edinburgh: Constable, 1907.

23. J.F. Annand, 'Progress of forestry work on Culbin Sands, Morayshire', *SFJ* 42(1): 1928.

24. *Forres, Elgin and Nairn Gazette*, 18 June 1925.

25. Sir John Stirling-Maxwell, 'A decade of state forestry and its lessons', *SFJ* 44(1): 1930

26. *PJ*, 4 Oct 1930.

27. *PJ*, 10 Sept 1932.

28. *PJ*, 20 May 1939.

29. M.E. Hardy, 'Afforestation in Lewis and Harris', *SFJ* 45(1): 1931.

30. Sir John Stirling-Maxwell, 'Turf nurseries' *SFJ* 50(1): 1936.

31. *PJ*, 31 May 1931.

32. Lovat obituary, *SFJ* 47(1): 1933.

33. J. Hunter Blair, 'The present position of private forestry', *SFJ* 45(1): 1931.

34. Curran, 1987.

35. *PJ*, 5 April 1941.

36. *PJ*, 15 June 1940.

37. Wonders, 1991.

38. Ford, 1985.

39. J.P. Tait, 'Women labour and forestry problems', *SFJ* 56: 1942.

40. *IC*, 15 Aug 2008.

41. J. McEwen, 'Wartime logging camps in Scotland' *SF* 17(4): 1963.

42. *PJ*, 15 Sept 1945.

43. *PJ*, 22 Sept 1945.

44. *PJ*, 27 April 1940.

45. *PJ*, 24 July 1943.

46. *HN*, 11 May 1946.

47. Scottish Home Dept, *A Programme of Highland Development*, HMSO, 1950.

CHAPTER 3:

'afforestation has injected new life into the community'

1. *IC*, 9 Aug 1946.

2. *PJ*, 2 Feb 1946.

3. *SF* 8(1): 1954.

4. MacKenzie, 2001.

5. *PJ*, 8 July 1950.

6. *PJ*, 26 April 1947.

7. *SF* 1(3–4): 1948.

8. W.C. Wonders, 'Forestry villages in the Scottish Highlands', *SF* 52(3–4): 1998.

9. Quoted in Stewart, 2007.

10. MacDonald, 1960.

11. G. Forrest, 'Multi-purpose land use in a forest park', *SF* 20(1): 1966.

12. *PJ*, 12 June 1948.

13. *HN*, 31 Jan 1950.

14. *HN*, 22 Nov 1952.

15. Sillar and Meyler, 1973.

16. Department of Agriculture and Fisheries for Scotland, Advisory Panel on the Highlands and Islands, *Land Use in the Highland and Islands*, Edinburgh, 1964.

17. *PJ*, 19 June 1948.

18. *SF* 58: 1944.

19. *SF* 1(1–2): 1947.

20. *HN*, 4 Aug 1951.

21. *IC*, 11 March 1975.

22. J. Keenleyside, 'The Forestry Commission's Dublin Bothy in the 1950s', *FCA Today*, Nos. 30–33, 2006–07.

23. B. Denoon, 'Forestry in the fifties', *IC*, 28 Dec 1993, 31 Dec 1993, 4 Jan 1994.

24. J.H. Alexander, 'The forest nursery trade in Scotland 1854–1953', *SF* 8(2): 1954.

25. *OSA* VII, Dunrossness, Shetland; *OSA* VII, Kirkwall and St Ola, Orkney (Barry); *OSA* VIII, Canisbay, Caithness; *OSA* XIX, Barvas, Ross and Cromarty.

26. S.A. Neustein, 'A review of pilot and trial plantations established by the Forestry Commission in Shetland', *SF* 18(3): 1964.

27. Letter by M.T.T. Phillips, *SF* 48: 1994.

28. A. MacDonald, 'Trial plantations established by the Forestry Commission on the island of Hoy, Orkney.' *SF* 21(3): 1967.

29. *SF* 40: 1987.

30. A.L. Sharpe and S. Jacyna, 'The potential for tree growth and woodland creation in the Western Isles of Scotland', *SF* 47(4): 1993.

31. J.W.L. Zehetmayr, 'Experimental plantations in the far north of Scotland,' *SF* 7(3): 1953.

32. J. Cotter-Craig, 'Forestry on Ardross estate 1848–1855,' *SF* 30(2): 1976.

CHAPTER 4:

'It'll never take over from the horse'

1. D.G. Pyatt, 'Long-term prospects for forests on peatland,' *SF* 44: 1990.

2. S.A. Neustein, 'A history of plough development in British forestry', 30(1): 1976. Pt 25.

3. J. McEwen, 'Wartime logging camps in Scotland,' *SF* 17(4): 1963.

4. R.E. Crowther, 'Extraction of thinnings by horse,' *SF* 14(1): 1960.

5. See, for example, Alan Glen, 'The forester's janker', *Scots Magazine*, March 1953.

6. N. Deveria, 'Wyssen crane work in Argyll,' *SF* 20(3): 1966.

7. Stewart, 2007.

8. J.A. Drummond et al., 'The place of short distance cable cranes in British forestry,' *SF* 26(2): 1972.

9. Obituary of James Fraser, *SF* 13(4): 1959.

10. O'Dell and Mackintosh, 1963.

11. *SF* 15(3): 1961.

12. *SF* 28(1): 1974.

13. *SF* 25(2): 1971.

14. *SF* 17(2): 1963.

15. *HN*, 11 Feb 1966.

16. Steven, 1970.

17. Gemmell, 1990.

18. Tompkins, 1986.

19. Crowe, 1966.

20. E.J.M. Davies, 'Cumbernauld Forest,' *SF* 22(3): 1968.

21. J.F. Ogilvie, 'Forestry in mid-central Scotland,' *SF* 39: 1985.

22. McEwen, 1977.

23. Denoon – see note 23, Chapter 3.

24. See, for example, *HN*, 22 Jan 1960.

25. *HN*, 29 Jan 1965.

26. B.R. Feaver, 'The gale damage of 31/1/53', *SF* 7(2): 1953.

27. A. Whayman, 'The gale of January 1953,' *SF* 9(4): 1955.

28. *OSA* I, Kiltearn, Ross and Cromarty.

29. *SF* 14(3): 1960.

30. *HN*, 11 May 1946. More data on fire and fire risk are in J.R. Thom, 'Fire and the forest,' *SF* 5(2): 1951.

31. *Perthshire Constitutional and Journal*, 6 Aug 1919.

32. *PJ*, 19 June 1920.

33. *PJ*, 25 May 1946.

34. Millar, 1909.

35. R.S.D. Ogilvy, 'New developments in fire fighting,' *SF* 37: 1983.

CHAPTER 5:

'a central part of our culture, economy and environment'

1. *HN*, 11 Aug 1951.

2. *SF* 9(1): 1955.

3. J. Edwards, 'Forestry recollections', *SFJ* 47(1): 1933.

4. Audio-visual presentation, Drumlanrig Castle Visitor Centre.

5. *SF* 35: 1981.

6. *IC*, 19 Aug 1975.

7. A. Evans, 'The growth of forestry and its effects upon rural communities in north-east Scotland: the case of Strathdon', *SF* 40: 1987.

8. *SF* 46: 1992.

9. *SF* 47: 1993.

10. *SF* 40: 1986.

11. *SF* 53(3): 1999.

12. *Aberdeen Press and Journal*, June 1999.
13. J. Fenton, 'Native woods in the Highlands: thoughts and observations', *SF* 51(3): 1997.
14. Mutch and Hutchison, 1980.
15. Scottish Crofters Union, *Crofter Forestry Experiences*, Broadford, 1998.
16. See, for example, J.S.R. Chard, 'Highland birch', *SF* 7(4): 1953; and D.G. Cumming, 'Integration of agriculture and forestry: over-wintering cows with calves in a Scottish plantation', *SF* 35: 1981.
17. See www. forestry.gov.uk for information on all the current policies of FCS.

BIBLIOGRAPHY

Anderson, M.L. (1967) *History of Scottish Forestry* (London, Nelson)

Blackie, W.G. (1882) *The Comprehensive Atlas and Geography of the World* (London, Blackie and Son)

Cregeen, E.R. (ed.) (1964) *Argyll Estate Instructions 1771–1805* (Edinburgh, Constable) (Scottish History Society)

Crofters Commission (1992) *A Guide to Crofter Forestry* (Inverness)

Crowe, Sylvia (1966) *Forestry in the Landscape* (London, FC Booklet 18)

Curran, T. (1987) *They Also Served: The Newfoundland Overseas Forestry Unit 1939–1946* (St John's, Newfoundland, Jesperson Press)

Darling, F.F. (1955) *West Highland Survey: An Essay in Human Ecology.* (Oxford, Oxford University Press)

Darling, F.F. and Morton Boyd, J. (1964) *The Highlands and Islands* (London, Collins)

Davies, J. (1979) *The Scottish Forester* (Edinburgh, Blackwood)

Elliot, W. (2004) *Working the Land, Harvesting the Forest* (Selkirk, Borders Traditions)

Ford, A.A. (1985) *Telling the Truth: The Life and Times of the British Honduran Forestry Unit in Scotland (1941–44)* (London, Karia Press)

Fowler, John (2002) *Landscapes and Lives: The Scottish Forest through the Ages* (Edinburgh, Canongate)

Fraser, Donald (2004) *Highland Reflections: The Reminiscences of a Forester* (Coupar Angus)

Gemmell, A. (1990) *Discovering Arran* (Edinburgh, John Donald)

Graeme Robertson, J. (1988) *Skye Rural Land Use Survey* (Portree, Habitat Scotland)

Grant, E. (1898) *Memoirs of a Highland Lady 1797–1827*, ed. A. Davidson (London, John Murray, 1972 edn)

Gray, Affleck (1998) *Timber! Memories of Life in the Scottish Women's Timber Corps 1942–46*, ed. U. and J. Robertson (East Linton, Tuckwell Press)

Grigor, J. (1868) *Arboriculture* (Edinburgh)

Guthrie, W. (1812) *A New Geographical, Historical and Commercial Grammar and Present State of the Several Kingdoms of the World* (London)

Hamilton, G.J. (1975) *Forest Mensuration Handbook* (London, FC Booklet 39)

Hustwick, I. (1994) *Moray Firth Ships and Trade* (Aberdeen, Scottish Cultural Press)

Johnson, Samuel (1775) *A Journey to the Western Islands of Scotland in 1773* (Paisley, Gardner, 1906 edn)

Lindley, F. (1935) *Lord Lovat: A Biography* (London, Hutchinson)

MacAskill, Don (2007) *Listen to the Trees* (Dunbeath, Whittles)

MacDonald, C.M. (ed). (1960) *The County of Argyll* (Glasgow, Collins) (Third Statistical Account of Scotland).

McEwen, John (1977) *Who Owns Scotland* (Edinburgh, Polygon)

McEwen, John (1998) *A Life in Forestry*, ed. D. Hatvany (Perth, Perth & Kinross Libraries)

MacKenzie, K.C. (2001) *A Glance in the Rear View Mirror* (Inverness)

MacKenzie, K.C. (2005) *Three Points North* (Inverness)

McKirdy, A., Gordon, J. and Crofts, R. (2007) *Land of Mountain and Flood* (Edinburgh, Birlinn)

Macnab, P.A. (1970) *The Isle of Mull* (Newton Abbot, David & Charles)

Meldrum, E. (1970) *Forestry in Scotland* (Edinburgh, HMSO)

Millar, A.H. (ed.) (1909) *A Selection of Scottish Forfeited Estates Papers* (Edinburgh, Constable) (Scottish History Society)

Mitchell, Joseph (1884) *Reminiscences of My Life in the Highlands* (Newton Abbot, David & Charles, 1971 reprint)

Mutch, W.E.S. and Hutchison, A.R. (1980) *The Interaction of Forestry and Farming* (Edinburgh University Department of Forestry and Natural Resources)

New Statistical Account of Scotland, 15 vols, 3rd re-issue, Edinburgh, 1845.

O'Dell, A.C. and Mackintosh, J. (eds) (1963) *The North-East of Scotland* (Aberdeen, Central Press)

Omand, D. (ed.) (2004) *The Argyll Book* (Edinburgh, Birlinn)

Pringle, D. (1994) *The First 75 Years: A Brief Account of the History of the Forestry Commission 1919–1994* (Edinburgh, Forestry Commission)

Rampini, C. (1897) *A History of Moray and Nairn* (Edinburgh, Blackwood)

Reid, John (1683) *The Scots Gard'ner*, ed. A.H. Hyatt (London, 1907 edn)

Report of Her Majesty's Commissioners of Inquiry into the Condition of the Crofters and Cottars in the Highland and Islands of Scotland (Napier Comm.), London, 1884.

Report of the Royal Commission (Highlands and Islands, 1892), London, 1895.

Roy, William (2007) *The Great Map: The Military Survey of Scotland 1747–55* (Edinburgh, Birlinn)

Ryle, G. (1969) *Forest Service: The First Forty-Five Years of the Forestry Commission of Great Britain* (Newton Abbot, David & Charles)

Scottish Crofters Union (1998) *Crofter Forestry Experiences* (Broadford)

Scottish Executive (2006) *The Scottish Forest Strategy* (Edinburgh)

Sillar, F.C. and Meyler, R. (1973) *Skye* (Newton Abbot, David & Charles)

Sinclair, Sir John (1795) *General View of the Agriculture of the Northern Counties and Islands of Scotland* (London)

Sinclair, Sir John (ed). (1791–99) *The Statistical Account of Scotland* (*OSA*) (London)

Smout, T.M. (ed) (1997) *Scottish Woodland History* (Edinburgh, Scottish Cultural Press)

Stell, G.P. and Hay, G.D. (1984) *Bonawe Iron Furnace* (Edinburgh, HMSO)

Steven, C. (1970) *Glens and Straths of Scotland* (London, Robert Hale)

Steven, H.M. and Carlisle, A. (1959) *The Native Pinewoods of Scotland* (Edinburgh, Oliver & Boyd)

Stewart, M. (2007) *Smell of the Rosin, Noise of the Saw* (Edinburgh, Forestry Commission Scotland)

Stewart, M. (2008) *The Forest Is a Beautiful Place to Be* (Edinburgh, Forestry Commission Scotland)

Stitt, L. (1977) *Ae Village Celebrating 50 Years* (Ae)

Thompson, F. (1974) *The Highlands and Islands* (London, Robert Hale)

Tompkins, S.C. (1986) *The Theft of the Hills: Afforestation in Scotland* (London, Ramblers Association)

Wonders, W.C. (1991) *The Sawdust Fusiliers: The Canadian Forestry Corps in the Scottish Highlands in World War Two* (Montreal, Canadian Pulp and Paper Association)

INDEX